Charles Maclean

The Wolf Children

Allen Lane

For my mother and father

Allen Lane
Penguin Books Ltd,
17 Grosvenor Gardens, London SW1W OBD

First published in 1977

Copyright © Charles Maclean, 1977

ISBN 0 7139 1016 X

Set in Monotype Ehrhardt

Printed in Great Britain by
Cox & Wyman Ltd
London, Fakenham and Reading

Contents

List of Illustrations

Acknowledgements

Many people have helped me in gathering material for this book and without their cooperation, encouragement and generosity it would not have been written. I can never hope to thank all of them or express my gratitude adequately to clear a debt that in most part can neither be measured nor repaid. If (in attempting to do so) I overlook anyone, my gratitude and obligation to them are no less felt.

In America I was given valuable help and warm hospitality by Dr Louise Bates Ames, Madge Beamiss, Margaret Beamiss, Mrs Charles Bohlen, Richard Cooper, Charles W. Dunn, Rex Gerold, Kate Grimond, Tom O'Laughlin, Christine Merchant, Edward M. M. Warburg, Mary Warburg, Emma Zingg and Henry Zingg.

In India I received great kindness from Yulin Chen, to whom I am especially grateful; and from Dr P. K. Dhowmick and Dr Ashok Ghosh of the Department of Anthropology at Calcutta University, who helped me with every aspect of my research and by enlisting the welcome aid of the Government of Bengal enabled me to travel in otherwise inaccessible places. In Midnapore the headmaster of the Collegiate School, Haripada Mondal, was my tireless guide, interpreter, teacher and friend and without his assistance I could have achieved little. I am also indebted to Ashok Mozumdar and Ajit Kumar Ghosh who accompanied me on two expeditions into the jungle areas of Bengal and Orissa, and to Biduhuti Bhusan who finally led us to the village of Denganalia. In particular I would like to thank Dr B. B. and Mrs M. Mohanty for their unforgettable hospitality.

Among those who gave interviews and helped with my research in other ways I owe a special debt to Mrs Preeti Lota Jana, a daughter of the Rev. Singh, and to Mrs M. M. Singh, his daughter-in-law. I would also like to thank Miss Sipra Banerjee, Barbara Barnes, Narayan Baska, Sureshkar Bhanj Deo, M. Bhaumick, Dr Biswamoy Biswas, Birendra Nath Bose, K. C. Bose, the Rt Rev. R. W. Bryan, Bankim Chaulia, A. K. Chowdhury, Kunja Mohan Chowdhury, the Church Missionary Society, Father Ian Clarke, Louise Mani Das, Monindro Das, Naren Nath Das, Ragunath Das, A. K. Dash, Abanikanto Dey, Surendra Mohan Dey, Mrs Ganguly, P. C. Ganguly, B. K. Ghosh, S. K. Ghosh, Ram Chandra Biri, Sir Percival Griffiths, Captain M. Guin, Nangi Hembron, the Rev. Lionel Hewitt, Jageswar Khatua, Timothy Khatua, Ghambir Mahato, S. Maity, Sunaram Maji, Mrs Gita Mallik, Lasa Marandi, Dr B. K. and Mrs Mohanty, D. Mukerjee, Dr K. M. Naha, E. G. Nathaniel, Dr D. Nyogi, the Oxford Mission, Mr Pal, Umakanta Pattanaik, Bimoy Roy, Dr D. S. Roy, Mrs Ranjana Roy, Rashbehari Roy, Dr Santra, Dr K. C. Sarbadhicari, Dr Jyotimoya Sarma, N. E. Seager, Dr U. Sengupta, Gajendra Shankar, Ajoy Kumar Singh, A. R. Singh, Niren Singh, S. C. Singh, S. K. Singh, the Rev. Krishna Swamy, Father Peter Thorman, the United Society for Propagating the Gospel and the Rev. Michael Westall.

My thanks to the principal and staff of Bishop's College, Calcutta and the staff of the Library of Congress Manuscript Division, the Centennial Museum of El Paso, the India Office Library and the London Library. I am grateful too to Diana Cookson and Jane James who typed the manuscript with such skill and perseverance. I owe more than a professional debt to Peter Carson of Allen Lane for believing in this book from its early, unpromising beginnings and subsequently for his encouragement, patience and editorial exactitude.

I would also like to thank the following for the use of copyright materials quoted in this book: the Gesell Institute of Child Development, the Library of Congress, Gerhard A. Gesell and Mrs Preti Lota Jana.

Finally I would like to thank Edward Goldsmith, who introduced me to the subject of feral man and suggested that I write not the book I have written, but one something like it.

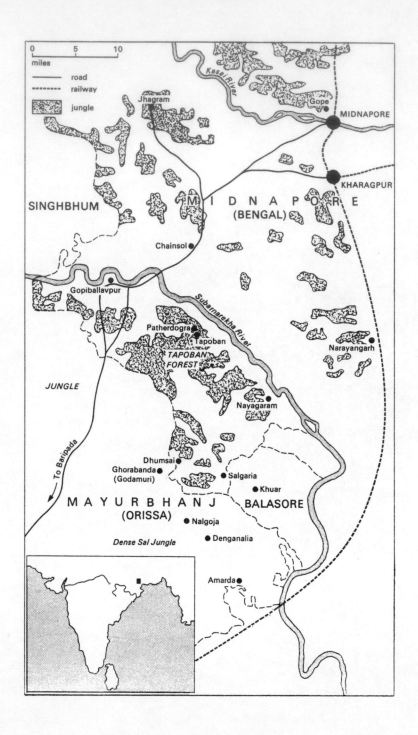

Kasai River

Jhagram

Gope

MIDNAPORE

KHARAGPUR

SINGHBHUM

M I D N A P O R E
(BENGAL)

Chainsol

Gopiballavpur

Subarnarekha River

Patherdogra

Tapoban

*TAPOBAN
FOREST*

JUNGLE

Narayangarh

Nayagaram

To Baripada

Dhumsai

Ghorabanda
(Godamuri)

Salgaria

Khuar

M A Y U R B H A N J
(ORISSA)

BALASORE

Nalgoja

Dense Sal Jungle

Denganalia

Amarda

Introduction

In 1942 Harper and Brothers of New York published a book called *Wolf-Children and Feral Man*. Although a work of some academic pretensions, represented as 'a definitive review by a well-known anthropologist' of the extant literature on extreme cases of isolation, 'wild' men and animal-reared children, it anticipated a wide public by the incorporation of a unique and sensational document. Held to be the true account by an Indian missionary of his attempts to rehabilitate two children recently found living with wolves in the jungles of Bengal, *The Diary of the Wolfchildren of Midnapore* by the Rev. J. A. L. Singh, available for the first time in print, promised to supply the reader with 'a series of facts such as no novelist's imagination could have invented'.

The many legendary heroes from Romulus to Tarzan, known to have been suckled by wild beasts and to have acquired in consequence the more desirable qualities of their foster-mother's species, failed to find a place in the book alongside the Midnapore wolf children on the grounds that they belonged to the realms of mythology – a different province of study. The author of *Wolf-Children and Feral Man*, Robert M. Zingg, an associate professor of anthropology at Denver University, preferred to concentrate on 'historical' cases, classified by the eighteenth-century naturalist, Carl Linnaeus, as *homo ferus* or feral man – an altogether less appealing creature, which ran about on all fours having gained the habits, bodily strength and sharp senses of an animal, but lost the human faculties of speech and reason. To give perspective and background to the Midnapore diary, Dr Zingg included in his collection of feral oddities the famous accounts of the Wild Boy of Aveyron, Caspar Hauser and Wild Peter of Hanover (victims of extreme isolation, though not thought to have been raised by animals), as well as numerous stories of children for whom some feral connection had been established with a variety of animal species including leopards, wolves, bears, sheep, pigs and cattle.

Of the forty or more case histories rounded up by Zingg, mostly from Europe and Asia and dating from the fourteenth century to the more recent past, a high proportion dealt with wolf children. 'An account of Wolves nurturing Children in their Dens', published in 1852 by Colonel William Sleeman, who travelled widely in North India and took an amateur interest in the subject, provided Zingg with much of his best material. However, the evidence in support of wolf and other animal-reared children, if only due to the remoteness or antiquity of most cases, was far from conclusive. Since the time of Linnaeus the subject had been a focus of controversy, with most scientists regarding stories of feral children as the stuff of myth rather than experience. Dr Zingg's book, although labelled an impartial review, was clearly aimed at removing their doubts and, in presenting *The Diary of the Wolfchildren of Midnapore* as the first case that fulfilled 'all the primary conditions for an acceptable scientific datum', at raising feral man to the status of scientific respectability.

When I first read the Reverend Singh's diary I was already aware that Dr Zingg had failed in his mission. On publication, *Wolf-Children and Feral Man* had caused a small stir in academic circles: a number of respected authorities had accepted it as true, others equally respected had not been convinced, while still others had dismissed it as rank nonsense: the controversy had flared briefly, then burnt itself out. I was, nonetheless, fascinated by the diary and despite its evidential limitations I felt certain that it contained some truth. On the strength of that conviction, without knowing any more about the subject, I decided to investigate the Reverend Singh's story and his world and try to find out what happened.

Although the events described in the diary took place fifty years ago, I believed that I should be able to produce enough evidence to satisfy myself and others whether or not a human being had ever been fostered by wild animals. There were more recent cases, as I soon discovered, which might have been easier to investigate: a gazelle boy of the Spanish Sahara, allegedly still running about the desert in 1966, Ramu the wolf boy of Lucknow, monkey children from Teheran and Ceylon, even Patrick, the chicken child, whose parents had kept him in a hen-house from the age of two to seven-and-a-half; but, apart from this last and gruesomely domestic case (from the records of the N.S.P.C.C.), on *prima facie* evidence they all seemed suspect for one reason or another. Last year an ape boy from Burundi with apparently respectable credentials was revealed by an American psychologist to be a fake, his monkey-like features and mannerisms diagnosed as the result of mental illness.

There were also better documented cases of feral children, in particular the Wild Boy of Aveyron, who in some ways had a more interesting story than the Midnapore wolf children. The accomplishments of the boy's teacher and benefactor, Jean-Marc Itard, whose careful observations and skilled experiments on 'Victor' made a small but significant contribution to sensory education and the study of human development, cannot in fairness be compared to the untrained efforts of an Indian missionary. But, for reasons that were no doubt more profound than I appreciated, I was captivated by the idea of a connection between children and animals, and the question of whether it had ever happened seemed to me as a non-scientist more important than the conclusions which might be drawn from a similar case in which animals were not involved. In the beginning it was this optimistic and perhaps naive quest for the truth that sustained me along the trail of the wolf children.

Although Zingg and Singh were both dead, my investigations began bravely enough with the assumption that the original of the missionary's diary and a collection of papers belonging to the anthropologist must still exist. The search for these documents took me on a wild goose chase across middle America from Kentucky to El Paso and back. In Washington D.C., under the quiet ceilings of the Library of Congress, I discovered that the papers had indeed existed, but had since been lost. During the war a box containing all Dr Zingg's materials on feral children had been sent from Denver to Yale where, on the recommendation of Dr Arnold Gesell (who had himself written a book on the subject), they were to be housed in the medical library. The documents, it seemed, had arrived at Yale, but mysteriously disappeared before reaching their final destination.

In Yale I checked with every library on the campus, but there was no record anywhere of a wolf-children deposition. Somewhat despondently, for the more I pursued the missing papers the more significant and graillike they became in my imagination, I went to see Dr Louise Bates Ames, co-director of the Gesell Institute of Child Development, who had assisted the late Dr Gesell in his work on the wolf children. Since she could do no more than confirm the unfortunate loss of the papers, I resigned myself to asking rather pointless questions about what the Zingg collection had contained. I was hardly surprised in the middle of this lugubrious interview to notice that Dr Ames's attention was beginning to wander. Suddenly she rose to her feet. There was a box-room in the roof of the Institute where bits and pieces, mostly old junk, were stored, but just possibly some other materials

4

might have reached up there by mistake. It took us a few moments to get from her office to the top of the stairs. Arming ourselves with torches, we pulled down a folding ladder from the ceiling and climbed up into the attic. Almost at once, in a dark corner under the rafters, I came upon the box. Beneath the layers of dust and grime I could just make out by the circle of torchlight the name of Robert M. Zingg.

The Reverend Singh's diary was not among Zingg's papers (only an edited manuscript of the published version), but the box contained a wealth of correspondence, amounting to several hundred letters, about the wolf children of Midnapore. The collection was to form the basis of my investigation; and, although the search had only just begun, it is difficult to see now, on looking back, what I could have hoped to achieve without it. Indeed, the success of my research into the wolf-children saga ultimately depended on this one lucky find.

My original intention had been to give a complete account of the research, to allow the reader to follow every turn of the investigation, to share every break-through, setback and dead end, but by the time I returned from India the story of detection had grown so long and complex that I had to abandon the idea. I decided instead to recreate the events of Singh's extraordinary diary from all the sources at my disposal, but to exercise my judgement in the choice of material and with no less respect for the truth. By this method I hoped to bring more light to bear on the character and background of the Reverend Singh, who soon enough emerged as the key to any understanding of what really happened. It is to his memory that I dedicate this journey into one of the stranger and more remote regions of human experience.

Chapter One

In a shimmer of heat the Down local from Kharagpur, trailing a pall of black smoke from the efforts of pulling its overloaded coaches up the gradient, slowly swept into the embankment straight and came towards the station. The sun glancing off its engine plates seemed to galvanize the small crowd on the platform, breaking the spell of lethargy cast over them by the excessive heat. They began to move all at once, collecting their belongings, rising from their hunkers and pressing forward to the edge of the platform, mobilized for the arrival. The *sais* from the orphanage, still squatting with friends under the platform awning sipping green coconut water, waited until the train was well into the station before leaving the shade for a strategic position opposite the parcels *godown*, where the last carriage usually stopped. He stood smiling up indiscriminately at the passing squash of faces that strained from every opening in the iron-red carriages, grimacing as the train squealed to a halt. At the sight of the tall figure in white standing at the doorway of the First Class compartment he put his hands together and, making a steeple of his fingers, lowered his head in a particularly elaborate display of reverence, a greeting which the Bengalis usually reserve for images of the divine.

Mr Singh acknowledged his servant with an impatient wave and waited for the roar of the final release of steam to die away before stepping down from the train, one hand holding up the skirt of his long summer cassock, the other proffered to a young tribal boy in *gamchas*, whom he was trying to coax down the steps of the neighbouring Third

Class carriage with an encouraging smile. The boy seemed as much afraid of the missionary as he was of the train.

A giant beside native Bengalis, Mr Singh stood two inches over six foot and was broad in proportion, confirming the Hindu prejudice that Christians only grow so big and strong because they eat beef. He was dark-skinned, as dark as the jungle boy himself, which combined with a military bearing and the rather fierce set of his features to betray his Rajputani ancestry. As a younger man he had been thought handsome, 'a jolly fellow' who sported a twirlable moustache and dressed to fashion, cutting a dash among his Indian contemporaries at Calcutta University. Now at forty-two, growing heavy about the jowls and proud to wear only the simple habit of his calling, the epithets of his youth were no longer apt. A dignified manner, solemn voice and deep-set, thoughtful eyes – their serious, even stern, expression reinforced by the uncompromising line of the mouth – told of a complex and embattled character, not without humour or kindness but driven with religious certainty, pressed into the service of a foreign God as much by his own inclination and ambition as any accident of birth.

The *sais* took over from Mr Singh and without ceremony pulled the boy out of the train; then, making a quick second obeisance to the padre, he turned and led the way along the platform, clearing a path through the throng of passengers, porters, hawkers and *gariwallahs* with a rim-fire invective that had the desired effect without causing offence to his master. A broken-down old man in *dhoti* and regulation red shirt that hung in tatters from his insufficient shoulders struggled with the baggage, dragging after him a tin steamer trunk that set up little dust devils in its wake, which the boy, recovered from the ordeal of the train, idly stamped on with his bare feet.

The *sais* had kept the horse and *tom-tom* waiting in the full sun. Mr Singh reprimanded him sharply as he gathered his cassock and swung himself up into the driver's seat.   8

Even in the hot weather he always preferred to drive himself unless the occasion demanded a different sort of
dignity. The servant threw a few *paise* to the porter, then
he and the boy squeezed into the cab alongside the baggage
as the horse took the strain and the orphanage rig lurched
forward on to the streets of Midnapore.

The town lay on the far side of the railway tracks. Here
the land is quite flat and the buildings so well camouflaged
by greenery that even from the vantage point of the
embankment there is nothing to be seen beyond the
impressive façade of St John's Church, an ochre eminence
solid against the sea of brilliant vegetation. From the air
Midnapore might appear as an emerald caught in the coil
of a slow brown snake, for on three sides the river Kasai
takes a protective loop about its limits; but its true character only reveals itself on closer inspection. Like so much
of British India it was readily divisible in two: the western
half, sometimes called 'the clerks' quarters', with red
brick public institutions and Government officers' bungalows neatly laid out within extensive compounds and
protected by avenues of shade-giving trees: and to the
south, the town proper with its narrow streets, twisting
lanes and crowded bazaars full of old crumbling houses,
brackish *tanks* and ramshackle *bustees*, where for want of
adequate drainage and ventilation cholera was endemic
until the pilgrim traffic shifted to the railways at the end
of the last century. Yet the teeming squalor in which most
of its 30,000 inhabitants lived, then as now, repeating the
daily rituals of an existence unchanged since medieval
times, doing business with each other or talking politics
in the bazaars over cups of sweet milky tea, had more of
life to offer than the salubrious and sedate enclave of their
European administrators.

A place of consequence, as its name 'the city of the
world' suggests, Midnapore had always been the administrative centre of the district – a high proportion of

lawyers, clerks, teachers and educated *babus* contributing to an unusual degree of sophistication and political awareness among its people. In earlier times 'administration' had a distinctly military flavour and the names of town quarters, like Colonelgola and Sepoy Bazaar, as much as the massive ruin of an old Mogul fort that occupies the centre of the town, bear witness to its unsettled history. Midnapore, being a border district and commanding the main road to Orissa, was constantly disputed by successive dynasties from the ancient Mauryans to the wild and bloodthirsty Marathas. Among the oldest settled districts of British India – finally secured for the East India Company by the middle of the eighteenth century after a prolonged struggle – it seemed to Robert Reid, a young district officer posted there that same year of 1915, to be 'full of ghosts'.

In the green and spacious western half of the town, 'the station', as the British liked to refer to what they once regarded as no more than temporary encampments, though everywhere in India they built massively and with a view to permanence, Mr Reid occupied a huge white barrack of a bungalow, said to have been used by Warren Hastings as a country residence, now infested with termites and snakes. At the bottom of his compound, guarded by the decaying tomb of an Indian athlete saint, an old racquet court (often a feature of British occupation before lawn tennis became fashionable) and a disused racetrack choked by lantana bushes, reverberated the echoes of a more leisurely and distinguished past. In the infantry lines the officers' quarters of a regiment that once fought insurgent tribes on the Orissa border had been taken over by American Baptists; but between the orderly rows of huts, there still stood the rusted 'bells-of-arms' from the days of the Mutiny – relics that must have seemed haunted enough to a Government contingent, reduced now to a handful of men who rattled about the station in a slightly unconvincing manner.

The 'native' town was less troubled by ghosts, for there decay and growth kept each other in check, while its own not uninteresting history was constantly assimilated and submerged in the daily struggle for existence. Since 1905, Midnapore had been at the centre of sustained resistance to the partition of Bengal, which at Lord Curzon's insistence had divided a province and people united since earliest times, apparently for the sake of administrative convenience. A political blunder that would have repercussions down the forty years that remained to the Raj, it had the immediate effect of precipitating Indian nationalism in Bengal to the revolutionary phase. In Midnapore there had been an unsuccessful attempt in December 1907 to blow up a train carrying the Lieutenant-Governor of Bengal at Narayangarh. Three months later and two hundred miles away in Mozufferpore, a bomb of identical design, intended for the District Judge, had killed the wife and daughter of Mr Pringle Kennedy, the leader of the local bar.

The ladies had been returning from a bridge evening at the club in a carriage similar to the Judge's, when two men ran up out of the shadows, one with a silver object held high above his head which he threw into the open victoria. The bomb struck Miss Kennedy on the side, blowing her backwards against her mother and leaving what remained of both women's bodies hanging from the shattered rear portion of the carriage, hair trailing in the dust as the frightened horse dragged the wrecked conveyance down the road.

Lurid press descriptions of how the innocent women died fuelled the sense of outrage that swept India; though at Simla, an editorial in the *Statesman* hastened to reassure its readers, discussion of the bomb attack was characteristically phlegmatic: 'It is not the British way to raise eyes and hands to heaven, or to waste much time in useless though pertinent interjection.'[1] In Midnapore the reaction could hardly be so contained, for the perpetrator of the outrage, arrested a few days afterwards, turned out to be one of her own sons, a young nationalist called Khudiram Bose. At the same time investigations into the Narayangarh train-wrecking attempt had revealed the existence of a revolutionary cell in Midnapore, which was planning to assassinate the District Magistrate and every other European in the district.

The police had acted swiftly. On 3 September 1908 the town was thrown into panic by the arrest of more than 150 people, among them several prostitutes and two Rajahs, on suspicion of conspiracy. There was protest from nationalist quarters, but a meeting at the Bayley Hall in Midnapore to pledge loyalty to the Government and express outrage at recent terrorist activity was attended by five hundred of the local gentry – among them Mr Singh, at that time Headmaster of the local Mission High School – who sang the National Anthem and moved a number of confident and loyal resolutions to protect their town, and indeed Bengal and the Empire, from the brutal crimes of the revolutionary movement.

History, past and future, would find their confidence, if not their loyalty, misplaced. Ever since Macaulay had publicly slandered the Bengalis by calling them a race of cowards and the Government had subsequently excluded this cleverest and most passionate of Indian people from the army on the grounds that they were not sufficiently tough or war-like, they had taken deep and lasting offence. Partition had added injury to insult. Some said it was done deliberately, that Lord Curzon had seen trouble coming and was out to crush the Bengalis first; but in any event he succeeded only in strengthening the resolve of the revolutionaries and their supporters against the British. Midnapore would remain in the front line of their sometimes overt but mostly surreptitious war.

The village of Tantigoria, where the Singhs had moved on their return from Calcutta just before the outbreak of the Great War, lay outside the municipal limits to the north-west of Midnapore, a mean cluster of huts backing on to scrub jungle, barely half a mile from the railway station. Their house stood well apart from the rest of the village on the right hand side of the road that leads to Gope, set back in a large tree-filled garden, hidden from view by a brushwood fence and a handsome pair of gates. A wooden plaque advertised the house, which could be seen gleaming whitely through the trees, as 'The Home'. Singh had chosen the name because it seemed particularly suitable for a mission-house and orphanage combined, and whenever he stopped there in front of the gates, as now, waiting for the *mali*, hopefully alerted by the barking of the dogs, to come and open them, he felt a certain pride in its simple appeal. He was proud, too, of the association with that great missionary institution, The Society for the Propagation of the Gospel in Foreign Parts, which had sent him here as a Deacon of the Anglican Church with a licence in his pocket sealed and signed by the Metropolitan of India 'to preach and extend the word of God as a Missionary'. The document, dated 18 January 1913, hung now above the desk in his office and he knew its solemn wording by heart. Although he recognized and often repeated that his work here 'in the Lord's Vineyard' had hardly begun, in four short years he had built up 'The Home' from a half-ruined farmhouse on the edge of the Narajole estate to an establishment worthy of the good name he had given it.

Taking the *tom-tom* between the gates and up the drive at a fast trot, he swept round the circle of grassless lawn in front of the house and pulled up opposite the portico under the shade of a magnificent jack-fruit tree which dominated the compound. He climbed down and stood there for a moment enjoying respite from the sun while the *sais* took the reins and began to lead the horse away to the stable. The boy remained by his side looking about in furtive wonder.

The Reverend Singh's eye was more critical. The orphanage buildings, consisting at present of his own house, a square stone bungalow lime-washed white with green louvred shutters, and two wings of thatched huts built on behind for the children, forming an agreeable courtyard, which served temporarily as an open air school, playground and kitchen, still fell short of his ambitious plans. The front of the house, owing to lack of funds, had not yet been completed; both the portico and the prayer room beyond, which led on to the drawing room, were open to the sun and rain; but the need for improvement to the Singhs' own quarters could not be regarded as a priority. From the far end of the compound the impression was of an imposing and comfortable residence.

It was pleasant to be in the garden. Mrs Singh, waiting in the shade of a pillar on the front steps, came over to meet them under the tree carrying a glass of water for her husband. They greeted each other with customary reserve. Introducing the boy, Jageswar, to his new 'mother', the Reverend Singh explained to her in Bengali that he was a Santal, the son of Bhagobat Khatua of Salgaria. He was twelve years old and had come to live with them at the orphanage for a few years because it was his father's wish that he should receive the benefits of schooling and upbringing in truly Christian surroundings. Although she could not speak Santali, Mrs Singh, who knew Bhagobat, her husband's most valued Reader in the south of the district and stalwart of his mission to the Santals, from his occasional visits to Midnapore, received the boy warmly and, urging her husband to go and take rest, led him away to the back of the house to meet the other children.

Although tired from the journey – it had taken them four days by bullock cart from Salgaria to Kharagpur – Singh ignored his wife's advice and after washing off the dust of *kutcha* roads, settled down at his desk to write a 14 long overdue report to the District Board of Missions. He had to have it ready by the morning as tomorrow they were expecting a visit from the Bishop of Calcutta, the Right Reverend George Lefroy. The visit, itself a rare and prestigious event, on this occasion was something more: Mr Singh believed his future and that of the orphanage depended on it. He knew that his work had met with the approval of both the Diocesan Council and the S.P.G. and that they were pleased with what he had achieved at the orphanage, but he needed more than their praise and encouragement – he needed the assurance that his work would be allowed to continue. He wanted them to recognize that the orphanage was not merely a charitable institution, but an effective way of spreading the Word, that those who had been brought up in the Christian atmosphere of 'The Home' would one day go back to the jungles and convert their heathen brothers. Some of the boys and girls in his care, like the newly arrived Jageswar Khatua, were not orphans at all, but had families who either could not afford to feed them or wanted them schooled. He took in widows and destitutes and child prostitutes; but most of the children, as he put it in his report, were 'picked up from the streets in Santalia and Kharagpur and taught the priceless Love of Our Lord from their infancy'.[2]

These reports never varied much, giving pride of place, after the obligatory parish news, to the orphanage; detailing the number of children (which stood usually in the low twenties), listing the names of the Managing Committee, praising the good work of the teachers and generosity of 'the sympathetic Church members, both European and Indian, in the Station, who have been the chief supporters of the institution'.[3] He always rounded off with a somewhat naive vote of thanks to Mrs Singh, 'the Honorary Lady Superintendent' as he dubbed her, 'who is the life and soul of this establishment and has nobly given up her home and compound to the orphans'[4]

– as if he himself had had nothing to do with it. And then came the inevitable request for more money. The orphanage was permanently in financial distress. Because it lacked various facilities, it was not recognized by the education department. It failed, therefore, to receive substantial grants from the District Board and the Municipality, which meant that the money collected from charity, the S.P.G. and the Church was spent in running the orphanage instead of being set aside to make the necessary improvements to qualify for Government aid. What Singh hoped for from his Bishop was the promise of a large enough sum to buy the parcel of land, for which he had been negotiating with the Rajah of Narajole for several months now, so that he could establish the orphanage in its own buildings.

As it happened, Singh's work had recently received some favourable publicity: a visiting missionary had published his impressions of 'The Home' in the diocesan magazine, painting an idealized picture of the Indian Christian institution at work.[5] The article did not mention the financial difficulties of the orphanage, but in stressing the importance of such institutions it expressed concern that they should be allowed to founder. The appeal would undoubtedly strengthen Mr Singh's hand. And there were others who had visited the orphanage during the last year, offered advice and encouragement and talked enthusiastically of Singh's achievement on their return to Calcutta. He had made every effort to earn their praise, conscious after four years in the Diaconate that he was due for advancement to the priesthood, and that the Bishop's support for the orphanage would depend to a large extent on whether or not he thought him ready for ordination. Although priests were always in short supply in India and native recruits usually welcomed with open arms, because the accusation was often levelled that Indians only turned to Christianity for what they could get out of it in the way of jobs and improved social status, greater care was taken in selecting and sorting candidates than might otherwise have been the case.

Joseph Singh's credentials, before he ever showed any interest in becoming a priest, were held to be above reproach. His ancestors came from Bundelkhand in Rajputan and belonged to the Kshatriya or warrior caste. Traditionally they had always served in the military until his grandfather, Joseph Hiralal Singh, at the time also a soldier, had fled from the Sepoy Mutiny in 1857 and settled in Bengal. He was the first Christian convert in the family and in later life became a priest and a missionary, devoting his considerable energy and a substantial part of his inheritance to founding and running the Local Mission High School and, setting a precedent for his grandson, opening a small orphanage in Midnapore. One of Hiralal's sons, Luther, followed him into the clergy, but Joseph's father, Timothy Singh, entered Government service as a clerk, later becoming Sheristadan (inspector) of the Moonsiff's Court in Bankura. Joseph, the eldest of five children, was brought up there and educated at the Wesleyan Mission School. He did well at his studies, developing a talent for oratory and languages, and in 1893 became the first member of the family to pass the entrance examination for Calcutta University, entitling him by the terms of his grandfather's will, who died that same year, to a large sum of money to be spent on further education in England. But much to his family's dismay, Joseph, who had fallen in love with a police inspector's beautiful daughter from Murshidabad and wanted to marry her (love matches were not the convention even among Christian Indians), rejected the offer on the pious grounds that, if he accepted, he would be depriving his poorer relations of the money which would otherwise be distributed among them.

After six years of study at Bishop's College, still accredited in those days to Calcutta University, Joseph Singh received a Faculty of Arts Diploma at the second attempt and was awarded a gold medal for coming first in English recitation, though he failed to get his B.A. While still at college he had married Rachel Mninmoye Singh against his parents' wishes and with only the grudging consent of his parents-in-law, who disapproved of the match because he was dark-skinned. On graduating he found that they could not return home since his mother, a formidable woman, from whom he had inherited a violent temper, would not allow Rachel in the house. The young couple moved to Hazaribagh, where Singh taught mathematics at the Dublin University Mission School for two years and then returned to Calcutta and another teaching post, which qualified him for the Head-mastership, recently fallen vacant, of the Local Mission High School in Midnapore, founded by his grand-father. In spite of his rejecting the Reverend Hiralal's generous bequest, Singh had always admired his grand-father and was delighted to follow the path he had trod. He accepted the appointment and, with his wife and three children, came to Midnapore in the summer of 1906.

He took his new job seriously, working hard to raise the academic standards of the school and never failing what he considered his first duty as a Christian preceptor. Dr Kshitish Sarbadhicāri, whose father became the Singh's family physician, remembers him as a kind and useful teacher, something of a disciplinarian, yet popular with the children because he made jokes and in May always distributed the fruit from the school's mango trees among them. But when it came to religion he found him distinctly over-zealous: 'Every day before school we used to gather in the Hall and he would stand solemnly in front of us with his hands together – the palms turned up, one over-laying the other – forming a circle below the waist; the children, most of whom were non-Christian, would all have to do the same while we prayed for at least five minutes – that can be a long time for a small child. Every day we did this.'[6] Out of school, the headmaster also found time to help the local padre as catechist, teaching the life of Christ, preparing converts for baptism, visiting Indian Christian families, and every Sunday travelling over to Kharagpur to conduct a service in Hindi for the railway's migrant workers who did not know Bengali. There was no doubt that Singh had a natural propensity for this kind of work and the issue arose whether he might not better serve his God from within the Church rather than as a lay teacher.

The question was ultimately resolved in 1910 by the sudden closure due to financial difficulties of the Mission school in Midnapore. An invitation arrived from the Bishop of Calcutta for Singh to study theology at Bishop's College for the Diaconate. At the same time he was offered another Headmastership by the Education Department; but he had no difficulty in making up his mind in favour of the Church. He would write later of having received 'the Call', of persistent dreams wherein mysterious figures in shining white robes led him across 'a big yawning grave' and brought him face to face with 'the Altar'. And no doubt he did have a vocation, though there were other considerations too.

During his four years as a teacher at Midnapore one event in particular may have decided the course of his career. Certainly it is given momentous significance in Singh's own accounts of his life, where he tells in loving detail how by application of Chlorodyne and prayer he had once cured a young tribal boy attending his school of cholera. The boy's relatives and friends were so impressed by his teacher's magical Christian 'mantras' that they came to him to learn more about the power of the 'Great Healer'. By the end of the year Mr Singh could take credit for some forty Santal baptisms. After being escorted by his new friends on a three-week tour of their villages in the jungle he was able to claim even more. On that trip, enjoying the extraordinary beauties and freedom of jungle life, he discovered his missionary vocation:

We felt that it was a direct call from the Lord Jesus, and fully believed that the Lord had actually called us to these people, His disciples to unfold the Gospel to them while they were so eager to accept the Master ... it was clear they did believe in the prayers and supplications to Our Lord Jesus and were willing to accept Him as their Lord in place of their Gods and Goddesses called 'Bongas'.

In all this we found the reverse principle of Evangelism. The Missionaries and the Preachers generally go to the people to preach unto them the Gospel of Our Lord. But here the principle is different. The people themselves came to seek the Lord and found Him.[7]

As soon as he had finished his report to the District Board of Missions the padre began to clean and oil the two guns he always took with him on his trips to the jungle, calling through to his wife to prepare tea for the arrival of his first visitors, the Brothers of the Poor, a charitable society which he had started in Midnapore to succour the lepers, cholera victims, prostitutes and untouchables of the town, whom no one else would help. A group of young volunteers met regularly under Reverend Singh's presidency at 'The Home' to discuss and plan their work. Because they had no religious or political affiliation, their work was recognized by all and did much for Singh's reputation among the people of Midnapore. It would be false to suggest that he deliberately cultivated the esteem in which he was beginning to be held for selfish reasons, but he believed his position as head of a Christian community that numbered only 150 Bengalis and a handful of Europeans in a town of 30,000 pagans, required him to set an example that could be seen by Hindu and Moslem alike as the embodiment of Christian faith and morality in action. This sometimes meant, as in the case of the Brothers of the Poor, suppressing the Christian interest in favour of his own, but for political rather than for personal reasons, since Christianity was regarded by many Indians as the religion of the conquering race, an extension of the power of the Raj, and derided as such. The Reverend Singh could not hope to avoid censure altogether. In many ways he did not want to, for in political terms he saw Christianity and British rule in India as supporting and justifying each other, and if he did not always distinguish too carefully between his loyalty to the Raj and his duty to the Church, it was because he loved both with equal passion.

Standing on a chair, he placed the guns on a shelf above his desk out of reach of the orphanage children and his own son, Daniel, who was almost twelve years old now and at boarding school in Hazaribagh. He had forbidden him to touch them on pain of chastisement, although he knew there was little danger of his doing so, for somewhat to his father's disappointment the boy showed little interest in fire-arms or hunting. They shared a fondness for animals, but that was spoiled by Singh's greater love of *shikar*. Apart from the excellent opportunities for sport afforded by his long missionary tours in the jungle he often used to shoot with friends nearer home. There were *shikar* parties organized by the Rajahs of Narajole and Jhagram, informal expeditions with the British officials and the simple pleasure of going out with a gun behind the house and walking up snipe, hare and other small game for the pot. But he took care not to become too well known as a hunter. Although he could easily be persuaded to tell the story of how he got his 'stripes', as the Bengal tiger was affectionately known, he kept few trophies other than some rather poor specimens of chital and black buck, which gathered dust high on the walls of his office. There was nothing in the drawing room which might have offended visiting parishioners or ecclesiastics. Not that most missionaries did not hunt, and were even obliged to on occasion, but he had to think of the devout Hindu who was opposed to the killing of any animal and of his missionary superiors who might accuse him of spending too much time with a gun under his arm in lieu of a bible. The European community, however, understood his predicament and sympathized, for now that pig-sticking and polo were beyond the purse of most district officers, hunting was their chief outdoor recreation and if an Indian could share the pleasures of this manly pursuit, the enlightened among them welcomed the chance of fraternization on the safe social ground of jungle and *jheel*.

For Reverend Singh there were other points of contact with the British that he prized more highly, not the least being his university education and command of the English language, which allowed him to tender with pleasure and a certain pride his services as interpreter to the District Judge and the Collector in difficult or import-ant cases. But it was through the Church that he came most into contact with the 'Twice Born' and was able in some cases to establish relationships that he believed trans-cended the racial barrier in a way that would have been impossible for a Hindu or Moslem. Probably his finding favour with the British had as much to do with the fact that he came from Rajputan and belonged to the Kshatriya warrior caste, which in their eyes made him 'a man', as acceptable as the loyal, honest Pathan or Punjabi and raised him above the level of the Bengali *babus*, whom they regarded as shiftless, untrustworthy, effeminate and always 'too clever by half'. Over the years to come Reverend Singh would pay court to each successive District Magis-trate, a policy exercised as a matter of course by all the leading loyalist citizens of Midnapore, but in his case not so much because he needed their cooperation in his work but because he believed that his education, social standing, his very 'Britishness' entitled him to their company. In reality his success would depend largely on the devoutness of the individual magistrate and the interest he showed in Church matters, but pride would never allow Reverend Singh to admit that he occupied any but a special place in the heart of his British masters. There were a few, of course, who within the limits of propriety accepted and returned his friendship, not merely for professional expediency, but because they liked him and respected, him. In spite of his short temper and schoolmaster's pompous manner they saw Singh as a reliable man of some charm and sophistication, who held strong, over-simple and rather rigid convictions, but lived more or less according to the principles on which they were founded; and if his attempts to be more British than the British were a little galling at times, it was a common enough fault among educated Indians, and he made up for it with a sense of humour more highly developed than most, whose comic disposition had been nurtured by a climate in which irony would not grow.

In Kharagpur, where he and the boy, Jageswar, had spent last night on their return from Salgaria, Reverend Singh had attended a *café chantant* at the Railway Institute. The evening had been organized by his supervisor, the Reverend G. Reynold Walters, in aid of Church Funds, but Singh may have had an ulterior reason for being there. Godfrey Walters had taken over the chaplaincy at Kharag-pur nearly five years ago and was talking of retiring, though he had threatened to leave so often during his residence that nobody really knew whether to believe him or not. In those early days Kharagpur, a growing railway town eight miles south of Midnapore, was an onerous and unhealthy parish. Walters' wife had died in the first year they were there. At the time he had been too ill himself with malaria and dysentery to realize what was happening. When he returned to consciousness after a long bout of fever, he had met his loss with the fortitude expected of a man in his position. But gradually loneliness had eroded his strength and as it became clear to him that he needed a replacement for his wife and had little chance of finding one in Kharagpur, he grew morose and bitter. He became prone to eccentric outbursts, and would sometimes call out in the middle of Evensong 'Soul of my soul! I shall clasp thee again', whereupon his congregation would look away or clear their throats in sympathy. They knew well enough what he had suffered, but the cemeteries of Bengal were full of young Englishwomen who had survived the rigorous passage out, only to succumb to the deadly climate soon after arrival.

After his wife's death, Walters went into a decline. A difficult man to work with, always finding fault and complaining to his superiors in Calcutta, he had become obsessed by the quality of his living arrangements and would dash off letters to the Archdeacon, scribbled on the backs of First Communion cards, scored by heavy underlinings, pointing out the inadequacies of his bungalow, which he claimed was unworthy of him. In fact the bungalow was large and comfortable, but Walters' obsessions were revenants that could not be laid. That night at the concert he had complained about it to Singh, who had heard his colleague's views on the subject many times before, but knowing that he might need Walters' recommendation to the Bishop, listened patiently, hoping it was for the last time.

Although in his reports over the years Singh had expressed nothing but the warmest gratitude for the co-operation and help shown by Walters, the two men did not get on. When Singh was ordained Deacon at Advent 1912, placed on the list of S.P.G. Clergy and sent to Midnapore, a new district had been added to the Diocese of Calcutta, but because he was only a Deacon and a 'native' clergyman, he had to remain for the time being under the wing of the European Chaplain at Kharagpur. The Midnapore Church Committee, however, were opposed to the idea of throwing in their lot with Kharagpur because they 'were frightened of being swamped by so large a place'[8], as they put it, though it later emerged that the real reason for their desire to remain independent of Kharagpur had more to do with their low opinion of the wretched and slightly mad Reverend Godfrey Walters. When Walters happened to discover what the Church Committee thought of him, after seeing a letter they had written to the Bishop, he refused to have anything more to do with Midnapore and for a long time associated Singh with his persecutors.

Not that Walters' voice was likely to be decisive on Singh's candidature for the priesthood. He was after all not a missionary but a railway chaplain and the future of the Church in India barely concerned him, whereas on Joseph Singh it rested. Unlike the Government chaplains who had been sent out to care only for the souls of the white-skinned population (sometimes refusing to minister to non-Europeans), the Missionary Societies looked ahead to a self-supporting, self-governing Indian Church with Indian Clergy under Indian Bishops as the end aim of the work that they sustained. The Metropolitan of India had the difficult task of reconciling both often opposed camps. In that sense Singh's being sent to Midnapore and put in charge of a large new district was a political appointment and his advancement to the priesthood, although he did not know it, was only a question of timing. As it turned out it would coincide with Walters' retirement.

'I remained a Deacon till the year 1917,' Singh wrote some years later in a letter to America, 'and the Metropolitan, Bishop Lefroy, visited us and was very much pleased to see the Orphanage and our parish work. He carried a very healthy impression of our endeavour and spoke very highly in the D.B.M. Committee and advised them to strengthen our hands. It was done and the Reverend Gee, the then Secretary, visited us and sympathized with us in various ways and granted us all we wanted. Dr Lefroy had made it implicit on me that I should be ordained a priest . . .'[9] At the beginning of the rains, a month or so after the Bishop's visit, a telegram arrived from Father Ernest Brown, the Superior of the Oxford Mission, inviting J. A. L. Singh to come to Calcutta and be prepared by him for ordination.

Although he had been awaiting a summons, it was a special and unexpected honour, for Father Brown was one of the most distinguished and revered missionaries of the day. Having founded the Bishop's College School in Calcutta and reorganized the S.P.G. Mission to the Sunderbans, the vast tiger-infested delta area above the Bay of Bengal, he had practical experience and understanding of the sort of work in which Reverend Singh was engaged at Midnapore. A man of intellectual vigour, kindliness of heart and simple piety, he was well known and loved about Calcutta, where he cut a somewhat bizarre figure because of his enormous size and eccentric habit of pedalling through the meanest districts of the city, loudly singing and whistling as he disbursed old Christmas cards from a basket attached to the handlebars of his bicycle to bewildered urchins, who soon learnt to cheer and chase the gigantic 'Padre Sahib' through the streets in the hope of making him fall off.

The Reverend Singh stayed with him at the Oxford Mission on the outskirts of Calcutta from 1 August till the end of December, making monthly visits to Midnapore to see his family and minister to his parishioners, but otherwise living in retreat among the Oxford Brethren, devoting his time to prayer and study. Father Brown, whose lectures he had attended as a student at Bishops' College before the war, became his teacher, his spiritual counsellor, and moreover a friend, who would turn out to be a useful ally in the difficult times that lay ahead. At the end of the year he witnessed his pupil's 'letters testimonial' to the Bishop, proclaiming him in all conscience 'to be, as to his moral conduct, a person worthy to be admitted to the sacred office of priest'.[10] At 8.30 a.m. on 23 December, a bright cold-weather morning, in St

Mary's Church, Calcutta, Joseph Amrito Lal Singh, dressed for the last time in Deacon's cassock, surplice and stole, before a congregation of his family, friends and those clergy of the Diocese who would take part in the Laying-on-of-Hands, was ordained to the priesthood.

Chapter Two

The land of the Reverend Singh's missionary forays
against the heathen lay to the west and south of Midnapore, a natural border country where the alluvial plains
of Bengal meet the rolling waves of laterite rock that push
down from the highlands of central India to the coast,
creating a more broken and picturesque scenery. The
fertile black earth of flat, neatly cultivated rice swamps
gives way to red murrum and laterite outcrops covered by
scrub jungle and, towards the frontiers of the province,
by great tracts of sal forest. The undulating countryside
appears almost park-like, with stately, well-spaced trees,
areas of dense grass, bamboo or cane brakes and pleasantly
unexpected views; but the land is barren and poor,
traversed by fast-flowing rivers and water courses, some
deeply eroded with steep banks, others spread out in wide
expanses of sand and shingle, which flood rapidly but as
soon fall away and go to nothing in the dry season. The
moment it rains, everywhere luxuriant growth burgeons
forth, yet the soil is never closely clothed, the grasses and
vegetation remain rampant and sparse and, underneath,
the red skin of earth can still be seen. The naked gauntness
of the land, common to much of India where the gentle
contours of more intimate landscape are hardly known,
gives it a dramatic beauty, primordial and harsh.

In summer a hot wind blows steadily from the south.
The bare soil of the *khas* dries hard as the undergrowth
withers away, leaving often stunted trees starkly revealed.
It is as if the jungle had been devastated by fire – the
brilliant scentless blossoms of flowering shrubs and bright

wing flashes of silent birds, residual flames flickering in the autumn heat. An arid, inhospitable land, it is nonetheless densely populated; villages, hidden discreetly behind green clumps of bamboo, guarding their wretched clusters of paddy-fields, emerge frequently from the pervasive scrub; but as the scenery changes and the sal forest begins to predominate, signs of human habitation become increasingly rare. 'The further one goes from the town,' the Reverend Singh wrote, 'he finds the scattered Jungle becoming thicker and thicker. About forty miles off, this Jungle becomes very dense and gloomy. Here and there only footpaths are visible to go into the Jungle, and cart ruts are seldom found. A few miles beyond, no footpath or cart rut can be seen. The vast area of this dense jungle is impenetrable, the big sal trees being heavily entwined with thick creepers of enormous size spreading over the trees a beautiful canopy of chequered foliage . . .'[1]

The shade of a sal forest appears almost continuous. As the species is gregarious and thickets of its saplings grow extremely close together, other varieties are mostly excluded, which imposes a remarkable uniformity and architectural beauty on the formation of the forest. The sal itself, a magnificent tree, tall and straight with a pale smooth bark, soars up branchless to its head, which spreads out into a shock of refreshingly green leaves, something like those of a Spanish chestnut. Much in demand as timber, the old sal forests have mostly been cleared now, but in the Reverend Singh's day, although felling had already been going on for a considerable time and the Santals had cleared large areas for cultivation, substantial tracts were still standing in primary splendour. Like most people who travel through them the padre was not able to resist their fascination. In an account of his early missionary voyages, he wrote lyrically:

The scenery is so beautiful and enchanting that it is difficult to describe. In the forest the sun could not be seen . . . only a ray of sunshine . . . here and there during mid-day, peeping through the trees, bathing its focus with a golden hue glorious and superb. In the open you could see at times a pack of deer grazing on the luxurious grass, but as soon as they came to know that we were approaching, they sprang up in a body and vanished, leaving only the dust in a smoky form covering the whole place. It was a glorious silence inside the Jungle and the serene calm pervaded the whole area bespeaking the Divine presence in the wood. On a cloudy day you could see the beautiful Peacocks dancing on the trees and on the creepers forming like swings from one tree to another. It was a pleasant scenery, and I dare say it is only in the lot of the Sikaries to see and realize such beauty in the Jungle.[2]

In many respects Singh's early missionary tours had as much to do with hunting as they did with evangelizing, for not only was he a keen sportsman himself, but his Santal guides, often thirty or forty strong, accompanied him, as well he realized, 'for the love of wild game'. He excused them on the grounds that they had to eat and that skins and trophies were a useful way of supplementing their income. 'This was a grand opportunity provided by the Lord Himself,'[3] he declared staunchly, mindful no doubt of his readership in the diocesan magazine. On tour he always carried with him two guns and a good supply of cartridges, but on long expeditions ammunition sometimes ran short and he would have to resort, not without pleasure, to the weapons of his companions, which usually included an arsenal of bows, knives, battle-axes, flintlocks, spears, horns and hunting drums. Where the Santals went on foot the padre, who was a strong walker, always accompanied them, while his servants followed with the bullock carts. They travelled mostly by night when the animals gave a better performance and there was no need to make stops for feeding. An empty kerosene can fixed under each cart and a stick tied to one of the wheels served as a primitive ratchet that made a noise as they went along to avoid any unexpected encounters with leopard, bear or tiger, all of which preferred to walk by night along roads

30

and cart tracks to spare their pads the roughness of the jungle floor. The men carried long torches made of bamboo poles with a wick of rags stuffed down one end and soaked in oil for the same reason, and if the party had to spend the night inside the forest they would always sleep within a circle of protective fires.

As well as the tools of his trade – bible, leaflets, religious pictures, magic lantern slides – the Reverend Singh carried with him the usual accoutrements of camp life, from galvanized tub and canvas *chagals* for carrying water to the obligatory medicine chest containing quinine and Epsom salts for malaria, and in case of snake bite permanganate of potash. But the practical advantages of keeping equipment light were reinforced by the necessity, due to the extreme shyness of the more remote tribal people with whom Singh was attempting to make contact, of avoiding giving the impression of an invasion. On his earlier voyages he discovered that the aboriginals often ran away and hid in the jungle when they heard he was coming. Assured by his Santal guides that it was his missionary canonicals and *sola topi* which frightened them, he took instead to wearing a simple *gamcha* or loincloth: 'We had to give up our costume, changing it into their mode of dressing and making ourselves just like them in appearance. This went on for several years till they got accustomed to us, and understood us to be their friends.'[1] It was a slow process and a hard, even dangerous life that at times might have seemed unrewarding had not Singh's true missionary zeal and enterprise been compounded by his great love of the jungle, which the more he learnt of its ways and its inhabitants grew accordingly. It was a common enough syndrome, shared by any number of British District Officers who were devoted to their jobs for the days they could hope to spend under canvas, and who, when they talked of loving India, really meant her forests and her jungles. But their work did not suffer on account – in fact, rather the opposite – and neither did the

31

Reverend Singh's, whose impressive though probably exaggerated bag of 700 Santal converts testifies that he did more with his time in the jungle than shoot tigers.

The Santals were by no means the only tribe or scheduled caste to receive the benefit of his missionary intentions, but theirs was the strongest, most pervasive culture in that part of the district and at the same time the most receptive to Christianity; besides which Singh admired them as a simple, carefree and independent people, with whom he imagined rather wistfully that he enjoyed a special affinity. His attitude towards them was nonetheless paternalistic, approving the Santal character for being honest, open, gentle and brave, while deploring its childlike hedonism and enslavement to superstition. He had no doubts about the fitness of his cure, no compunction in supplanting the Santal story of Genesis with his own, in forbidding their favourite pastime of getting drunk on rice beer, when they would sing and dance all night, in banning recitals of their erotic love poems; nor indeed did he have any understanding that by impugning their Gods and institutions he was undermining the whole structure of their society; yet he was not above learning from them and always showed interest in the customs he was so earnestly and righteously engaged in destroying. Through them he discovered many secrets of the forest; and for knowledge of how to call up red jungle fowl by handclapping, or take advantage of a sloth-bear's partiality to the intoxicating fruit of the mohua tree, or mark the passage of time by the withering of a sal leaf – the Reverend Singh became a better *shikari* and perhaps too a more effective missionary, for the Santals, as much impressed by the padre's physical appearance, by his fearlessness and stamina and strength as any offer of salvation, appreciated his unfeigned interest in things they knew and loved.

The early missionary tours were voyages without destination. Guided by his companions, the Reverend

Singh wandered through the forest moving on from village to village, here and there preaching the gospel in Santali, but always concentrating on preparing the ground for return visits. Whenever possible he persuaded a handful of men from each village to accompany them a short while for the sake of hunting, and then allowed them to return home where hopefully they would spread the Word or at least create interest among their friends and relations. It was hardly an aggressive campaign and as a result hostility was rarely encountered. Once shyness had been overcome the band of Christians was everywhere received with the hospitality for which the Santals are famous. Embarrassed sometimes by the effusion of their welcome, and especially by the ancient Santal custom of washing the feet of any stranger who crossed the village boundaries, the padre soon got used to what he interpreted as a potentially Christian mark of respect and humility. Whenever the Santal women approached him with brass pitchers balanced gracefully on their hips, their white saris not unlike the robes of neophytes and their raven black hair tied behind in a thick knot, decorated with flowers and a twist of red silk, he would return the compliment by giving them his blessing.

Santal villages, although they vary in size, consist of identically built adobe and thatch houses arranged to a more or less fixed pattern along a single wide and neatly-kept 'street'. Consequently the Reverend Singh had difficulty in distinguishing between them and, since one part of the great sal forest was very much like another, he often had only a hazy idea of where his travels were taking him. There was no clearly delineated border inside the forest between Bengal and Orissa and sometimes he crossed over, inadvertently at first, into the neighbouring feudatory state of Mayurbhanj, which lay beyond the bounds and jurisdiction of his parish; but, knowing that apart from rival missionaries no one would really object if he were to extend his mission field to include Santal villages on both sides of the border – he could always plead disorientation – the padre soon took to working in Mayurbhanj on a deliberate and regular basis. One of the villages he visited there, a remote hamlet called Denganalia, which lies on the edge of dense forest due south of Salgaria and the Bengal border some four miles into Mayurbhanj, although in no way different to other small villages in the neighbourhood, was yet to play a significant part in the extraordinary saga with which the Reverend Singh was about to become closely involved.

In Denganalia the Santals gave the following account[5] of what happened in the forest not far from the village one bright moonlit night in late November – the year was 1914, or thereabouts. Whether the Reverend Singh visited Denganalia between 1914 and 1920, and whether he heard this story from the Santals then or at any other time is not on record, but there can be little doubt that the Santals' story is directly connected with the events that would take place a few years later in the same part of the forest and which would change the missionary's life.

As it rose beyond the tops of the sal, throwing irregular plumes of black and silver crested leaves into relief against the sky, the moon reached down where it could find breaks in the canopy to the floor of the forest. Over open ground it drenched the earth with a flat brilliance that defined stone and thorn and each tuft of grass by a sharp monotone shadow, the intensity of its illumination restricting movement beyond the protective shade of the trees to the fleeting disturbances of minute life. Regular patterns of animal activity had been suspended, leaving the deserted glades and clearings ominously still. In the jungle even a slight change in conditions affecting survival will usually weigh to the advantage of the predator.

Driven from the savanna where they had fed from dusk until moonrise on the thin autumn grass, a herd of chital moved off through the forest in search of safer pasture. In the dim light their shadowy movements were almost indistinguishable as they passed between the serried trees and thick brakes of rattan and bamboo, cropping rapidly at the scant vegetation, now and then pausing to lift their heads and test the air for scent of danger. The pallor of rufous-fawn coats spotted with white, the lowest series of spots on their flanks arranged in longitudinal rows like broken stripes, camouflaged them well against the dappled undergrowth. But in leaving the open edges of the forest for the protection of heavy cover they were risking much, limiting their chance of rapid flight, which ultimately is their only effective defence against attack.

A light wind rose in the tops of the trees. The herd drew in under the mantle of an ancient pipal inhabited by a colony of langurs and began to feed on the leaves and fruit which the monkeys carelessly let fall from its high branches. The langur's wasteful habits foster a common interaction between the two species, whereby the deer repay the vigilance of the monkeys, on whom they can rely to give early warning of an approaching enemy, by drawing off an attack should one develop – chital being the preferred prey. The langurs were sitting warily, as they always sit to roost, not on the thicker parts but towards the extremities of the branches, with long grey tails curving down through the leaves to balance their hunched bodies. Intermittently they scanned the surrounding jungle, their watchfulness increasing as the shadows cast by the moon grew shorter.

Approaching down wind of the chital the wolf rapidly closed the gap between them and came to a halt a hundred yards out from the tree. Lowering its head to the ground it laid back its ears, then pricked them up again and peered intently, all its senses straining towards the deer. It moved on again displaying growing excitement, quickening its pace and then slowing down, wagging its tail, seeming anxious to rush forward yet managing to hold itself in check, restrained as if by an invisible leash. The distance closed to less than seventy-five yards. Under the tree, standing close to its buttressed silvery trunk, the chital, although still unaware of being at risk, were beginning to show signs of restlessness, infected by the nervous chattering of the langurs who had already sensed danger. A prelusive hush swept the jungle like a bow-wave in the path of the advancing wolf. At sixty yards one of them saw it break cover and gave the alarm – a noise like a sneeze followed by a cry of 'Khok, khok, khok', which was taken up briefly by the rest of the troop as they vanished about the byways of their roosting tree, hiding behind heavy boughs and knots of foliage, skilfully drawing branches together to screen themselves from view. Although they had little to fear from the wolf, some of them fled the pipal altogether, springing away from branch to branch and, with flying leaps between trees, disappeared up into the high canopy.

At the first note of warning the chital, uncertain of which way to run, made a sudden headlong dash through the undergrowth, and headed straight towards the enemy. If they had kept going then, they might have got away, but their first scent of the wolf when they were almost on top of it, stopped them in their tracks. A grey shadow swiftly detached itself from the indefinite line of scrub and crouched down in front of them, not fifty feet away, blocking their path. The two leading stags with antlers under velvet raised their stubbled heads in gestures of defiance; amid the soft bleating of fawns and the grunts of anxious mothers they stood their ground and returned the wolf's impassive stare. Inhibited by the gaze of its prey, a wolf needs the stimulus of a running animal to attack. But the chital could only delay the inevitable: in the end they would have to run just as surely as the wolf would give chase.

Already it had singled out its victim, a withered old buck standing a little away from the herd. Darker in colouring than the others, with two false points on each brow tine where it joined the main beam of his antlers, he was long past his prime and a pack of wolves would have made short work of him; but a lone animal, grown accustomed to hunting for hares and bandicoots and other small fry, stood less than an even chance of a kill. The confrontation began to draw out, tension easing as the wolf turned its head more often to avoid the eyes of the deer; both seemed ready to relax their guard when, unaccountably, the buck wheeled and charged off through the trees, and the wolf went after him. The rest of the herd bolted, scattering in every direction, plunging through the undergrowth, offering easy targets at each twist and turn of their laboured flight. The wolf concentrated on the buck. This was the critical stage of the hunt: if it failed to get close in these first few seconds it would lose its only chance to attack, for unsupported it could never hope to run the buck down. At full tilt, bounding after its prey, it made a lunge for the flank and missed, its teeth snapped on air with a noise of boards being clapped together, the buck swerved, jinked and with an extra burst of speed showed his assailant a clean pair of heels. Disadvantaged by the loss of momentum, the wolf quickly fell behind and made no attempt to recover the ground. It ran on a little way before slowing to a trot, then, giving up the chase altogether, turned back on its tracks.

Panting a little after its exertions, but otherwise un-affected, the wolf fell into an easy rhythmic gait, loping along purposefully with elbows held in and paws turned outward, its forefeet swinging in the same line as its hind feet on each side, in that smooth gliding motion which characterizes the species and, notwithstanding its slightly crouched hindquarters, makes it one of the most graceful of animals. Smaller, of slighter build and with a thinner shorter coat suited to its tropical habitat, the Indian wolf (*canis lupus pallipes*) differs in outward appearance from its northern relatives, but not enough to be classified as a separate species. Superficially the Indian wolf has more the look of a jackal or a dog: the mane, ruff, hairy cheeks and bushy tail which distinguish the grey wolf of the arctic tundra are scarcely evident, though the pale yellow eyes, permanently alert expression and deadly arrangement of teeth quickly dispel any illusions of domestication. Its colouring can vary from a light ochre to rusty brown with darker guard hairs evenly distributed over the neck, back and tail and whitish underparts (which have earned it the epithet, 'pale-footed wolf'), creating from a distance an overall impression of greyness.

Behaviour, hunting methods, denning habits and character, though necessarily adapted to a different environment, are very similar to those of northern wolves. Formerly a predator of wide open spaces evolved to hunt the herd animals of the plains, the Indian wolf was driven through competition with man to take refuge in the mountains (a Himalayan sub-species – *canis lupus laniger*) and in the forests and jungles of the lowlands. Although it still prefers to hunt in packs over open ground, in the forest, where it could not make such good use of its speed and stamina for the pack tactics of running animals down, the wolf soon learned to live off smaller prey and mostly hunted singly or in pairs. Its range became more limited and its diet more varied, but its innate sociability, the strength of family bonds and capacity for emotional attachments, which are evolved features of a hunting pack's life, remain unchanged. The wolf family, born as early as November or December, in a litter of three to eight cubs, usually stay with their parents, with periods away from home, until they reach full adulthood at two or three years, when they will leave to mate and start their own families. If they do not succeed in pairing off they may return to the family in the role of uncle or aunt; a widowed wolf, who will not usually take a second mate (wolves being strictly monogamous) may do the same, so that the number of wolves living together at any time may be high, but numbers will always be regulated according

38

to the food supply. On the whole, the forest environment encourages small families.

Shortage of food sometimes forces the wolf to make depredations on domestic stock, earning it the infamous reputation which it has enjoyed for centuries throughout most of its range. In India, however, men did not come to fear and hate wolves or to attribute to them the evil characteristics for which the European wolf is so well known in folklore and mythology; and this despite the fact that the Indian wolf, according to district records, was held responsible for the deaths of more human beings than any other animal after the tiger. Contrary to popular opinion wolves, it is now thought, have rarely attacked men, but in India they were known – particularly in times of famine, which threatened the survival of both men and animals – to prey on defenceless human beings, becoming bold enough to enter villages and attack the sick and elderly or steal children. In 1926 in the districts of Bareilly and Pilibhit, United Provinces, ninety-five people were killed by wolves. The victims were mostly young children, favoured because of their size and availability: Indian mothers would take their young with them when they went to work in the fields, leaving their babies in baskets close by, but often without proper supervision and on the very edge of the jungle. No obstacles were placed in the wolf's path: on the rare occasion when a child was seen being carried off, little or no attempt was made to go after them, for Hindus believed that even one drop of wolf's blood shed anywhere near a village would make their fields infertile. The Santals, however, were bound by no such taboo and wolves, like most other animals of the forest, were considered fair game.

The wolf broke stride and stopped, lowering its head to investigate a new scent. A hind left cover close by and made off hesitantly in the direction of the pipal tree, halting every few yards to look back over her shoulder. Apparently forewarned, the wolf ignored her and continued along its path; not far from where the dam had been standing in the lee of a dense thicket, it came upon her fawn hopelessly entangled in a wreath of blackthorn. Without altering its pace it sprang at the struggling creature, dragging it free from the thorn and pinning it to the ground in a single fluid movement. It tore out its throat, lapping quickly at the blood that gushed from the wound, and ripped away a large chunk of flesh from the neck, which it bolted with a few convulsive shakes of the head. The fawn's spindly white legs flailed for a moment in defensive reflex as its belly was slashed open and its lights spilled smoking on to the ground, then it lay still. With furtive glances all about, the wolf crouched down beside the carcass and began to eat more discriminately, tearing off long strings of fat from the intestinal membrane and chewing them with the nice deliberation of a dog champing stems of grass. The muscles on the back of its neck rippled unevenly with the excitations of its jaws, the delicate guard hairs of its mane quivering under a band of light that fell almost vertically through the trees and seemed to chain the animal to the roof of the forest.

The harsh cry of a jungle fowl sounded the all-clear. Life in that quarter of the jungle had received the next temporary reprieve. While the wolf fed, immediate danger was allayed. Gradually the familiar sounds of the night and other noises, peculiar to forests, often unexplainable, returned. The wolf pulled the half-eaten carcass into the thicket, scraped earth over it and made off.

Not far from the kill, as the crow flies perhaps two or three miles – the Santal method of measuring distance by the length of time it takes a fresh sal leaf carried in the hand to turn brittle is never very accurate – the wolves had made their den in the enlarged burrow of a porcupine. From under a flat piece of laterite on the edge of a clearing the main entrance, partly concealed by a plum-bush, commanded a limited view across the dried up *nullah* of a   40 stretch of open scrub bounded on one side by a tamarind grove, marking the site of some long-deserted village or cultivation, and the forest wall on the other. There was a second entrance, a tunnel running back into the jungle immediately behind the den, but the two young Santals from the near-by village of Denganalia, who kept watch on their activities, had not seen the wolves use it since they first moved in soon after the end of the rains. For more than three weeks the female wolf had not left the den at all, coming only to the entrance to receive the food, brought by her mate, and either eating it there in the den-mouth or taking it back inside, alone. The male made no attempt to follow her – had he done so he would certainly have been rejected – but remained in the vicinity, lying up in the undergrowth close behind the den during the day and ranging more freely by night. After the birth of the whelps some fifteen days ago he had become more wary and it was only due to their exceptional tracking skill that the Santals had been able to keep up their observation of the animals without disturbing them. Since then they had stepped up their own campaign of waiting for the moment when the female would first leave the den to a nightly vigil.

In position, squatting in the broad fork of the tamarind tree since well before dark, they were wrapped in lengths of cotton, thicker and longer than those which made up their ordinary loin-cloths, to protect them from the sudden chill of dew-fall: in a sal forest, the drop in temperature at night can be a serious hazard; and, as a safeguard against snakes, panthers, and perhaps the wolves themselves, each carried his *kudi*, an instrument combining the virtues of axe, hoe and spade, tucked into his waistband. From where they sat overlooking the *nullah* not more than thirty yards from the entrance to the den, by the insidious glare of the moon they could make out every detail of the den-mouth and beyond it see far enough back into the jungle to locate the opening of the second entrance. Their view of the clearing, however, framed by a careful arrangement of the feathery leaves and long sickle-shaped fruit of the tamarind, was restricted to the area immediately surrounding the den: they had to be constantly on the alert in order not to miss anything.

When the wolf finally came that night there was no warning. Distracted a moment by a slight disturbance behind the plum-bush that covered the den mouth, they looked back and he was there already, standing immobile in its shadow, calling with a low whine to his mate, whose head had appeared beyond the fringe of the dark hollow. She emerged fully and stood crouching in a submissive posture to greet him, wagging her tail as she swung her hindquarters sideways against him. Keeping her ears pinned back she pushed up at his muzzle with her nose and, lifting one forepaw in a playful gesture, began nipping and licking excitedly at his mouth as if begging for food. The wolf had brought nothing with him. He often came back empty-handed, but this time it was clear from the behaviour of the female, who continued to lick greedily at his teeth, that he had certainly eaten and probably killed in the last hour. The significance was not lost on the two men watching from the tamarind. The wolf might have made a kill and then been interrupted while eating or even driven off by a rival predator; but there was another possibility – that he had cached it somewhere and wanted his mate to leave the whelps and return with him to feed on the carcass. If this was the case, however, and that moment which the Santals had been waiting for so patiently had at last arrived, the wolves showed no signs of breaking their routine of the past few weeks. When the reunion was over, they went their separate ways, the female back inside the den and her mate into the jungle, leaving the tree-bound onlookers to their disappointment. A second visit from the wolf seemed unlikely but they could not risk abandoning their post before morning; while one of them slept, the other continued to keep watch.

If the moon had been less bright, he would probably have seen nothing. As it was he could not be certain, but half asleep, staring over at the den and beyond it into the trees he thought he saw a shadow, a spirit rather, some *bonga* of the tamarind grove, rise out of the ground and melt back between the grey stanchions of the forest. Only after it vanished did he realize that the apparition had manifested itself in the very spot where the second entrance to the den had its opening. With the realization that they had almost been outwitted, fear evaporated and he woke his companion. They waited for a long time before climbing down, and they waited again at the foot of the tree. But there was no sign of movement. They unhooked their *kudis* and advanced quickly towards the den. One of them slipped on the steep bank of the *nullah* dislodging a little earth. Nothing stirred, no reaction to the noise, no wolf leaping from the den mouth or charging out of the undergrowth to challenge them. They approached the entrance and with a few blows of a *kudi* cut back the plum-bush. Inside they could hear the whimpering of the pups. They began to dig out the opening. Luckily the passage was not more than a few feet long and the earth soft and loose. Cautiously at first, for they had heard of she-wolves remaining in the den with their cubs to the very last, one of them crawled into the widened mouth and without difficulty retrieved the six struggling pups, handing them one by one to his companion, who placed them in the deep basket they had brought along for the purpose. As soon as they had secured their prize, the two men hurriedly kicked some of the earth back into the gaping den mouth in a token attempt to cover their traces and ran from the clearing, and all the way back to the village, constantly looking over their shoulders to see if they were being followed. They knew well enough that a wolf would only attack under extreme and direct provocation, but they were aware, too, that any animal suddenly deprived of its young may behave erratically. It was not until they had reached the palisades of the village that they felt safe enough to be a little elated by their success. In two days' time, they would take the cubs to the local '*hat*', the weekly fair and market at the village of Kuarh, some two-and-a-half miles north of Denganalia, where if they were lucky enough to avoid competition from leopard, bear and even tiger cubs, they would sell them for a few annas apiece. It was not much of a return for all the long cold nights spent sitting up and watching from the tamarind tree, but Santals from a small jungle hamlet, finding money hard to come by at the best of times, could be happy with little in these lean war years. They celebrated with a jug of rice beer.

Later that night they heard prolonged howling from the jungle and knew that the wolves had finally discovered their loss. They checked again that their huts and the compound, in which they had put the whelps, were secure. They had heard a story about a Santal from another village who had stolen the cubs of a tigress in similar circumstances, only she had come to the house in the middle of the night and taken her cubs back, leaving the man's wife, who had woken and cried out in alarm, so badly mauled that she died from her wounds. Sometime just before dawn the howling sounded very close. It came in short bouts, every half-an-hour or so until first light, when it ceased and was not heard again until the following evening. For several nights, even after the cubs had been taken and sold for a poor price in the market, the wolves came and howled outside the village. During the day sometimes they were heard by women gathering roots and herbs in the forest and occasionally they were seen. On the first day, somewhere not far from the village, a party of women were followed and pestered by the she-wolf. The animal behaved in a strange, distressed manner, rolling over as if in pain and dragging her belly along the ground, emitting short plaintive cries. At one point she came so close that the women had to drive her away by throwing sticks at her. 44

They noticed that where she had been lying the earth was made wet by milk streaked with blood.

After a few days the wolves moved away to another part of the jungle and, as far as anyone can remember, were not seen or heard again near Denganalia. Some years later when the village was haunted by another she-wolf in rather different circumstances, none of those who had seen the mother with the gorged and lacerated teats roaming the forest in search of her cubs, would be able to say whether or not it was the same animal. Indeed, it would not occur to them to make a comparison between a wolf and a creature of the spirit world.

It happened in 1916, during the long summer months of April and May when the Santals' tiny paddy fields that skirt the edge of the jungle are baked iron-hard by the sun and the men work all day in the heat and dust breaking up the earth, to make it ready for sowing by the first rain. The previous year in Mayurbhanj the harvest had been disappointing and rice stocks, intended to last until October, were already running low: if the rains came late they could expect severe hardship by the following season. But though rice is the staple food, unlike his Hindu neighbours whose diet is restricted by religion, the Santal may eat almost anything and can survive where even a rat will starve. All the produce of the forest, the roots, berries, leaves and grasses, the meat of tiger, bear and porcupine, of crows, snakes and frogs, even ants and termites, may be a source of nourishment to him, and where no fresh meat is available he will eat carrion.

While they waited for the monsoon to break, searching the sky each evening for the sign of a barred cloud in the west, propitiating the tribal deities as the days grew steadily fiercer and the food supply dwindled, the Santals turned as they did every year at this time to their traditional occupation of hunting. Towards the end of the hot weather conditions were particularly favourable, for as the jungle dried out and the undergrowth withered away the animals, deprived of cover, and being forced to travel further for food and water, were more often exposed to danger and generally in a weaker condition than at other times of the year. The Santals, who as a rule hunted individually or in small village groups, took advantage of their plight and organized cooperative hunting expeditions with neighbouring villages and tribes that often led to slaughter on a massive scale. A regular fixture in the tribal year, these expeditions involving the deployment of hundreds of men over vast tracts of jungle took place under the auspices of the state of Mayurbhanj, chiefly so that the Maharajah could have some control over the massacre of game and take part in the sport if he wished, but also because any large assembly of armed men presented, if not a threat to Government, at least the potential for some kind of disturbance. In the summer of 1916, as the preparations for Deshua Sendra, the most important tribal hunt of the year, got under way, that potential was realized.

The essential information about the hunt – when it would take place – had been carried through the jungle by the traditional means of a knotted string, known as *Gira gath*, brought by messenger from village to village and untied one knot at a time by each head-man, who always left the correct number of days in knots that remained until the date of the hunt before passing it on. Details that demanded less accuracy, such as the number of men required from each village, where the hunters should congregate at the start, and meet up again at the end, were left to the messengers. On this occasion they were also responsible for carrying some additional information that turned out to be the cause of all the trouble.

How the rumour got started is not known, but it was based on the news that the Santals, among other tribes, were soon to be recruited as coolies for the war effort. Although Mayurbhanj was a feudatory state and not part of British India, the Maharajah, Puri Chandra Bhanj Deo, 46 was a keen supporter of the Raj, and having himself served with distinction in the war, saw no reason why the aboriginals should not help save India from the Germans. The local *sardars*, or landowners, had been instructed to inform the headmen of the villages under their jurisdiction of the Maharajah's wishes and many had already done so; but the message somehow became distorted and by the time of Deshua Sendra a serious misunderstanding had arisen.

Convinced that they had been told a lie about their recruitment as coolies, the Santals had come to believe that the war was a great village somewhere far away which required each day countless human sacrifices in order to prosper, and that in reality they were to be sent to this village to provide the blood for which it thirsted. Naturally they were not disposed to go, and as this simple but horrifying picture of their fate accompanied the knotted string announcing the day of the hunt through the jungle, a mood of revolt spread among the Santals. And as the warm nights leading up to Deshua Sendra filled with the sound of drumming carried for miles on the still air, old and perennial grievances, chiefly against the rapacity of Hindu money-lenders and landlords, were recalled and the dances and songs of the 1856 Santal Rebellion were performed again with reborn enthusiasm.

On the appointed day the hunt took place as planned. After the customary sacrifice of a red fowl to the gods of the locality, columns of men arranged on four sides of a vast square of jungle, marshalled all at once by the deep reverberative notes of the *sakwa* horns, turned in to face each other and in long wavering lines began to converge on the centre. Behind the hunters and their dogs came the musicians, who set up a regular cacophony on *nagra* drums, bells and cymbals, commenting on the progress of the hunt with changing rhythms that announced the movements of the animals as they ran before them or sometimes broke back through the lines. It was during these

47

initial stages of the hunt, still early in the morning, that in the north-eastern section of the jungle area covered by the people of Denganalia, Topera, Bhadua Sol and other near-by villages, a couple of wolves were said to have outwitted the hunters by lying low until they had passed by and were then seen breaking cover and running off 'free and laughing'. They were remembered – though there may have been some confusion here with what occurred later – because one of the hunters claimed that the wolves had been accompanied by another animal; he had only caught a glimpse of it and could not give it a name, but what he had seen for some reason the man was unwilling to describe.

After the hunt was over the tribes returned to their villages to divide up the spoils. Later the women had brought the men rice beer and then left them to feast, drink, talk, sing and dance their way through the night; but discussion soon turned from hunting to politics and the mood of gaiety reverted to one of apprehension over the cruel edict that would send them away as sacrifices to the 'great village of blood'. The following day, instead of dispersing and returning to their villages in the usual way, several bands of tribesmen in the south of the district, still inflamed with drink and full of terror at the prospect of their imminent destruction, went on a rampage through one of the more prosperous Hindu villages, where an extortionate money-lender was known to live, causing considerable uproar and some bloodshed. The police and local militia were promptly called out, which resulted in a *mêlée*; though the Mayurbhanj government, anxious not to provoke the Santals into open rebellion as in Bengal during the 1856 uprising, withdrew its forces as soon as the leaders agreed to talk. After the grievances of the Santals had been aired and their fears of being sent off to war put to rest, the situation defused itself and everyone went home. There were no reprisals but the Deshua Sendra was banned for the following year and in future it 48 was made illegal to pass the knotted string as a means of calling together the tribes for any purpose whatever.

In Denganalia and other villages of the Muruda district, the troubles had been contained even before the hunt began, chiefly by the action of the local *sardar*, Gopabandha Pattanaik, who, being forewarned of the Santals' despair over the recruitment question, had visited on horseback as many as possible of the ninety or so villages in the locality for which he and his brother were responsible, to explain the misunderstanding. But those not involved in the rioting had nonetheless made common cause with their fellows in the south, for the bond of kinship among Santals is strong, and for several weeks a mood of dissent and resentment of Hindu authority that was still tinged with fear lingered on in the hearts of many.

Suggestible at the best of times, the people of Denganalia were perhaps more than usually predisposed towards the supernatural after the Deshua Sendra disturbances. When a small hunting party returning to the village through the forest one evening at sundown reported having seen a small creature that was neither animal nor human darting about between the sal trees until it vanished as if swallowed by the shadows, the village elders at once declared that this was a malevolent spirit, a *bonga* or *bhut*, come to haunt them and to succeed where the Hindus had failed in carrying them off to the village of blood. A second apparition in another part of the jungle some days later did nothing to dispel their fear and when it was revealed that on both occasions the '*bhut*' had been accompanied by a female wolf, although it was agreed that this must be the same animal sighted during the hunt, the wolf, too, was given supernatural status and from then on there could be no connection made between this wolf-spirit and any living animal. No attempt was made therefore to hunt or drive off the creatures and the places in the jungle where they had been seen were given a wide berth. The villagers placed themselves in the hands of their *naeke* or priest

49

who led them to invoke the aid of Maran Buru, the presiding Deity of the Santals, to make sacrifices of blood at the sacred grove at the junction of the two roads north of the village, to leave offerings of rice beer for the boundary deities and pray to the gods of the forest to protect and deliver them from the *bhuts*, and confound their evil intentions.

In different circumstances the villagers might have appealed to their local *sardar*, Mr Pattanaik, for temporal help; but in the aftermath of the Deshua Sendra *débâcle*, there was little wish for contact with an authority which many still believed wanted to send them to the war. At that time the Santals believed the malevolent power of the demons, which none could doubt who had been unfortunate enough to set eyes on them, was so strong that it could only be countered by magic.

The 'demons' continued to be seen about the forest by the people of Denganalia until the monsoon broke, when the dreadful apparitions suddenly ceased. With the release of tension brought by the rain, as the jungle quickly grew green and luxuriant again and the paddy sprang up in the sodden fields, came relief from persecution by evil spirits and the threat of war alike. They were left in peace, the magic of the *naeke* was held to have been effective and for the time being at least the episode was forgotten.

Chapter Three

By late September of 1920 the same grey sullen mass of cloud that gathers morning and evening with monotonous regularity to lower over, then inundate, the Bengal country-side for more than three months of each year, had at last begun to break up, giving way with intermittent down-pours to ever longer periods of clear sky. The rains, never before time, were coming to an end, and it was with a feeling of release, shared by anyone who had spent the long sticky summer cooped up in some office in the plains, that the Reverend Singh, accompanied by Karan Hansda, his driver and cook, and Daniel, his bearer, leaving orphanage and church behind them, set out from Mid-napore by bullock cart to visit the Santal villages in the cool forests of the south.

Although he prided himself on his stamina and fortitude when it came to working in 'the Lord's Vineyard', the padre generally preferred to wait a month or so for the cold weather to come in before starting off on tour, as in September many roads would still be impassable, most rivers dangerous or difficult to cross, and the jungle, fresh and appealing in the mind's eye, would be a dank un-healthy wilderness. A few weeks before, however, he had received a message from Bhagobhat Khatua of Salgaria, still active as his chief reader and catechist among the Santals, asking that he should make an earlier start to his tour than usual. Whatever reason was given it evidently found favour with Singh, for although he stipulated that he had to be back in Kharagpur before the end of the month, he turned up as promised on 20 September in

Chainsole, a sizeable village lying some twenty-eight miles south-west of Midnapore on the north bank of the Subarnarekha. At that time Chainsole was one of the main Christian centres in the district, even boasting a small wattle and daub church which the Reverend Singh had built with the help of the local people several years earlier. The church was the present focus of a long-standing row between the S.P.G. and American Baptists, who over the last half-century had poached each other's converts with such zeal that mutual enmity had slowly communicated itself to their bewildered neophytes. It was most likely in this connection, to settle some dispute, that Singh was summoned there by his Catechist. Yet it can only have been a pretext, for Bhagobhat had a more pressing reason for calling him, which had nothing to do with mission rivalry or, for that matter, with Chainsole; but he had calculated, sensibly enough, that the Reverend Singh would not have come out to the *moffussil* in September on the strength of a ghost story.

Whether or not he revealed the true purpose of their journey before leaving Chainsole, Bhagobhat managed to persuade the Reverend Singh to extend the limited tour they had originally planned. Instead of remaining in the Chainsole area, where villages were accessible and the countryside relatively tame, they set off for the wilds of Nayagaram, taking with them Janu Tudu, one of Singh's Chainsole converts (hotly disputed by the Baptists) to be their pilot in the jungle. They travelled south along the east bank of the Subarnarekha until they reached Dhashragat where, after the usual haggling with the ferrymen, who always had to be reassured that the bullock carts would not sink the ferry, and the usual wait for the wind to turn in their favour, they were punted across the great brown sweep of water, carried and spun around by the current like the frail skiffs that plied the river night and day for the abundance of fish brought by the rains. They finally landed several hundred yards down-stream, a mile or so from the village of Nayagaram. From there they continued south along *kutcha* roads, rough tracks, thick with mud, barely negotiable even by bullock cart, as far as Salgaria, where they spent the night in Bhagobhat's home. The next day, after the Reverend Singh had celebrated before the assembled village, the party set off again, and heading due west crossed the four miles of open savanna and *khas* jungle that lay between Salgaria and the Mayurbhanj border. Half a mile on they came to their destination of Godamuri, one of three tiny hamlets set close together behind bamboo stockades and groves of tamarind, betel and palash trees on the edge of a wide expanse of sal forest. In Godamuri Bhagobhat had arranged for them to stay with a herdsman of the Kora tribe called Chunarem, converted to Christianity by the Reverend Singh some years ago and since become, under Bhagobhat's direction, one of their most reliable and stalwart 'workers in the field'. It was Chunarem, nonetheless, who had extracted a promise from Bhagobhat to do all in his power to bring the padre out to Godamuri as soon as possible to save his people from immediate destruction by evil spirits.

Late that evening, when the Reverend Singh and his party had prayed and eaten and were settling down for the night under the lean-to cowshed in Chunarem's courtyard, their host and his wife came to them in evident distress and, after the customary prevarication, told the padre about the *bhuts* living in the jungle close by the village. Chunarem, who seemed very much afraid, claimed to have seen these 'ghosts' himself at a place they frequented in the heart of the forest about seven miles from there, describing them as *manush-bagha* (man-beasts) with a human form and the head of a devilish animal. At first he could say little else about them that was coherent other than to beg the priest to come with him and exorcise the spot before death overtook them all. Prompted by the Reverend Singh's questions, however, he revealed that the *manush-bagha* had been seen off and on over some period of time at a great distance from Godamuri in the thickest part of the jungle; but because they were far away, apart from offering *pujas* to ward off evil whenever they happened to see them, people ignored the ghosts and forgot about them. Then three or four months ago, just before the beginning of the rains, the *manush-bagha* had begun to appear more frequently, usually at dusk and sometimes in the early morning, much closer to the village. Although *pujas* and sacrifices were offered to drive them away and Chunarem and other Christians had prayed to their God, the ghosts had remained in the vicinity and the people had become so frightened that they wanted to abandon their homes.

The Reverend Singh had been prepared for Chunarem's story by Bhagobhat Khatua, who had used it to explain the state of abject terror in which they had found the people of Godamuri on arrival. Although interested by Bhagobhat's claim that he had heard the same ghost story from reliable sources in other villages, Singh found it difficult to overcome his initial repugnance at what was clearly a case of reversion to primitive superstition. He had reprimanded Bhagobhat for his credulity and together in prayer that evening they had asked that the people of Godamuri should be 'raised from the slimy depths of heathenism, and brought from darkness into the glorious light of our Blessed Lord'.[1] Nonetheless, as Chunarem ended his story with a further desperate plea for help in which he was joined by his wife, the Reverend Singh, finding it impossible to doubt their sincerity, and by now not a little curious, agreed to go with him to the jungle the next day and see the ghosts for himself.

The expedition was not a success. Travelling mostly on foot, since the jungle was too thick for the bullock carts to pass, they ventured some six or seven miles into the interior to the south-east of Godamuri in the direction of Amarda Road. Arriving a little before dusk at the place supposedly haunted by the ghosts, identified by a very

54

large termite mound, they waited in vain for something to happen as the gloom of the forest gathered around them. At nightfall the Reverend Singh called off the vigil. 'We had failed to see any sign of it,' he wrote in his journal under the entry for 24 September. 'I thought it was all false and did not care much.'[2] But if he was feeling a little foolish for allowing himself to become involved in the ghost hunt, he considered that he had at least done his duty by Chunarem. The herdsman, however, was far from being reassured and although easily prevailed upon to lead the disgruntled and rather nervous party away from the haunted spot, he insisted that they should come back and try again the next day. The Reverend Singh refused him on the grounds that he had to return to Kharagpur and with that the party withdrew to the near-by village of Denganalia.

While they were setting up camp the padre received a visit from the village *mondhal* or headman, Mr Babusahu, and others known to him from earlier missionary visits, who again told him of the ghosts in the forest that were terrorizing the neighbourhood and begged him to rid the place of them. The *mondhal* claimed that he had reported the matter to the local *sardar*, Mr Pattanaik, and requested his help several times, but that nothing had come of it and that now they had given up all hope. Impressed, despite himself, by the powerful influence which the 'ghosts' seemed to exert on the imaginations of the villagers, the Reverend Singh reluctantly agreed to change his mind and to pay a second visit at dawn to the haunted part of the forest. In talking to the *mondhal* he had also learnt two interesting pieces of information that had not emerged from the garbled accounts of Chunarem and others. The *manush-bagha*, it seemed, for the last four months had actually been living inside the enormous ant mound, coming out and going in by the large holes in its base; and whenever they were sighted, more often than not it was in the company of wolves, albeit wolf-spirits.

The second expedition turned out to be as abortive as the first. They watched concealed behind trees for more than an hour, but saw no sign of wolf, ghost or any kind of activity about the ant mound. The Reverend Singh, however, had begun to entertain the possibility that the *manush-bagha* might not after all be a figment of the primitive imagination but some rare species of wild animal never seen before in those parts, and therefore like anything strange and new regarded by the aboriginals as enchanted. His curiosity as a hunter aroused and anticipating perhaps the addition of a unique trophy to the rather dim collection on his study wall, before leaving the place he ordered the villagers to build a *machan* or shooting platform in a large mohua tree, its trunk noticeably scarred with the clawmarks of bears, that stood about fifty yards away from the ant mound and commanded a fairly good view of the surrounding jungle. He advised them how to construct the *machan* and where to position it in the tree at a height of about fifteen feet above the ground, and warned against cutting the wood for the platform in the vicinity of the ant mound or making any disturbance which might frighten the animals or 'ghosts', as he was still obliged to call them, away from their lair. Although they were afraid to remain there without him the Santals agreed to do what the padre asked on the understanding that he would return as soon as possible and kill the ghosts. He gave them his word as a *shikari*.

Later that morning of 25 September the Reverend Singh caught the train to Kharagpur at the Flag railway station in Amarda Road some six miles south of Denganalia, taking with him his bearer Daniel, but leaving behind Bhagobhat, Chunarem and the others to look after the bullock carts and equipment which were still lying up in Godamuri. Since he was unable to give a firm date of return, he arranged with one of them to come back and wait for him there in a week's time. As it turned out he stayed away rather longer than anticipated, kept at home for more than ten days by parish duties and other commitments. During that time he said nothing of his adventures in the jungle to his family or friends in Midnapore, but took into his confidence two Anglo-Indians, who worked as fitters and guards on the railways in Kharagpur and who in the past had sometimes accompanied him on his missionary tours for rough shooting. Their names were Henry Richards and Peter Rose. Of the two he best knew Richards, a tall light-skinned man with a limp, who had lived in Midnapore for some time and been active in church affairs; but he probably first mentioned the story of the ghosts to Peter Rose, since it was to marry his son, Alexander Rose, that he had cut short his tour in Mayurbhanj.

The wedding took place on 28 September at All Saints Church in Kharagpur, and at the reception afterwards in the South Insitute the Reverend Singh was unable to resist telling his old hunting companion of his experiences in the forests of Denganalia which, he claimed, had nearly prevented him from attending the ceremony. Exaggerating a little no doubt, he managed to convince him, as he had by now convinced himself, that there really might be some strange animal living in the haunted ant mound, and suggested that it would be an interesting jaunt if all three of them were to go back there and try and bring it to bag. Rose and Richards needed in any case little persuading. Having arranged to take a fortnight's leave from the B.N.R., for they intended to get some shooting even if the other matter came to nothing, they met the Reverend Singh in Kharagpur a week later, equipped with rifles, camp kit and Mr Rose's field glass, and on the evening of 5 October the three men set off together for the Mayurbhanj border.

They reached Godamuri on Friday, after meeting up with Bhagobhat and the bullock carts en route, and stayed that night in Chunarem's yard. The next morning they went into Denganalia forest to take a look at the home of the ghosts and check that the Santals had built the *machan* according to instructions. The white-ant mound, which they examined through the field glass, taking care not to go too near, stood on the edge of a clearing a short distance from the by-path, which the villagers had used until recently on their way to collect roots and leaves and wood from different parts of the jungle, but had abandoned because of the ghosts. Between ten and twelve feet high (roughly twice average size although termite mounds of twenty feet in those parts were not unheard of), shaped something like a menhir, it reminded the Reverend Singh of a Hindu temple – perhaps the Juggernath in Midnapore with its tall fluted roof in rust-coloured stone corresponding to the red earth and bevelled surfaces of the termite structure. Evidently it had long since been abandoned by the termites else the dome, well-worn by wind and rain, and the cavities around the base of the mound would have been kept repaired; but it seemed possible that larger animals had since taken up residence, as they commonly did, for some of the holes appeared to have been widened and rubbed smooth and looked like tunnels leading to the centre of the mound. There was no telling, however, which of the holes might be the main entrance; the *machan* had been built to overlook the largest and the best worn. After inspecting the platform, sited so that if there was a moon its light would fall from behind the mohua tree on to the ant mound, the Reverend Singh declared everything in order and he and his companions left the place as quietly as they had come. The stage was set.

They returned at about 4.30 in the afternoon and mounted the platform by the rope ladder which hung down on the blind side of the mohua. The last man aboard pulled it up after him. Besides the padre and the Anglo-Indians there was Bhagobhat, Chunarem and perhaps one other on the *machan*. It gave them little room for manoeuvre. The three men with guns sat to the front enjoying an unrestricted view, while the others had to perch as best they could on the spreading branches of the tree. The two

58

railway men carried conventional rifles, the Reverend Singh his favourite 20-bore Westley Richards, which fired shot and ball over and under, but the padre soon handed his piece over to Bhagobhat and concentrated on using the field glass. They settled down to wait, trying to keep silent and still under constant attack from mosquitoes, flying beetles, white jute moths and a myriad of insect species attracted by the strong scent of the mohua – 'the tree of life', as the Santals call it, feeder of men, animals and birds, and supporter of parasitic plants like hoya orchids and climbing ferns, but also a frequent host to snakes. Without making any movement they checked the near foliage while it was still light for any unwelcome guest, looking out particularly for the beautiful but deadly emerald green tree snake: so thin it could easily be mistaken for a twig, its victims were mostly bitten in the face while walking under trees, having failed to spot its tiny lozenge-shaped head poised motionless among the leaves. From the point of view of comfort the mohua was hardly the most suitable place for the *machan*, but that was not the important consideration; the men were all hardened to jungle life and as they waited and watched and listened for any sign of movement from the ant mound, minor irritations were forgotten in the unreasonable expectation that something was bound to happen. The constant whirr of cicadas and other minute instruments in the familiar background music of the jungle, momentarily silenced by their arrival, had returned soon after they had installed themselves, at first to deafen them and then to fall away in their ears to a low generalized hum, almost a silence from which the least irregular noise stood out sharply defined. The soft whistling of green fruit-pigeon and steady whooping of langurs from a near-by wild fig tree would suddenly give way to the rattle of a porcupine's tail quills, a warning sign eagerly interpreted by the watchers on the platform; or a flock of jungle fowl scratching up dead leaves in the lantana would begin to sound like the movement of larger game and somebody's grip would tighten on the stock of a rifle, grown clammy in the cool, humid atmosphere. But nothing came. By half past five the light was fading fast; they felt the evening wind on their faces and heard it in the tops of the sal; it was the time when the animals begin to appear.

On the *machan* the tension rose. Scanning through the field glass the Reverend Singh followed the creeping shapes of pea-fowl through the long grass beyond the mound, here and there catching sight of a green-crested, periscopic head, alertly raised. A little further on he picked up a large grey shape moving slowly between the trees. He lost it in his excitement but caught up with it a moment later only to recognize the shuffling gait and cumbersome stance of a sloth bear climbing on to its hind legs to lick the ant-soil sticking to the trunk of a sal. Although it was a long way out of range he hoped his companions would not see it in case they were tempted to take a shot. They were sound enough men, but in the rather jumpy atmosphere on board the *machan* it was impossible to have absolute confidence in anyone holding a gun. It was almost dark. In the distance the chuckling call of a night-jar sounded like a stone bouncing away over ice. The Reverend Singh had his glass trained on the base of the white ant mound. The eerie form of a large, evil-smelling fruit bat sailed close by the platform on noiseless leathery wings, startling its occupants. Just then Singh saw a wolf emerge from one of the holes and run off into the undergrowth. It was followed in quick succession by a second wolf and a third with two cubs all coming one after the other, as the size of the hole would not allow two to pass together. Behind them he saw something else.

'Close after the cubs,' he noted in his journal,

came the 'ghost' – a hideous looking being, hand, foot and body like a human being; but the head was a big ball of something covering the shoulders and the upper portion of the bust leaving only a sharp contour of the face visible. Close at its heels there came another awful creature exactly like the first, but smaller in size. Their eyes were bright and piercing, unlike human eyes . . .

The first ghost appeared on the ground up to its bust, and placing its elbows on the edge of the hole, looked this side and that side and jumped out. It looked all round the place from the mouth of the hole before it leaped out to follow the cubs. It was followed by another tiny ghost of the same kind, behaving in the same manner. Both of them ran on all fours.[3]

As soon as they saw them, Rose and Richards raised their guns to shoot. The Reverend Singh, engrossed in watching, was only just quick enough to hold up their barrels; offering them the field glass, he said that he felt sure that the ghosts were in fact human children. When they had all had a look through the glass, although visibility was by now extremely poor and the 'ghosts' did not stay long before following the wolves into the jungle, everyone on the *machan* agreed that the creatures most probably were human – except for Chunarem, who could not be persuaded that they were anything but *manush-bagha* and was resentful that no one had tried to shoot them. The Reverend Singh could see that the man was still afraid and did not press the matter. After descending from the *machan*, the party rejoined the bullock carts, which were waiting on the nearest cart track a mile or so away, and returned to Godamuri by late evening.

The next day, 10 October, they saw the ghosts again from the *machan*. This time there could be no doubt about their human origin, but Chunarem, supported by the people of Godamuri and Denganalia, continued to deny the truth. When the Reverend Singh asked them if they would provide some men to help him dig out the white-ant mound and rescue the children, they refused flatly. 'You are only here for a day,' Chunarem told Singh, as he later recalled, 'but we have to live here. When you go away, these *manush-baghas* will play havoc with us and would kill us all.'[4] Retreating stubbornly into the darkness of superstition they left no room for discussion and Singh, who by now had thought of another plan, let the subject drop. Before leaving the area he paid a visit to the near-by village of Nalgoja, where the local *sardar*, Mr Gopabandha Pattanaik, received him with all the courtesy of a Hindu gentleman on the thatched veranda of his house and over light refreshment listened attentively while the padre recounted the extraordinary events of the past night. After hearing his story Mr Pattanaik made profuse apologies for refusing to take the matter seriously until now and politely regretted the unwillingness to cooperate shown by the local people. Offering to help in any way he could (although privately he may have retained some doubts), he suggested that the most sensible course of action would be to send word to Dibakar Bhanj Deo, the Maharajah's hunting officer, to come over from Baripada and organize a hunting party and, with the sanction of the Maharajah, to capture the children. Having already vetoed the suggestion of Rose and Richards, that they should shoot the wolves from the *machan* and try to recover the children themselves, on the grounds that it was too risky – the children seemed to be able to run extremely quickly and if they were not killed by a stray bullet would certainly disappear into the forest before they could catch them – the Reverend Singh felt at first somewhat doubtful about the idea of a hunting party. He was, however, personally acquainted with both the Maharajah and Dibakar, as he explained grandly to Mr Pattanaik; his brother-in-law, Iswari Singh, who had married his sister, Bimolla, worked in the office of the Dewan of Mayurbhanj; and, having shot with Dibakar on several occasions, he believed that he could be persuaded to cooperate in his plan. Insisting that the only safe way to capture the children would be to surround the termite mound and dig out the den, he revealed his intention of going to a distant village, where the people had never heard of the *manush-bagha*, and hiring some men to come back with him to do the job. He agreed to Mr Pattanaik's 62 sending for Dibakar on condition that, if he came, he should await his return before attempting any rescue operation.

The Reverend Singh left Godamuri on 11 October and was away for six days. Accompanied by Rose and Richards he travelled by bullock cart, crossing the border into Bengal and following the road north for some twenty miles or so through the forest of Tapoban until they came to the village of Patherdogra, not far from the old Hindu temple of Tapoban. It is not clear why Singh had to go so far to get help or why the journey took as long as six days. He may have put in some missionary work on the way, or Rose and Richards may have insisted on doing a little shooting; or it may have been that Patherdogra was the nearest village where he could be certain of getting help, since there was a Christian settlement there. The villagers mostly belonged to the Lodha tribe, a criminal caste who were much feared in the district, which was also perhaps an advantage in that they would not be easily influenced by the Santals of Denganalia. Singh often stopped by Patherdogra on his way to or from the villages in the south to visit the Reverend Kenan, who was stationed there and, although an American Baptist, a friend of his. Whether Father Kenan was at home on this occasion Singh does not say; if he was, he may not have told him about rescuing the children in case the story got back to the Lodhas, who as yet knew nothing of the ghosts. 'Here I spoke to the villagers,' Singh wrote, 'to do a job for us in the jungle by cutting for us an opening like a temple door in one of the white ant mounds. I promised them their daily wages and tip money for the work. They agreed and we started back the day following, straight for the haunt of the wolves. None of us told them anything with regard to the ghosts living therein.'[5]

When they reached Nalgoja the Reverend Singh found Dibakar Bhanj Deo, the Maharajah's hunting officer, and Bhaduri Singh, a well-known *shikari* from Baripada, waiting for him at the house of Mr Pattanaik. They had received the king's full permission to carry out the rescue. Dibakar had also managed to persuade the men of Dengan-alia, Kosdia and one or two other villages to take part in the hunt on the understanding that they would not have to go near the haunted lair. Everything was ready. Immediately upon the padre's return word was sent round to the villages. By eight o'clock the following morning, Sunday 17 October, the Santals had taken up their positions in the jungle, in a rough circle drawn at a radius of about a mile from the white-ant mound waiting for the signal. Lasa Marandi of Denganalia, then a young man of sixteen, held a place in the line alongside his father, Gita Marandi, and Motra Maji. He remembers how everyone felt afraid. 'Some of the older men were saying they would rather stand unarmed against the charge of a tiger than come face to face with the ghosts. But at the sound of the *sakwa* horns they raised a shout and we all began to walk towards the cave of the ghosts. It was a still beat and our drums were silent. Many of us believed we were going to our destruction but we also felt sure that Dibakar and the others would succeed in killing the ghosts with their guns and rid the place of them once and for all.'[6]

On board the *machan* Dibakar was less confident. Nobody knew for certain whether the wolves and children were inside the mound; if they were near by in the forest, it was hoped they would run before the beaters and take refuge in the den, but should they choose to double back he was doubtful that the Santal line would hold. On the ground beneath the mohua tree the Reverend Singh waited with the hired diggers, ready to supervise the rescue when the time came. He had told his friends on the *machan*, Dibakar, Bhaduri Singh, Richards and Rose, not to fire on the wolves or any other animals unless human life was in danger and at all costs to avoid risking the lives of the children. If possible he wanted to capture the wolves as well as the children alive.

There was no sign of movement from the termite mound. As the Santals closed in only small game, a few frightened hares and a bandicoot got up before them and ran to and fro across the clearing. Nobody paid any attention. The line of beaters drew to a halt about a hundred yards out from the mound. They stood in silence, just visible from the *machan*, their *gamchas* showing white between the trees and here and there a spearhead or sword catching a ray of sunlight. Dibakar signalled them forward but nothing would induce the Santals to come closer.

The Reverend Singh now stepped forward at the head of the little band of Lodhas and advanced warily on the termite mound. The Lodhas carried *kodalis* for digging, but many were also armed with bows and arrows: although they still knew nothing of the ghosts they had been warned that there might be wolves inside the mound, but instructed not to kill them unless they had to. While half of them began to hack away at the hard brittle surface of the abandoned termitary, the others kept guard. The Reverend Singh stood back a little to watch. Almost as soon as the men began digging two wolves came out round the far side of the mound and ran off towards the beaters. As Dibakar had expected, the line broke at once and the animals escaped. Then a third wolf appeared, a female, which Singh took to be the mother wolf, for instead of running off like the others she made for the Lodha diggers, scattering them to all sides before diving back into the hole. She came out again and raced round, growling furiously and pawing the ground. Lowering her head with bared teeth and ears flattened against her neck, her tail whipping threateningly from side to side, she refused to leave the spot. The wolf made a second charge at the diggers, only this time the bowmen were standing by at close range; before the Reverend Singh could stop them they loosed off their arrows and pierced her through, killing her instantly. In the circumstances it seems doubtful if the animal could have been captured unharmed, at

65

least without injury to the diggers, but Singh blamed himself for what happened. After the event he claimed somewhat dubiously that he was so enraptured by the mother wolf's brave defence of her young (who were still inside the mound) that he became 'dumb and inert' and did nothing. Although aware of the particular interest in preserving the life of the animal, he had failed understandably enough to realize just how important it would turn out to be. In the meantime the rescue of the children was his only concern. He ordered the men to lay down their weapons and return to work, lending a hand himself at digging out the ant mound, still unsure of what they would find.

'After the mother wolf was killed,' Singh wrote, 'it was an easy job. When the door was cut out, the whole temple fell all around, very fortunately leaving the central cave open to the sky, without disturbing the hollow inside . . . The two cubs and the other two hideous beings were there in one corner, all·four clutching together in a monkey-ball. It was really a task to separate them from one another. The ghosts were more ferocious than the cubs, making faces, showing teeth, making for us when too much disturbed, and running back to reform the monkey-ball.'[7] By now Dibakar, Rose, Richards and the others from the *machan* had joined them on the ground and everybody was crowding round to see the ghosts, making suggestions about how to secure them. One of the diggers had already been bitten on the hand and although the Lodhas appeared unafraid of the creatures there was a certain reluctance to handle them. Amid general confusion the Reverend Singh remained firmly in control of the situation. He had the idea of using a make-shift net. 'I collected four big sheets from the men, called in that region *gelap* (the villager's winter wrapper), and threw one of the sheets on this ball of children and cubs and separated one from the other. In this manner we separated all of them, each one tied up in a sheet, leaving only the head free.'[8]

Four struggling, whimpering bundles were laid on the ground a little way off from the body of the she-wolf while Singh and the others inspected their former den. A large cavity set below ground level with as many as seven tunnels leading up to the surface, it was shaped like the bottom of a kettle. The inside walls were smooth and of the same red sand used by the termites throughout the structure, though evidently the wolves or some previous occupant had dug out or enlarged the cavity beneath the mound for their own use. The Reverend Singh, seeing the interior of a wolf den for the first time, was surprised by how clean it was. 'The place was so neat that not even a piece of bone was visible anywhere, much less any evidence of their droppings and other uncleanliness. The cave had a peculiar smell, peculiar to the wolves – that was all.'[9] Dibakar, who had more experience in these matters, explained that wolves always voided their excretions outside the den and that when they were cubs the mother would lick up their faeces and urine until they were house-trained; but in the case of the human children he could only venture a guess. It was not an important question, but like a thousand others that came to mind, many of which they had already discussed for long hours and would continue to do so for years to come, it was un-answerable. They were looking at the only material evidence of the children's life among the wolves, an empty hollow that gave away no secrets. In a few days even the smell would have disappeared. The other witness, perhaps the only one who could have provided them with some explanation, still jerked a little as the Lodhas retrieved their valuable arrows from her carcass.

The bravest among the Santal beaters approached circumspectly to examine the captured ghosts, poking at the white bundles with the butts of their bamboo spears, but retreating in alarm as soon as the matted balls of hair began to twist and turn about and they saw the bared teeth and rolling eye-whites of their former tormentors.

Some expressed surprise that the creatures were so small and not half-beast as they had been led to expect. To others this was only natural since they were *bhuts*, the spirits of children who had died before the initiation ceremony of *chatiar*. It is through *chatiar* that a child becomes a member of Santal society: without initiation the dead cannot achieve the full status of a *bonga* spirit and therefore may not be offered sacrifices at the family altars by their relations. For the Santals, who see the afterworld in terms of relationships with their ancestors and descendants, becoming a *bhut*, a spirit outcast condemned to haunt the forests, an evil being that preys on mortal men, is the worst fate that could befall anyone. They regarded the two creatures wrapped in the *gelaps* with ineffable horror; it made no difference that the spirits had evidently materialized and been rendered harmless; many would not go near them, while others wanted them destroyed.

Ignoring these requests for retribution, the Reverend Singh paid off the diggers, took charge of the children and the wolf-cubs and returned to Denganalia, where he was promptly hailed by the villagers as their deliverer. After taking obligatory refreshment with the headman, he managed to procure two bamboo cages, to which he transferred his captives, paralysed with fear and offering little resistance, under the gaze of the equally frightened but curious crowd that had gathered round the bullock carts. By the early afternoon the party was ready to move on to Amarda village, some two miles distant, where Singh, Rose and Richards had arranged to stay the night at the dak bungalow. The *chowkidar*, Mr Mahato, and his son, Ghambir, greeted them enthusiastically, for the Reverend Singh was a frequent and popular visitor. He used Amarda as a centre for his missionary tours in that area and always stayed at the bungalow, a comfortable stone building, set upon a hillock overlooking an old Hindu temple on the edge of a large tank. Formerly a hunting lodge of the Maharajah it was on a grander scale than most dak bungalows and, in contrast to the simplicity of Chun-arem's cowshed and similar accommodation which they had had to put up with over the last ten days, the Reverend Singh and his friends found it a welcome change. After giving thanks to God for His great mercy in helping them to rescue the children, the three men rested up for a while. Sitting out on the veranda in planters' chairs, carefully arranged for their occupants' enjoyment of the view of the temple and banyan tree reflected in the silver waters of the tank and the smoky-green line of jungle beyond, they drank sweet milky tea brought to them by Mr Mahato and Ghambir, whom Reverend Singh chaffed gently as he always did about becoming a Christian, promising him a good marriage with a beautiful girl if he took the plunge. The *chowkidar* and his son, however, were more interested in hearing about the creatures on the back of the bullock cart, which had been left in the stables, closely guarded over by Karan Hansda and Janu Tudu. Already a small crowd had gathered at the bottom of the hill by the bungalow gate, anxious to see the mysterious ghosts the *shikaris* had brought out of the jungle. News of their capture had travelled before them, and here perhaps the Reverend Singh had his first taste of the inconvenience and even danger which publicity could cause. Only a select few, among them the village *sardar*, Kalandi Saranji, who had arrived rather more promptly than usual to pay his customary respects to the padre, were allowed to satisfy their curiosity.

After they had gone an attempt was made under Singh's supervision to bathe the children. Their bodies were encrusted with dirt and mud, smelt strongly of the wolves' den and appeared from their scratching to be full of fleas and other parasites. But the operation was not a success. The children reacted violently to being touched or to any contact with water. What dirt could be removed revealed a large number of small scars and scratches all over their bodies, and on their elbows, knees and the

69

heels of their hands, heavy callouses – presumably from going on all fours. Although thin, they were otherwise in good condition and apart from their matted hair, long nails that curled over like blunted talons and an inability or unwillingness to stand, they appeared at first physically no different from other human children. They were both girls, one aged about three years old and the other perhaps five or six; the Reverend Singh would sometimes change this estimate, but the consensus held to a two- or three-year age difference. They seemed very small to those who saw them at this stage, perhaps smaller than their actual size because they were constantly in a crouched position, but they could be picked up and carried in the arms without difficulty. There was a reluctance, however, to handle them for fear of being bitten or scratched, since it was considered more than likely that the children were rabid. At the time this may have seemed the most charitable explanation of their wild appearance and ferocious behaviour, which in apposition to a completely blank expression when their faces were in repose, might otherwise be seen to divorce them from the order of human beings.

Later that night there was a small celebration at the bungalow, attended by Dibakar, Bhanj Deo and Mr Pattanaik, and some say the Maharajah himself, who supposedly came over from Baripada to see the children and reward the Reverend Singh for catching them; but there is little evidence to support a royal visit. What is more certain is that the hunters enjoyed an excellent dinner prepared by the Mahatos and afterwards sat long at table in the bungalow's high-ceilinged dining-room, talking over the day's events.

On everyone's mind was the question of how the children ever came to be with the wolves. Dibakar and Mr Pattanaik had already made some inquiries among the villages, starting with Denganalia, to find out if any children had been lost in the last five years, or stolen by 70 wild animals, but there had been no positive response. The Reverend Singh suggested that the girls might have been deliberately abandoned and later picked up by the wolves in the forest, which meant that no one would dare come forward to claim them. Exposure among the Santals was extremely rare but some other tribes in Mayurbhanj still practised it and, although the children were clearly of aboriginal descent, there was no guarantee that they were Santals. Another possibility, suggested by Dibakar, was that the children came from farther afield, even as far as thirty or forty miles away, since wolves in some cases were known to range over a wide territory. The question of their provenance was also complicated by the inability of the people from Denganalia, Godamuri and other villages where the story of the ghosts was known, to associate them with real children or even with real wolves. The saga of the she-wolf, for instance, who had suffered the loss of her cubs five years ago in the forest near Denganalia was not mentioned by the villagers because it did not seem relevant. Around the dinner table, however, the theory was put forward that a she-wolf who had lost her cubs might have stolen a child, left alone by its mother while working in the fields or gathering roots in the forest, as a replacement for her own and taken it back to her lair and suckled it. Alternatively she could have stolen the child for food, a common enough occurrence in jungle districts, only neglected to kill it before reaching the den, where its scent had become confused with that of her cubs, encouraging her to accept it as one of her litter. The problem was complicated by there being two children. The girls, who did not appear to be sisters, were separated by an age gap of two or three years, which suggested that the wolf had taken them probably from different places and almost certainly on different occasions; in other words, the wolf had repeated its experiment in fostering. The possibilities seemed almost infinite. But all were agreed on one thing – if they had not been acquainted with the evidence at first hand, they would have found it un-believable.

Although it is not known for sure whether the Reverend Singh and his companions had heard or read about children being raised by wolves, other than in Kipling and myth-ology, it seems likely that at least one of them would have done so. As recently as 1912 a case of a wolf boy had been reported in the *Calcutta Statesman* and a number of popular books on hunting and jungle life in India contained accounts and references to children being raised by wild animals. Since the appearance of **Mowgli** in 1905 the sub-ject had enjoyed a revival of interest, but its appeal had always rested on unsubstantiated stories rather than fact. To be confronted by the reality of wolf children was as surprising and as shocking as if the phenomenon had never been heard of before, and everyone according to his lights was feeling unsettled and perplexed by what had happened. The Reverend Singh, a little pompously perhaps, tried to put the case for divine intervention, firstly in the original rescue of the children by the wolves (for he stuck to his theory of abandonment), and then again in what they themselves had achieved that day – the return of two of God's children to the human fold. His prayer of thanksgiving was joined in by all as they tried to ignore the long drawn-out howling that came intermittently from the direction of the stables. Later the men went outside on to the veranda to smoke a pipe in the cool night air. Below them the moon, reflected in the glassy waters of the tank, seemed to tremble to the distant pulse of the Santal drums that drifted up from the jungle, celebrating no doubt the capture of the ghosts. From the stables the howling continued unabated, each cry begin-ning on a hoarse and mournful note, and ending up with a shrill, high-pitched wail, not altogether like the howl of a wolf and yet not remotely the cry of a child. They tried to compare the sound with what some imagined were the answering calls of wolves from the jungle, but then Dibakar pointed out that they had been listening to jackals, and soon after the party went back inside and broke up for the night.

From the moment he first sighted the children through Mr Rose's field-glass as they emerged from the white-ant mound, the Reverend Singh had never been in any doubt that it was his duty to rescue them. Although he would come to question the wisdom of this course in future years, wondering if they might not have been happier left alone, regretting particularly the slaying of the mother wolf, he was quite certain at this time that he had taken the right decision. Indeed, it is hard to imagine in the circumstances how anyone in his position could have done otherwise. He was equally certain of his responsibility for the children now that they had been captured. His intention had always been to take them back to the orphanage with him, but immediately this presented a logistical problem since he was due in Midnapore on 21 October to perform the important christening of one of the European officials' children. Three days did not give him enough time to return by bullock cart, which meant he would have to take the train and leave the children and the bullock carts to be brought back by Janu Tudu and Karan Hansda. For obvious reasons he did not want to subject them to the train journey, but he was also doubtful that he could trust even Janu and Karan with two such unpredictable charges over the long road home to Midnapore. Finally, he decided to leave them for a few days in the care of Chunarem at Godamuri and as soon as possible to return and fetch them back himself.

The next morning he delivered them to their new keeper and after helping him to construct a barricade of sal poles in the corner of his courtyard, making a square of roughly eight feet, they released the children from their cage into this makeshift pen. Chunarem was given careful instructions on how to look after them. For food and drink two small earthenware pots, one containing rice, the other water, were placed on the inside of the barricade so that they could be replenished whenever necessary from without. Although the children had as yet shown no interest in either eating or drinking, it was thought that as soon as they recovered from the shock of capture, hunger and thirst would assert themselves in the normal way. The Reverend Singh saw no cause for alarm; the children, if somewhat cowed, seemed healthy enough and Chunarem and his wife, who appeared to have recovered from their earlier terror of the *manush-bagha*, gave their word that they would care for them as though they were their own. With such an assurance, the padre left Godamuri to catch the train at Amarda Road and, accompanied by Rose and Richards, returned that afternoon to Kharagpur.

Within five days he was back at Amarda, where he was met by Karan Hansda and Janu Tudu with the news that the children were in a desperate plight. He set off at once for Godamuri and found the village almost deserted. Terror of the ghosts had taken hold once again. Chunarem and his family had panicked soon after he had left the children at his house and abandoning them without food or water had gone away to another village, no one knew where. 'I found the situation very grave,' Singh wrote in his journal, 'but did not wait or indulge in that thought for long, but made for the barricade at once, broke open the sal props, and found the poor children lying in their own mess, panting for breath, through hunger, thirst and fright. I really mourned for them and actually wept for my negligence. I sprinkled cold water on their faces. They opened their mouths; I poured water in and they drank. I took them up in my arms one by one and carried them to the bullock cart.'[10]

The immediate probem was how to feed the children. 'They would not receive anything into their mouths. I tried by syphon action. I tore up my handkerchief and rolled it up into a wick. I dipped it in the tea cup; and when it was well soaked, I put one end into their mouths and

74

the other end remained in the cup. To my great surprise I found them sucking the wick like a baby. I thanked God most fervently for the great kindness in forgiving me my negligence in leaving the children under such care.'[11]

It is difficult to understand why Janu and Karan, who had looked after the wolf cubs in the back of the bullock cart, could not also have kept watch on the children during Singh's absence. The same might apply to Bhagobhat Khatua, who would certainly have made a more reliable guardian than Chunarem, but his movements after the capture are not known. Possibly they were all involved in some other work for Singh; or he may have thought it unnecessary to tell them to keep an eye on things; or again he may have been covering up for them and taking responsibility for their negligence as well as what he recognized as his own. One can only speculate. More certain is that if they had come any later they would have found the children dead. As it was they had to remain in Godamuri for several days nursing them back to health on a diet of milk, until the padre considered them strong enough to travel.

The journey back to Midnapore, with frequent halts on the way to rest the children, took more than eight days. Even so the constant jostling and lurching of the bullock cart did nothing to improve their condition, and they remained weak and unable to move. In some ways this was all to the good, since it meant that they did not have to be confined to their cage and could lie on a pile of rice straw in the back of the cart. When they finally reached Tantigoria on 4 November and pulled up in front of the gates of 'The Home', after nineteen days of captivity the children were so emaciated, feeble and wretched-looking that no one could have told anything from their appearance of their extraordinary background. As the Reverend Singh had already explained to Janu Tudu, whom they had left in Chainsole, and now told Karan Hansda and Bhagobhat Khatua, the two girls had been found abandoned by them in Santalia and as far as the world needed to be concerned they were the neglected off-spring of mendicant fakirs. He was determined that the true story of their capture from wolves in the jungle should remain a secret, hoping thereby to protect them and himself from the unwelcome curiosity, sensationalism and gossip which in a small town like Midnapore would otherwise shadow their lives. After prayers on the evening of his return in which he again gave thanks to God for the rescue and safe homecoming of the children, the Reverend Singh took his wife into his confidence, impressing on her the need for total secrecy. Mrs Singh gave her word and was to keep her promise faithfully. Others, however, would not find it so easy to resist the telling of a good if improbable story, and the children themselves would recover soon enough to provide the unmistakable evidence.

Chapter Four

During their first few days at the orphanage, the wolf girls were kept apart from the other children in a dark outhouse adjoining the residential quarters of 'The Home'. Mrs Singh attended to them herself and allowed none of the orphanage servants to go near them. They were given charpoys to lie on and blankets to cover them at night for by now the weather had turned chilly, but in spite of their general debility they rejected both, preferring to sleep on the floor on rice-straw. They showed no sign of feeling the cold, they neither shivered nor huddled together for warmth except when sleeping, and immediately tore off any clothes or covering they were made to wear. Mrs Singh, who considered it important that they should get used to wearing clothes as soon as possible, had the idea of tying loin-cloths around their waists with a detachable flap that passed between the legs, serving also as a nappy, and stitching them in place. They were unable to free themselves from these 'langotis' and made little attempt to do so until they recovered their strength, when the constant irritation of unaccustomed clothing would keep them busy for hours on end trying to reach their own and sometimes the other's and worry at them with teeth and nails until they had torn them off. In the meantime they lay in the straw completely inactive, except for their feeble efforts to escape when Mrs Singh came to feed them. They showed their fear of both her and the Reverend Singh and their dislike of being patted or stroked by drawing back their lips from their teeth and growling, but more often than not they accepted the milk offered them. Apart from water it was their only sustenance and had to be given in a baby's bottle since they were still too weak to take it in any other way.

As the days turned into weeks the health of the children began to cause the Singhs grave concern. Not only were they recovering strength more slowly than had been hoped, but they had both developed a large number of sores all over their bodies, which the Reverend Singh attributed to the filth in which they had been left lying in Chunarem's courtyard. As he recorded: 'These sores ate up the big and extensive corns on the knee and on the palm of the hand near the wrist which had developed from walking on all fours. The sores had a very fearful appearance and went deep into the flesh . . . Besides attacking the knee and the palm, they extended to foot, elbow and ankle. It was a dreadful sight to see.'[1] Instead of calling in the doctor right away, which they feared would lead to the exposure of the rescue story, the Singhs began by treating the children themselves, washing the sores with carbolic soap and lotion and bandaging them with boric cotton. As soon as granulations began to form they used iodine, zinc and boric acid and the sores gradually healed up over a period of about three weeks, though in the case of the elder girl they would come back several years later, which suggests, since there was no question of either girl being leprous, that the complaint may have had more to do with diet than sanitation.

About ten days after their arrival at the orphanage, when the children became strong enough to sit up and crawl about a little, they were given solid food consisting of rice and vegetables and a little meat, served on a plate and left on the floor of the room, but after sniffing carefully at the food they showed no interest in eating, preferring to stay with milk and water, which they now lapped noisily from a bowl. The two wolf-cubs, who had been kept in their original cage, were still young enough to survive on milk alone, but the children, it was felt, needed something more substantial. All attempts to make them eat, however, failed until one afternoon they were taken out into the courtyard at the time when the orphanage dogs were being fed – coincidentally, it appears, though the Reverend Singh must have been interested to see how they would act in the presence of animals. He tried to prevent both children from going near the dogs for fear that they would be harmed, but only managed to restrain the younger girl; the elder was too fierce and threatened him when he tried to control her. Showing no fear, although the dogs who could be quite ferocious at feeding time were squabbling among themselves and fighting over scraps, she went up to them and after submitting to their investigation of her scent and one or two stiff-tailed attempts to drive her off, joined in their dinner of meat, offal and bones. Astonished by the way the dogs seemed to recognize the child as one of them, as much as by the eagerness and complete lack of inhibition she displayed in going among them, Singh watched as the girl, on bandaged knees and elbows, darting glances askance at her new companions milling around her, lowered her face to the dog bowl, seized her food and bolted it with convulsive shakes of her upper body, keeping her head close to the ground. She secured a large bone and carried it off in her mouth to a corner of the yard away from the others, where she soon settled down, holding it under her hands as if they were paws, and began to gnaw at it, occasionally rubbing it along the ground to help separate the meat from the bone. Observing her behaviour with fascinated horror, shocked by so strong a reaffirmation of the instincts and habits she and the younger girl had no doubt acquired from the wolves, Singh was forced to face up to the reality of the children's true condition and wants. Although he could guess what their diet had been in the forest, during their illness he had perhaps deluded himself in thinking that on recovery they would lose some of their wolfish traits. He felt that this should be encouraged by trying to treat them as near as possible like normal human children, by making them wear clothes, by talking to them (although they had no speech and gave no sign of understanding what was being said), by showing them affection and by feeding them on a conventional diet. It was a policy that he would never abandon despite constant setbacks; but he understood now that, if the children were to survive, they would have to be fed on raw meat.

On Wednesday 24 November, the girls were thought strong enough to be given a proper bath. Although this did not include total immersion they resisted fiercely and had to be held down while water was poured over them and Mrs Singh soaped and scrubbed them down, taking care to avoid their sores. After bathing the children's long claw-like fingernails were cut; their toe nails, worn down from dragging their feet along the ground when going on all fours, were trimmed; and the matted balls of hair, which contributed not a little to the wildness of their appearance, were shaved off. The Reverend Singh was pleased to note that for the first time they almost looked like ordinary children and his wife, who had been considering what to call them, now suggested two Bengali names – Kamala, which means 'lotus', for the elder; and Amala, 'a bright yellow flower', for the younger girl. Although the names may have seemed a little ironical there was no question of calling them by anything that would draw attention to their background. The appellation 'wolf girl' was avoided, if indeed the Singhs were familiar with it – there is some evidence to suggest that at this stage they were not. With the cutting of their hair the difference in appearance between the two children emerged more clearly. Although both had the flat noses and large nostrils, high cheek-bones, thick lips and bushy eyebrows of the aboriginals, Kamala, the older girl, had a proportionately smaller head with a round face, little deep-set eyes and rather squashed features. Amala, though there is no very revealing photograph of her, seems to have had a more finely etched face, oval in shape, with a more pointed chin and a sufficiently different look about her to convince those who saw both children together that they were not of the same family. As to their tribal origins, nobody could be sure, but it was agreed that probably they were Santals or belonged to one of the related Munda-speaking tribes.

The most interesting aspects of their appearance were undoubtedly those where it was suggested that modification had taken place as a result of their living among the wolves. One has to take into account, however, that in his amateur and sometimes fanciful observations of the children, the Reverend Singh may have confused purely physical description with his impressions and interpretations of their behaviour. For instance, he described their jaw-bones as 'raised and high . . . Asiatic, no doubt, to all appearance but somewhat different . . . the jaws had undergone some sort of change in the chewing of bones and constant biting of the meat attached to the bone. When they moved their jaws in chewing, the upper and lower jaw-bone appeared to part and close visibly, unlike human jaws . . . When they used to chew anything very hard, such as a bone this separation of the jaw-bone was very distinct. Such chewing caused visible hollows at both ends of the jaw-bones on both sides of the cheek.'[2] Possibly the effect was caused by some unusual development in the musculature of the jaw-bone, but it is not difficult to imagine how the sight of a six-year-old child attacking a large, meaty bone with the practised skill of a wolf might make one think that the structure of the jaw itself had somehow become adapted to the child's unusual eating habits. The same goes for Singh's description of the children's eye-teeth, which he claimed were longer and more pointed than normal, although human canines, especially milk canines, are not known to grow beyond occlusal level. Other witnesses have said that their teeth were very sharp, which Singh also noted. This more than likely was true, but they denied that the canines were particularly prominent, or as the padre observed, that the colour of the inside of their mouths was blood red.

The ears of the children he considered to be particularly large and they do in fact appear so from the earliest photographs, though in Kamala's case they seem to have grown smaller as she grew older; but here again the ears may have appeared larger to the observer's eyes to explain their unusually powerful sense of hearing which, as Singh records, enabled them to detect the smallest sound – for example, of approaching footsteps – which drew their attention long before it was picked up by anybody else. When the children became excited for any reason, their ears and lips would tremble and they would pump out breath through their nostrils, making a harsh noise; along with their habit of dilating and contracting their nostrils when investigating a scent and sniffing rapidly at the same time, this no doubt led Singh to remark that their nasal 'openings were much largei than ordinarily found in men'.[3] From the photographic evidence it was hardly apparent.

Unfortunately Singh's tendency to exaggerate is common to all his writing. His letters and reports, written in the convoluted and extravagant style of Indian English, are full of hyperbole and (particularly in any religious context) histrionic inflation. The fault may be recognized and accepted for what it reveals – an inadequate command of the language, compounded by a certain cultural and, in Singh's case, characteristic need to make things out to be a little bit more important, more beautiful, more significant, more noble and more tragic than they really were. It is scarcely recommendation for a witness, yet in his logging of the wolf children's capture and progress, he seems for the most part to have made a conscious effort to appear restrained, concise and, to the best of his ability, objective.

The children were not deformed in any way and despite their emaciated condition the build of their bodies suggested strength and agility. They had short muscular

necks, broad shoulders, flat hips and slender waists that
were peculiarly flexible from side to side. Only their arms
and, in Kamala's case, hands also from wrist to fingertips,
appeared to the Reverend Singh somewhat awkward and
perhaps longer than usual. Unfortunately he took no
measurements for comparison. Yet they could neither
walk nor stand on two feet and, as a consequence of going
on all fours, it seems, the joints of the wrists, elbows,
knees and ankles had grown unusually thick and strong.
When lifted off the ground from under the arms their
legs remained bent at the knee and at the hip joints, which
unlike the joints of the elbow and wrist had lost the
ability to straighten out or make flexible movements
beyond a certain angle. Going on all fours, they had three
different styles of locomotion, either crawling on knees and
elbows, which gave them the use of their hands (though
this was limited to paw-like actions); or more often on
knees and hands in the manner of a nine-month-old baby;
or running with their bodies in a raised position on hands
and feet. This last method allowed them to move very fast,
as Singh would discover later. Observing Kamala running
around with the dogs in the courtyard, he noted in close
detail this more rapid mode of progression, with 'head
erect on the broad shoulders, the body straight, resting on
the hip joints; the thigh making an obtuse angle with the
leg at the knee and the leg resting on the raised heel; and
the front part of the foot resting on the ground with the
toes spread out to support the whole weight of the body.
The front part of the body rested on the straightened hand,
supported by the spread-out palm and fingers on the
ground.'[4] Whether crawling or running on all fours, the
hands were never bunched into fists but always opened
out, palms and fingers flat. Their toes, however, particularly the big toe, when the foot was placed flat on the
ground, stood up at an angle.

When they ran along in this way, whether slowly or fast,
the consecutive jerks of the head and then the hindquarters

rising and falling alternatively, made a sort of undulating movement, which the Reverend Singh compared to the action of a squirrel, especially when they were going at top speed. The progression of limbs, however, was more like that of a genuine quadruped than a squirrel's: 'At first the left hand was raised and placed on the ground, and immediately the right foot was similarly raised and placed on the ground, and then the right hand and immediately the left foot were raised and placed. In this way it was noticed that whenever any hand or foot was raised in progression the arm blade or the thigh blade, respectively, was depressed a little, but when running fast nothing could be seen. I cannot say that the progression was by leaping, but it was a motion of the whole body in a mass.'[5]

Not long after the incident with the dogs Kamala and Amala were moved from the dark and rather airless outhouse to a special enlarged cage, which the Reverend Singh had constructed for them out of wood and wire netting in a corner of his office. The immediate advantage of the move was that the children would now be close at hand for care, observation and, most important of all, increased human contact. It was part of the long-term plan to bring them gradually into the life of the orphanage, so that eventually they would be able to join the other children as ordinary inmates, for neither the padre nor Mrs Singh had any doubt at this stage that Kamala and Amala would regain their human faculties, temporarily eclipsed, as they believed, by habits acquired in the wild.

The Reverend Singh's office was a long, narrow, whitewashed room with a plain classical moulding and a high ceiling supported by iron beams and wooden cross batens. Two doors under ersatz roman arches on the same west wall connected it with the drawing-room and the Singhs' bedroom. The furniture consisting of a desk, chair, bookcase and bed (sometimes used by Singh or by guests) had been rearranged to make room for the cage, which was placed so that it received maximum light from the only window set high in the north wall. The children, however, always sat in the darkest corner and when the winter sun streamed into the room, illuminating the floor of the cage, they made every effort to avoid its rays. The Reverend Singh was aware of their fear of light; although difficult at first to distinguish from their greater terror of human beings, it had become apparent soon after their capture. A match struck in their presence or a hurricane lamp brought into the room, even when they had been too weak to move, produced signs of alarm – one of the few emotions their static features could register, or at least, which could be recognized by humans – and as they became stronger they showed an intense desire to get as far as possible from any source of light.

Fear registered chiefly in their eyes, which during the day were always heavy as if with sleep, often half-lidded; at night when they became generally more active, their eyes would be open wide, alert and piercingly bright. This brightness was noticed by a number of those who saw the children at the orphanage at a later stage in their lives, but the Reverend Singh also recorded a more remarkable phenomenon, claiming that sometimes at night a peculiar bluish glare could be seen in their eyes, similar to the reflection in the eyes of cats and dogs and certain other animals. It was first observed by Singh during their illness, when 'they could not bear the presence of any light in the sick room ... so the light used to be kept at the door keeping them in the shade. They used to crawl into the darkest corner of the room to avoid even the faint light. On such occasions when we used to approach them in the room, we noticed that as soon as they turned towards us, the shape of the bodies used to disappear showing only two faint blue lights in proportion to the strength of the light then emitting.'[6]

85 Singh seems to have believed somewhat naïvely that the

glare actually emanated from their eyes and states elsewhere in apparent contradiction that it could not be seen when there was a light in the room. However, if one takes the analogy of a cat's eyes, it is light falling on them at a certain angle that produces a reflection which can be seen against an unlit background. These, indeed, are the conditions that pertain in the description above. The phenomenon, which Singh linked to the children's undoubted ability at that time to see better at night than by day, became less the longer they remained at the orphanage and gradually adapted themselves to a diurnal pattern of existence. When the story of the wolf children reached the outside world some twenty years later, the detail of the 'blue glare', thought fanciful and unconvincing by some and downright impossible by others, remained at the centre of the feral controversy, although Singh would always defend his claim, strongly denying any exaggeration on his part. In the meantime he saw the importance of getting the children accustomed to living by day and subjected them, perhaps cruelly at first, to the harsh brightness that came in through his office window in an attempt to break the influence and rhythms of night.

They slept little, either by day or at night, though they would lie down for an hour or two at about midday and were often caught dozing while sitting in a corner. In the wild their sleeping habits would probably have been determined by how often they ate – wolves usually rest and sleep for long periods after gorging themselves on a kill – but the Reverend Singh does not mention whether Kamala and Amala slept after being fed, only that they rested sometimes in the late evening, when presumably they had just had their main meal. Singh is reticent about their feeding arrangements at this stage, possibly because of the taboo that surrounds the eating of raw meat and the ferocious and unnerving display which the children put on while devouring their food. Jageswar Khatua, however, the son of Bhagobhat, who was still boarding at the orphanage when the children were brought in, remembers that they were fed on alternate days. When they did sleep, it was usually lying one on top of the other, like puppies in a litter, although during their illness and when their sores were causing them serious discomfort they lay apart. Knees were always pulled up to the chest, even when they slept on their backs, and their hands and feet were brought together, as if they were crouching while lying on their sides. They were noisy sleepers, snoring, grunting, grinding their teeth and at times giving little cries, but they slept lightly and the least sound awoke them. At any hint of danger they were instantly alert, though generally they did not come alive until just before dusk, when they showed signs of restlessness and wanting to get out into the open. Singh deduced from this behaviour that they were affected by the sunset and that the reddish colour of the evening sky seen through the window of his office, as it might have been through the mouth of their den in the jungle, was the signal for them to set out on the prowl. If a little picturesque, it was a reasonable enough assumption for a man who had only basic zoological knowledge with which to interpret the behaviour of two human beings whose reflexes and reactions were predominantly animal.

After midnight the children never slept and were constantly on the move, prowling around, pacing to and fro, whether in their cage, the outhouse or in the yard where they were taken for exercise. Sometimes at night they howled. The first time it happened at the orphanage was on the night of 10 December, soon after they had recovered from their illness. 'This cry was a peculiar one,' Singh wrote in his diary. 'It began with a hoarse voice and ended in a thrilling shrill wailing, very loud and continuous. It had a piercing note of a very high pitch. It was neither human nor animal. I presumed it was a call to their companions, the wolves or the cubs . . . intended to make them aware of their whereabouts.'[7] But the cubs in their cage near by were too young to answer, though they would whimper and scratch at the bars of their cage in recognition of the children's voices. 'There was a difference of pitch in the two voices – Kamala's was stronger and bolder, more sharp and shrill. Amala's was weaker, changeful and thinner. But both had a fine thrill of reverberating notes, very high and piercing. It could be heard from a good distance, and more so on a still night when everyone was asleep and no other sound was audible except the screeching of the owl, the chirping of some night bird and the sounds of the animals prowling in search of prey or drink.'[8] The howling, always started by Kamala, though Amala would sometimes go on after the elder girl had stopped, continued at intervals through the night, and for a while the same pattern would be repeated almost every night until it gradually grew less regular, later becoming only an occasional outlet for whatever emotion it expressed. They always howled at night, never during the day, and to begin with the noise alarmed everyone at the orphanage: the children had to be comforted, and the servants, from whom some explanation of the girls' behaviour (not necessarily the right one) could no longer be kept, were given strict orders not to talk about it in the bazaar. If anyone from the near-by village of Tantigoria asked about the howling, they were to say it was one of the dogs or the wolf-cubs the padre-sahib had bought from the Santals, or else jackals in the field behind the house.

The problem of keeping the wolf children a secret was becoming more and more difficult. The Singhs' own children had come back home for their Christmas holidays; Daniel from a boarding school in Darjeeling and the two girls, Preeti Lota and Buona Lota, from St John's Diocesan School in Calcutta; and naturally they wanted to know about the strange creatures being kept in a wire cage in their father's office; especially after Preeti Lota had been bitten on the hand while attempting to pet Kamala. In due course they were told by their mother at least enough to satisfy their curiosity, but the story of the children's capture from wolves was probably withheld. The same tactics were used on other visitors to the orphanage including the family physician, Dr Sarbadhicari, a frequent caller, whose advice had finally been sought in the treatment of the sores. Although it is not known what explanation was given to Dr Sarbadhicari for the children's, to say the least, unusual condition and behaviour, it appears to have satisfied him. According to the Reverend Singh it would be another ten months before the Doctor would find out from him the true story of their provenance, but in that time many others would come to know at least a part of the truth from a different source.

In their endeavour to protect Kamala and Amala from the curious and at the same time develop their human potential, the Singhs had to face frequent dilemmas and even contradiction in the methods they employed. It was not always easy to know what to do and, although in his diary the Reverend Singh describes the procedure as straightforward and simple, it was more a reflection of his own optimism than an accurate depiction of the complex problems they faced. To take a scatological example, now that the two girls were recovered from their illness it seemed advisable that they should be taken out as frequently and regularly as possible, not only for fresh air and exercise, but in the interest of hygiene. At the moment they urinated and defecated whenever and wherever they felt like it; they had no notion of wiping themselves other than by occasionally rubbing their bottoms along the ground as dogs will – this may have had as much to do with local irritation caused by worms, as a desire to get clean; and had to be washed by Mrs Singh, which they strongly resented and tried to resist with growling, scratching and teeth-baring. But if they were allowed out three times a day, morning, noon and evening, it was felt that they would acquire, with appropriate scoldings and praise (both quite meaningless to the wolf children), the

89

habit of emptying their bowels outside the house. However, this presented some difficulty. If they were walked in the garden or the field behind the orphanage during the day – naked, on all fours and with a rope around their waists to prevent them trying to run away, or making off to hide under the nearest bush, for they did not like to be out in the open during daylight – there was the constant danger of their being seen and attracting attention. At night, of course, it was safer and, as the Reverend Singh soon found out, the children were more likely to respond to what he termed, appropriately enough, 'the calls of nature' after dark; for in the wild he presumed 'that the whole night they used to prowl about outside the cave and used to finish everything during that period, and came back in the cave to rest the whole day there'.[9] But it was precisely this, their habituation to a nocturnal existence, that he wanted to break, and yet here he was encouraging it. At length a 'compromise was reached whereby the children were taken out into the courtyard during the day and into the gardens and field under the cover of night; but their excretory habits did not change and if, as sometimes happened, they were left in at night, they made no attempt to hold out until the next morning.

Another instance of the difficulties the Singhs had to contend with can be found in their attempts to bring the children into contact with the other inmates of the orphanage. At this stage, two months after their capture, there was still little sign of progress in Kamala and Amala's behaviour. Their reaction to any attempt at fraternizing by either children or adults was either to put on a threatening display or else to hide away in a corner of their cage and refuse to look round, as if the very sight of human beings was obnoxious to them. 'The presence of others in the room prevented them from doing anything, even moving their head from one direction to the other, or moving about a little, changing sides, or turning about. Even a look towards them was objectionable. They wanted to be all by themselves, and they shunned human society altogether.'[10] On the other hand they had shown interest in the orphanage dogs and, on the rare occasions when they were allowed to see them, in the wolf-cubs, whose company (along with that of the wolves left behind in the forest of Denganalia) the Reverend Singh believed they sorely missed. But the symptoms of their distress – the howling, sniffing the ground and searching the corners of their cage or room – might equally have been a protest against captivity and a reconnaissance for escape. The purpose of keeping the wolf-cubs separate from the children was to destroy the bonds of their former association. Less clear is why the cubs were retained in the first place, since no attempt was made to compare their behaviour with the children's, or make use of them for any other purpose; and, apart from the attentions of Daniel Singh on his return from school, they were generally neglected. Daniel, who was a keen animal lover, used to play with them for hours at a time and sometimes take them on leads to his father's office, which could be depended upon to elicit a strong and amusing reaction from Kamala and Amala. The padre, afraid that his son might interpret correctly the rapport that existed between the cubs and the caged girls, ordered them to be taken out on the pretext that they were upsetting the children; but he had not failed to notice that Kamala and Amala's interest in the cubs had predominated, if only for a moment or two, over their fear of Daniel. If this gave Singh the idea of using the cubs as a means of establishing a relationship with the children, it was over-ridden at this time by the considered danger of reviving the animal associations of their life in the wild; besides which the cubs did not live long enough for any experiments to be carried out. However, they had already set in motion the long and awkward process by which, ironically, their former den-mates would eventually regain some of their human faculties.

91   The Singhs noticed that when Kamala and Amala were

hungry they would approach the corner of the cage or room where their food was usually left and sit there for some time; then they would move away and return again, and go on doing this, with Amala making little whining noises and occasionally a 'hoo, hoo' sound (Kamala was silent), until they were given something to eat or drink. If the bowl or plate containing their food was put in an awkward place, high up on a table or chair, for instance, they would make considerable efforts to reach it, standing on their knees, scrabbling and pushing at the bowl with their noses. Their attitude towards eating remained ferocious; as soon as their food was placed before them they would smell it carefully, then plunge their faces into the bowl and with somewhat grotesque sound effects and hideous grimaces, glimpsed whenever they lifted up their heads, bolt it down in a matter of seconds. Yet, like recalcitrant children, they always left the rice and vegetables that Mrs Singh had carefully mixed with the meat, except where particles had adhered to its raw and sticky surfaces. Convinced that the diet of raw meat was contributing to the children's fierceness and making them more unmanageable, the Singhs tried them with cooked meat and then a purely vegetable diet, but even when noticeably hungry, after a preliminary sniffing investigation, neither child showed any inclination to eat. Nonetheless their voracious appetite for raw meat was a constant; indeed, apart from the wolf-cubs, it was their only interest in life; and although it seemed to the Singhs almost as retrogressive as allowing them to associate with the cubs, meat was the medium through which they chose to work on their limited susceptibilities, when everything else had failed.

For some time Mrs Singh had been bringing groups of the orphanage children into the office and talking and playing with them in front of Kamala and Amala in an attempt at drawing their attention. She would approach them, point out something of interest – a child's rattle, a rag doll or perhaps a flower – and, repeating its name offer, it first to one of the children and then to the wolf girls. But neither of them showed the slightest interest. As the Reverend Singh put it, 'They simply bestowed a forced look, as if looking at nothing, and would quickly turn their eyes again to the corner,' where they would crouch together in a trance-like state sometimes for hours on end, 'as if meditating on some great problem'.[11] Meanwhile the other children would be playing games, running about the room and making a lot of noise. Kamala and Amala could not be distracted, but Mrs Singh felt sure they were nonetheless aware of what was going on around them and were keeping a stealthy watch for any movement that might have been a source of danger.

Once when she brought in a tin of biscuits and distributed them among the children, she noticed that the wolf girls reacted to the sound of the children eating and caught them turning their heads to look. It was only for a second and then they turned away, but soon afterwards when more biscuits were given out they did it again. Mrs Singh approached the cage and offered the girls a biscuit each. They retreated showing their teeth and averting their eyes. She left the biscuits on a low stool inside the cage and went away. The next day the biscuits were still there. She repeated the experiment, only this time when Kamala and Amala again betrayed an interest in seeing the children eating, she came over to them with two small chunks of raw meat instead of biscuits. Again she tried unsuccessfully to make them take food from her hand, but as soon as she put the meat down on the stool and began to move away, they pounced on it and ate it up. From then on, each time they were offered meat in these circumstances they would take it and, although the Singhs knew well enough they would accept meat in almost any circumstances, the practice was continued for a time in the belief that at least some sort of link had been established between the wolf children and other human beings. Any attempt, however, at substituting

93

the meat for biscuits or inducing them to take it from the hand or in any way developing this slender contact, met for the time being with conspicuous failure.

The wolf-cubs were dead, their wasted bodies consigned by Daniel to the flames of a funeral pyre on the rubbish heap in the field behind the house. But the Reverend Singh had not forgotten. Willing to try anything now, he allowed the introduction of puppies belonging to one of the orphanage bitches into Kamala and Amala's cage. His earlier doubts about the wisdom of encouraging their association with animals were overridden by the exigencies of the situation, for understandably he was worried that the wolf children, like the cubs, would die of loneliness through virtual isolation. Their reaction to the puppies was encouraging. They sniffed at them and allowed themselves to be sniffed at in return, bristling a little at first and showing their superiority by feigned indifference, but they made no attempt to harm them and tolerated their playful and unruly presence in the cage. The puppies were then removed and put among the orphanage children, who were made to play with them in the same room, so that Kamala and Amala could see that they had no fear of the children or the Singhs. It was hoped by the puppies' example to create an interest on the wolf children's part in associating with humans. To begin with, the Reverend Singh's original fears were borne out and the girls, occupied with their new-found companions, paid less attention than ever to the other inmates of the orphanage. But Mrs Singh persevered. Whether the puppies were around or not, as often as she could, she would sit by Kamala and Amala's cage, usually with one or two of the younger orphanage children on her lap or playing at her feet, and talk alternately to them and to the wolf girls, as if they, too, were babies just learning to talk and walk. Although there was no change in their behaviour she then arranged with her husband to let them come out of the cage and spend a part of each day in 'The Home's'

94

nursery quarters, where the youngest children were cared for. At some risk to herself and the babies, she redoubled her efforts to approach the wolf girls and talk and coax them into some sort of response, but as soon as she came near, Kamala and Amala would quickly move away and go to take up position in the opposite corner of the room. If she followed them they would move again to another corner, and so it went on, until they became irritated by the 'game' and showed their resentment by baring their teeth and making a peculiar high-pitched growling noise. Then Mrs Singh would give up and sit with the babies and puppies in the middle of the room, going on talking and playing with them as if she had forgotten that the wolf girls were still there. Kamala and Amala remained indifferent, but now, whenever one of the babies or puppies crawled away from the central group around Mrs Singh or did anything unusual, they would quickly look round from their corner to see what was going on. Gradually they were becoming accustomed to the presence of other children and, in the Singhs' estimation, beginning to recognize perhaps that they were not so very different from themselves.

The break-through, if it can be called that, came a few days before Christmas. One of the orphans, a little boy of about a year old, called Benjamin, crawled over to the wolf children's corner and before anyone could stop him sat up beside them quite unconcerned. To Mrs Singh's surprise and relief, instead of moving away or trying to see him off, even when he boldly reached out and touched them, they showed neither anger nor fear and remained where they were. It was the beginning of an association which might be compared to the wolf children's relationship with the puppies: they tolerated Benjamin and allowed him to come up to them whenever he felt inclined, though this favour was not extended to any of the other children. Why they had made an exception in Benjamin's case even the Reverend Singh was at a loss to say. However, Mrs Singh was full of hope that the wolf children would learn from the boy, especially as he was just beginning to walk and make articulate sounds and, without forcing them to be together, she encouraged the friendship. But about ten days after the initial contact, on 31 December, the wolf children suddenly turned on Benjamin and savaged him. He was rescued just in time by the vigilant Mrs Singh, but had received a severe biting and scratching and been badly frightened. After that he never again made any attempt to approach them. There was no apparent reason for the attack, though the Reverend Singh believed that 'when they found some difference and understood that he was quite different in nature to them, then they commenced to dislike him',[12] which scarcely rates as an explanation. More likely Kamala and Amala, who by now had fully recovered their strength, were simply indulging in a little rough play of the kind they must have become accustomed to while living with the wolves. Indeed, it is surprising that the instance did not occur sooner. Ironically, it may have marked the beginning of a fuller recognition and trust of Benjamin, but it was interpreted, understandably enough, as retrogressive behaviour and the two wolf girls were confined once more to their cage.

By the middle of January 1921, almost three months after their capture, the Reverend Singh was obliged to admit in his diary that the wolf children had made no progress towards the recovery of their human faculties and as yet shown nothing but aversion to human beings and their ways. He recognized in their morose, apathetic behaviour the repercussions of complete disorientation and a desperate loneliness which he interpreted rather romantically as a longing for their former life in the jungle and the lost companionship and protection of the wolves, but which touched him deeply nonetheless. Yet neither he nor Mrs Singh gave up hope and at morning and evening prayers, together with the staff and children of the orphanage assembled in the unroofed chapel which gave on to the office where Kamala and Amala were caged, they asked God to speed their recovery. Sometimes during silent moments of devotion, the wolf girls could be heard making some inappropriate noise and inevitably the children would dissolve into giggles, which earned them an angry reprimand from the Reverend Singh and an extra prayer. But regardless of their progress or lack of it, life at 'The Home', with all its little routines, visits, duties, lessons and games, went on much as before. Although Mrs Singh devoted a considerable amount of her time to tending the wolf children, the padre could not afford to neglect the obligations of his parish, or indeed of the social round, where his presence at such functions as a tiffin party given by Mrs Cook, the collector's wife, to arrange linen and clothing for the needy patients in hospital, or the Christmas Treat, held in the Church compound for the poor children of the town, was thought by him at least to be indispensable. But out of deference, perhaps, to the wolf children, that year he did not take part in the Midnapore Zamindari Company's Boxing Day shoot.

His parish work, as he explained at a meeting of the Diocesan Council in Calcutta later that month, was at the present time unhappily restricted to preaching to the converted. The political agitation that prevailed across North India was coming to a head in Midnapore over the proposed partition of the district; there was a general reaction against all things British and that included the Church. As a result he had been forced to cut down on open addresses and bazaar preaching and for the time being had left off visiting the temple of the goddess Kali in Chirimarshai, where the more fervent Hindu *babus* and pandits of the old school met every afternoon, and where in the past he used to confront them in evangelical mood, Bible in hand, in an attempt to explain away their shastras in the light of the Gospel and make them understand that true Salvation could be obtained only through Jesus

Christ. Since Kali had been adopted by the revolutionaries as their patron, however, it was not a wise place for an Anglican priest to be airing his 'loyalist' opinions. One of Singh's rivals, the Reverend Long of the American Baptist Mission, had recently had an open air lantern-lecture in Ghatal broken up by political rowdies shouting 'Gandhi-gi jai'. Although they had eventually been thrown out by some low-caste sweepers who wanted to see the slide-show (a scriptural drama entitled *The Beheading of John the Baptist*) Mr Long had received a nasty fright. It was a lesson learned, but a strong element of competition existed between the two missionaries and the Reverend Singh was far from being a coward. He was yet to be seen in the bazaars distributing religious tracts and Epiphanies and visiting the educated Hindus in their houses or provoking religious discussions at the Public Library, where the English-speaking and more enlightened *babus*, the Sub-Judges, Deputy Magistrates, lawyers, schoolmasters, clerks, engineers and wealthy *zamindars* would meet and socialize most evenings of the week. But true missionary work, the conversion of souls, was becoming increasingly difficult due to the political situation.

It was the main theme of the council meeting. Among the different points of view expressed stood the old optimistic belief that, whereas in the past most Christians had been drawn from outside the pale of Hindu heritage, the time was now at hand when the bulk of India's middle classes were about to break into the Church. This drew the cynical reply that under *Swaraj* (Home Rule) mass movements of outcasts into Christianity would diminish and the middle classes would find little advantage in turn-ing to Christianity if it ceased to be the religion of the ruling race. The most cogent arguments supported the view that the new wave of nationalism which had swept over India since the war had accentuated the feeling of dissatisfaction among educated Christians and the growing estrangement between missionaries and the community. 98

The failure of the spread of Christianity was attributed to over-dependence on foreign missionaries and the more radical among them claimed to look forward to Home Rule, when Christianity would no longer be identified with the Raj.

The Reverend Singh listened to the argument without enthusiasm for it was basically the same case that the S.P.G. had been putting forward for the last quarter of a century, that the aim of missionary work was to create an indigenous Church and to remove the European missionaries in favour of the native clergy as soon as feasible. But with whatever degree of self-criticism and conviction the idea was expressed, it was difficult not to connect the Society's anxiety to withdraw itself in favour of diocesanization with lack of funds due to waning public interest at home in the missionary ideal. The balance was redressed by Bishop Westcott,who pointed out that the mission to the Sunderbans had all but collapsed due to the withdrawal of European missionaries before the Church had been sufficiently well established there, and that in these times of hardship the poverty of so many parishes made it impossible for the missions to be self-supporting. Foss Westcott, who had succeeded Bishop Lefroy to the office of Metropolitan in 1919, as a liberal and forward-looking Churchman, was aware that the chief disability of the Anglican Church in India lay in its intimate ties with the Government, by which a Bishop could not be consecrated or a Diocese divided without the sanction of the Viceroy and Letters Patent from the King-Emperor in England; in its foreign and bureaucratic image, and in the official and social bearing of its senior clergy, who lived in an opulent style which Indians found hard to reconcile with religious leadership. He had already set an example in this last respect by himself living a conspicuously simple life at Bishop's House – he refused to call this magnificent palladian building, which lies opposite the Cathedral on Chowringhee and where the Council was now assembled in the library, by its proper designation of 'the Palace' – but he was also obliged by the Government, of which he was a senior official, to maintain the impressive dignity and detachment which was held to be the lodestar of British rule in India, and had to equilibrate the responsibilities of high office with his role of helping to build a self-governing Indian Church.

In the Reverend Singh's opinion the new Metropolitan was leaning too far too fast towards reform. Along with a few other clergy he was incensed by what he took to be the Bishop's tacit support for Gandhi when Westcott had described him as 'the outstanding personality in India at the present time' and urged the Council that 'we ought justly to recognize the principles for which he is standing'.[13] The Reverend Singh had little time for Gandhi whom he regarded as a dangerous troublemaker, far more dangerous than the terrorists because of his undoubted mystique which enabled him to hold sway over the superstitious mentality of the Hindu masses and which he extended to all his ploys, from the magic nonsense of *khadi* (homespun) and the boycotting of foreign cloth, to what he considered the fundamentally dishonest doctrine of *ahimsa* (non-violence), which in the last two years of his civil disobedience campaigns had led to little else but violence and rioting over most of India. At St John's in Midnapore the Reverend Singh had preached thinly veiled sermons against the 'mahatma' and his disruptive nationalist politics, impressing upon his congregation that it was their duty to support the Church and remain loyal to the government in these troubled times. With Home Rule in all men's thoughts the position of Indian Christians in the community was a delicate one, but Singh reminded them that persecution could only temper the steel of a true Christian's faith.

His own loyalty was beyond question; as an Indian he could not ignore the 'liberal' arguments being put forward by some of his colleagues for the Indianization of the

Church – for one thing they favoured his own advancement; but he would not accept that reform at the present time was either wise or necessary, and felt strongly that instead of discussing its own future in terms of India without the British – a state of affairs he believed would not come about for a long time – the Church should concentrate on giving all its support to the Government. It was a reactionary point of view, shared by more Government chaplains than missionaries, but it was founded in the Reverend Singh's absolute confidence in the Pax Britannica, a confidence which even the massacre at Amritsar two years before, although he strongly disapproved of General Dyer's action, had left unshaken.

After the Council meeting the Reverend Singh remained in Calcutta for a few days staying at his sister-in-law's house on Blondel Street in Ballygunge. He was a popular visitor there and Dr Nathaniel always kept a bed ready for him, warned only of his coming by the sound of his voice booming up from the courtyard below, the heavy clack of his wooden *kharom* (slippers) on the stone stairs and the delighted screams of her little boy, Sonny. He enjoyed these visits to the city and after completing his priestly duties, which might involve preaching a sermon at St Thomas's or St Mary's in the hope of raising money for the orphanage (never failing to point out that the cost of living in Bengal had more than doubled since the war), giving a talk on the missionary life at his old school and sometimes lending a hand for a day or two at the Oxford Mission, he would always find time to call in at Bishop's College, where he still had friends on the teaching staff, though he kept going back for a different reason. His days there first as a student and then as a trainee for the priesthood added up to almost seven years of his life. As he walked now in the empty grounds of the college between the faded yellow ochre buildings with their familiar peeling green shutters, admiring the spring flowers in the neatly-kept borders and tubs, watching the open-beaked Calcutta crows drink from the emerald waters of the tank and observing how the lawn in the main quadrangle was still well-worn where the students played netball, he rejoiced in how little it had all changed since his day and so nourished the comforting ache of his nostalgia.

The chapel bell began to peal on the same solemn note he would always remember. It seemed to relegate the brash noise of native traffic in the busy Lower Circular Road to another world as the white-cassocked figures of the students appeared along the galleries of their cloistered dormitories, passing like ghosts in the shade of the green louvred sun-blinds and converging from all sides of the quadrangle in pious streams flowing towards the chapel. He joined them at prayer and afterwards, declining the Principal's offer to share their supper, returned on foot through the back streets of the city to Blondel Road, feeling somehow relieved, as if chastened by the necessity of leaving the past and all its securities behind him.

During his stay in Calcutta, however tempted he may have been to tell the story of their rescue, Singh said nothing to any of his friends about the wolf children and although he considered carefully whether he should perhaps report the matter to his Bishop, finally decided against it. It was not that he entertained any doubts of Foss Westcott respecting his confidence, but he did not enjoy the same rapport with him as he had with Bishop Lefroy, who had always looked on him as a favourite son; Westcott was not so convinced of the value of his orphanage or, indeed, so complimentary about his work in general. He was afraid the Bishop might require him to get rid of the children, to hand them over to some Government authority, and take him to task for the manner of their capture, which was likely to suggest to him that one of his priests had been out to the jungle on another hunting expedition when he should have been attending to his parishioners. Perhaps if Father Brown of the Oxford Mission had not been in England on sick leave at the time,

Singh might have consulted him, but in his absence there was no one in whom he could confide and he returned to Midnapore pleased at not having divulged his secret.

Outside the gates of the orphanage a small crowd of children had gathered; some had jumped the roadside ditch and were clinging on to the brushwood fence for a better view of the grounds; others were squatting in the dust, playing or milling around aimlessly, as if they were waiting for something to happen. The Reverend Singh, who was short-sighted, thought at first that the children were his own; it explained the reluctance of the *sais* on their way up from the station to answer his questions about the state of the orphanage while he had been away in Calcutta. He cracked the whip over the horse's meagre rump and drove the *tom-tom* up the incline at a brisk trot ready to be angry with whoever was responsible for this breach of discipline, but as they approached he saw his mistake and a little group of children, who had nothing to do with the orphanage, ran off shrieking and laughing down the road. The padre's reputation for possessing a short temper and dispensing summary justice was widely appreciated, but some of the older boys stayed their ground and others were still extricating themselves from the fence when Singh drew rein in front of the gates. By now he suspected the worst and it came as no surprise to him when a spokesman for those that remained asked politely if they might see the two wolf creatures that the padre-sahib had brought back from the jungle. Instead of becoming angry, as might have been expected of him, Singh tried to make a joke of their request, rebuked them mildly for believing the gossip of servants and, dismissing it all as a web of fantasy woven by the bazaar spiders, packed them off home. But as soon as he reached the house he gave way to his true feelings and calling together first his family and then the orphanage staff, reprimanded them in turn, with exaggerated regret, for breaking their word to him, for offending God and for endangering the very lives of two of His most unfortunate children. He did not pursue the matter, however, and made no attempt to find out which of his household was responsible for giving the show away, realizing, as soon as he had sufficiently calmed down, that in the end somebody was bound to talk and that it did not really matter whether it was the fault of the cook or of Daniel, his own son – the damage was done. But it was not yet irreparable.

Over the weeks that followed the children came back day after day and hung around outside the gates in the hope of seeing something that measured up to their notion of a wolf creature. Now and again they were kept company in their vigil by a few curious adults, but while these were easily persuaded to depart by the padre, who denied categorically even the possibility of such a phenomenon, the children had to be driven away at regular intervals by one of the orphanage servants, or sometimes by Singh himself, who only needed to appear in the driveway, a huge menacing figure in his winter-black cassock, to scatter their troops. In the end it became no more than a game, in which the idea of wolf creatures featured less and less as the children grew weary of repeated disappointment and eventually abandoned their siege of the orphanage. For the moment the secret of Kamala and Amala's past was as safe as a hundred other improbable rumours, some true, others not, that float up on the currents of bazaar talk either to be forgotten or dissipated by the Hindu's love of turning what might have been into myth, a blur across the vision which grants a limited but depreciatory credence to almost anything.

It was only a temporary reprieve, however, and although he would deny it later when he had become thoroughly enmeshed by the lies he had chosen to tell in his endeavour to protect the wolf children, the Reverend Singh knew well enough that in a small town like Midnapore there was little hope of keeping their secret safe for ever. Already visitors to the orphanage, remarking on the irksome presence of the children outside the gates, were asking if there was any truth in the stories that were going round, and under pressure the Reverend Singh would tell them about the two little idiot girls in his care, the daughters of a mendicant fakir, who had been deprived from birth and later abandoned, and of whom it was said – because they were a little retarded in speech and movement – by superstitious, over-imaginative servants, that they must have been raised by animals. His account was brief, convincing, dismissive and while Kamala and Amala scratched about at the bottom of their cage in the office next door, the visitors would take their tiffin in the drawing room and feel a little embarrassed at having appeared susceptible to kitchen gossip. As a result they never asked to see the children and went away satisfied, but the Singhs' luck could not last for ever. Towards the end of January that year an incident occurred within the family, unforeseen and almost tragic in outcome which, although it temporarily diverted their attention from the problem of the wolf children, finally brought home to them the impossibility of the task they had set themselves.

It happened one afternoon when Daniel Singh, recently turned fifteen years old, was searching for guinea-fowl eggs in one of the orphanage outhouses. A number of birds, kept for food as well as decorative purposes, were allowed to run loose in the grounds, always available for the pot. Their eggs, however, which guinea-fowl lay in one place and keep carefully concealed, were not so easily found and it was something of a triumph for Daniel to come across an enormous cache of them under a pile of rice straw used for thatching in the corner of the store room. He was so excited by his find that he did a little victory dance round the eggs and threw himself down on the straw, rolling over and laughing with delight at his good fortune. He flung out a hand to steady himself for fear of smashing the eggs and caught hold of a niche in the wall where the brick had crumbled away.

A cobra lying inside the cavity bit him on the thumb and then again in the join between his first and second fingers, leaving part of its fangs embedded in the second wound, broken off by the boy as in fright and pain he pulled back his hand, bringing the snake with it. The cobra fell to the floor hissing angrily and slithered away under the straw. Daniel ran out into the garden screaming for help.

Fortunately the Reverend Singh was near by and able to drive into town at once to fetch Dr Sarbadhicari. They came back together within an hour and the fight for the boy's life began. Tourniquets were tied and retied, anti-snake bite serum injected, poultices of permanganate of potash applied, a second doctor sent for; but Daniel, who was not as robust or healthy as his father, grew progressively weaker. He lay pale and drenched in sweat under a blanket on the drawing-room settee, attended by his mother and two sisters, while outside the doctors debated with his father whether he had taken the full sac of the cobra's venom, and if he had, what his chances were of survival. The doctors were not particularly hopeful: the full bite of a cobra, unless treated immediately, is usually fatal. When there was nothing more they could do, they went away leaving instructions for the boy to be kept warm. The padre, distraught with grief, called together the staff and children of the orphanage and, asking them to put their faith in God, led them in prayer for Daniel's recovery. Meanwhile Mrs Singh, who as a child had seen her own father die of a snake bite in Murshidabad, had as a last resort, without asking her husband's permission which she knew would not have been given, sent one of the servants out with a message for her brother-in-law, Jotin-dro Lal Singh, to come at once.

Joti Babu, as he was familiarly known, had a reputation for being able to cure snake bites. The youngest of the   106

Singh brothers, he had come to Midnapore soon after his eldest brother's ordination and much to the latter's dismay had settled and stayed, for although he managed to hold down a decent job as record keeper at the Judge's Court, Joti Babu was not a good advertisement for the Anglican Church. Nominally a Christian, it was well known that he preferred to worship Kali in strange Tantric ceremonies down by the burning *ghats* of the Kasai river, casting spells which he had learnt as a boy from an old man in Bankura, as he squatted beside the half-burnt bodies on the funeral pyres, and, as the stories went, ate rice from their smoking skulls. An eccentric, lonely and reputedly miserly character, who wore a belt of Victoria sovereigns around his waist and kept a brand new Raleigh cycle in his shed, which he never allowed himself or anyone else to ride, but from time to time would dust down and lovingly polish, Jotindro Lal was not welcome at the orphanage except once a year as a guest on Christmas Day. It was said that he kept a pair of milk-white cobras in a wooden box under his bed; yet he had never been known to harm anyone and as a herbalist enjoyed a certain reputation for curing specific diseases and afflictions in cases where the doctors had failed; but as far as the Reverend Singh was concerned his brother was a Tantric, a dabbler in black magic, and that necessarily put him beyond the pale.

Jotindro Lal came as soon as he received Mrs Singh's message and for once the padre's protests were overruled by his wife, as she led her brother-in-law to the sick-room, where after turning everyone out he took charge of the patient. First carefully removing the splinters of fang from between his fingers he made Daniel hold a black bean-shaped stone (said to have been taken from the head of a male toad) against the wound. Then, placing cowrie shells and red peppers on the boy's eyes together with a lock of Mrs Singh's hair – good Christian though she was, she gave it willingly – he cast a spell which he claimed would induce the snake to return under the cover of darkness and suck out its own poison. Acting directly against the doctors' instructions, he made Daniel sit up, threw off the blankets and helping him to his feet walked him backwards and forwards across the room for hours on end until the boy was so tired he could no longer move. But somehow Joti kept him awake and kept him walking all through the night. Whether or not the cobra came back for its venom, by dawn the worst was over. Daniel continued to be seriously ill for a day or two and weak for some time afterwards, but apart from shedding his skin in places he recovered without any ill effects.

The Reverend Singh refused to accept that Jotindro Lal had had anything to do with saving his son's life, which he ascribed to the power of snake serum and the grace of God. Nevertheless, he allowed him to return once or twice to the orphanage during Daniel's convalescence. It was on one of these occasions that he found him in his office, standing quite still and watching the wolf children cowering in a corner of their cage. No explanation was sought or given. Jotindro, it appeared, already knew the children's history and merely asked his brother if he might be allowed to treat them. The padre was incensed, as much by his offer to help as by his calm revelation that he also knew their secret. Resentful of Jotindro's suddenly respectable standing in the family after the triumph of Daniel's recovery, a state of affairs complicated by his own ambiguous feelings towards his son, who had grown up to be a constant source of worry and disappointment to him, he felt threatened by what he saw as a new attempt by Jotindro to extend the influence of magic and superstition over his household. The idea of Kamala and Amala being subjected to the obscenity of Tantric spells was more than he could bear, and in a sudden access of temper he ordered his brother out of the house, never to return. It was only later, when he realized that he had forgotten to ask Jotindro how he had found out about the wolf children, that it occurred to him that, instead of offending his brother, he should have begged him not to spread the story; but he need hardly have worried, for Jotindro was a man without friends who spoke little to anyone and rarely bore a grudge.

Chapter Five

With the arrival of spring, a barely differentiated season, which produces its refreshing crop of brief-lived flowers and new vegetation, but in everyone's minds merely adumbrates the fast approaching hot weather, life at the orphanage moved outdoors. The large 'English' garden surrounding the house, often compared to an oasis in the wasteland of the Gope countryside by grateful visitors sitting out in front of the porch sipping tea in the generous shade of the ansh tree, became a centre of activity. Although there were no lawns or flowerbeds to speak of, the garden covered some three-and-a-half acres with different varieties of mango, palm, tamarind and jackfruit trees, countless flowering shrubs and row upon row of large earthenware tubs spilling over with the tropical exuberance of ipomea, croton, coleus, poinsettia, and the delicate tendrils of passion flower, convolvulus and jas-mine. All of which made plenty of work for the *mali* and the orphanage children, who were taught to help with watering and tending the plants and keeping the paths and borders of the compound tidy. The Reverend Singh, whose proud creation the garden was, typically enough preferred to grow English flowers, violets, nasturtiums, phlox and other varieties, which, if they did not do as well as the exotic local species, carried a far greater cachet. Although gardening was a habit recently acquired from the British, and not much favoured by the Bengalis, for whom the virtue of a flower lay in its scent and its religious signifi-cance, some of the educated *babus* had learnt to admire and even to copy the neatly ordered compound that was the hallmark of the Sahib residence in India, an acre or so of would-be Surrey, defiant against the hostile climate of a foreign land. In their enthusiasm for the English garden some got carried away, forgetting that a highly cultivated and tree-filled compound was apt to make the house airless and unhealthy, but the Singhs' garden was big enough for its profusion of growth not to create a suffocating atmosphere and all who knew 'The Home' remember it first and foremost for the cool, luxuriant beauty of its grounds.

The garden also served a practical purpose, providing fruit and vegetables for the orphanage as well as fodder for the horse and cows. A kitchen allotment lay between the stables and the servants' quarters at the rear of the main building, protected along its north border by a high, dense growth of lantana bushes, which cut it off from the open field that lay beyond. Here in a secluded corner under the shade of a jackfruit tree, a large open-air pen had been constructed for the wolf children, where they could be left for an hour or two without the need for constant surveillance. It was in accordance with a new plan to give Kamala and Amala more freedom, which their guardians felt would help develop their trust of human beings. Although they were put back in the cage in the Reverend Singh's office at night, during the day now they were allowed to run loose in the courtyard, but always under the supervision of Mrs Singh or one of the older children. Their initial reaction to not being so confined was to spend their time finding ways to escape, restlessly patrolling the courtyard like zoo animals. And it was not long before they understood enough of their new surroundings to concentrate their efforts on the gate which led out of the courtyard into the kitchen garden.

One Saturday they were left in the charge of the eldest among the orphans, a girl called Khiroda, who had been abandoned as a baby on the Singhs' doorstep under a pile of old rags soon after they had come to live in Midnapore.

She had grown up a responsible and conscientious child and, as instructed, kept a watchful eye on Kamala and Amala. They were sitting close by her in the shade of the wall with their eyes half-shut, their tongues hanging out and breathing loudly through their mouths, for it was a warm afternoon. Khiroda had failed to notice, however, that one of the other children had left their circle and run out of the courtyard, leaving the gate into the garden open. Whether they had observed what had happened (possibly at this stage of their development the wolf children were more perceptive of movement than form) and intended to follow, or were simply making an exploratory investigation, Kamala and Amala suddenly started towards the gate moving rapidly on all fours. Khiroda looked round and saw the danger. She leapt to her feet and ran to head them off, but the wolf children were too fast and too strong for her. The moment she tried to lay a hand on them they turned and bit and scratched her so fiercely that she was obliged to let go, both arms streaming with blood, and could only watch in horror as they ran out into the garden and disappeared into the lantana bushes. The alarm was raised amid general confusion by one of the children who came rushing into the house screaming that Kamala and Amala had attacked Khiroda and escaped into the jungle, which brought the Reverend and Mrs Singh and all the orphanage staff hurrying to the spot. While Mrs Singh attended to Khiroda, the padre organized the search for the wolf children, sending a back-stop round to the far side of the lantana bushes in case they came through and tried to make off across the field, but concentrating his main forces on a frontal assault. Reminiscent of beating up tiger or pig in the jungle, it was not an easy job. Lantana, owing to its low, dense growth and the shark-skin abrasiveness of its tendrils, which earns it the nickname of 'Forest Officers' Curse', is practically impenetrable; and yet Kamala and Amala had found their way through the worst of it with apparent ease. After some time they were spotted lying low in the middle of a dense thicket, not making a sound; nor did they attempt to move away as their captors slowly cleared a path towards them; only their eyes glinting through the undergrowth gave any indication of the fear or the resentment which Singh sometimes imagined they felt, before they were finally recaptured.

The incident resulted in the construction of the pen under the jackfruit tree, but otherwise no attempt was made to restrict their freedom. As before they were allowed to move about inside the courtyard and continue to be with the other children, only now they were kept under the constant supervision of one of the orphanage servants, or Mrs Singh herself. The children, however, having seen what had happened both to Benjamin and to Khiroda, gave Kamala and Amala a wide berth. Only the very youngest in all innocence made occasional attempts to approach them or involve them in their games, which usually resulted in a threatening display by the wolf girls, howls of alarm from the other children and Mrs Singh having to come to the rescue. If they were given toys as an encouragement to play among themselves, they would ignore them or chew them up as though they were bones. Any remaining hope of bringing about even the most basic relationship between Kamala and Amala and the other orphans quickly evaporated. But although the wolf girls still showed not the least interest in people and tried to avoid both children and adults whenever possible, human contact was still regarded as an essential part of their rehabilitation. If they were unable or not inclined to learn by imitation, the Reverend Singh believed that they would gradually claim back their human nature by a sort of osmosis. But he had few illusions about their progress so far. It was nearly four months since he had brought them in from the jungle and they were still in all their immediate needs, actions and reactions no more than animals. His earlier, somewhat overbearing confidence in his own and his wife's ability to effect the speedy recovery of their human faculties, as it were through the Lord's will, had given place to a humbler, more pragmatic approach. Through careful observation, thought and prayer, he had come to understand the complexity of the wolf children's situation and how difficult and painful it was for them to adapt to the conditions which he must take responsibility for imposing upon them. 'They had cultivated the animal nature and condition of life almost to perfection in the animal world,' he wrote in his diary.

To change that, meant to change an acquired, and so far a permanent habit, which was not easy for them. We failed to understand them practically, as we had no experience like them. But this is certain, that they had to undergo a good deal of hardship and inconvenience in their set habits to permit such change to come about . . . if they were to grow in humanity, they would have to fight with their fixed animal character, formed during those years with the wolves in their cave and in the jungle, i.e. the whole animal environment. Theirs was not a free growth as in the case of a human child of that age . . . it was a hampered growth, consequently very, very slow in all its progress.[1]

Out of this refinement in his appreciation of their predicament grew a willingness on the part of the Reverend Singh to allow Kamala and Amala to develop in the directions which they seemed to favour and to do so in their own time, rather than try to impose his own structure on their development. It meant renouncing his earlier, often muddled and contradictory policy of discouraging those aspects of their behaviour - whether it was the association with the orphanage dogs, or recently discovered habit of pouncing on cockroaches, lizards and mice on the floor of their cage and eating them up while still alive, or their unchanging preference for living by night - which he disapproved of because they seemed to him retrogressive, and giving them instead more freedom to do whatever pleased them. Unfortunately, there was very little in their lives, apart from the satisfaction of eating and drinking, which they could be said to enjoy. Although an involuntary

rictus sometimes disturbed Kamala's features, which might
have been compared to a grin (Singh called it 'a smiling
face'), it was not an expression of pleasure or happiness
and behind the distortion her face remained mask-like.
Neither she nor Amala had ever been seen to smile or
heard laughing. The only time they gave any sign that
they might be enjoying themselves was when they were
taken out walking, at night or in the early morning in the
field behind the orphanage, and like dogs allowed off
the leash for a little while: 'When they went with us in the
open field, if they could perchance get away from us a
good distance which gave them the assurance of freedom,
we could see them stealthily moving about, and at times,
playing between themselves: running about, jumping on
feet and hands, looking at one another in a different
manner altogether. All this spoke of a peculiar joy among
animals only.'[2]

On one of these nocturnal jaunts in mid-February they
were almost too successful in evading their keepers, making them play hide-and-seek around the field and grounds
of the orphanage from eleven until two, taking advantage
of their remarkable ability to travel easily over difficult
and unfamiliar terrain in pitch darkness. At night they
were not afraid and, in contrast to their generally furtive
and apathetic behaviour during the daytime, their whole
demeanour became one of alertness. 'After dark, the least
sound drew their attention. They looked round very
sharply and watched if it was near. If at a distance, they
adjusted their ears by a little jerk every now and then and
listened attentively . . .'[3] They enjoyed a kind of confidence
in the night; darkness was their element; and to see them
at home in it, prowling about in the courtyard after the
children and servants had gone to bed, bold and unafraid,
was to appreciate the only successful aspect of their lives.
And yet, as the Reverend Singh found, believing that day
and night are divided between men and animals 'by God's
sanction and approval', there was something deeply

shocking about the change that came over them after dusk.

They continued to be able to see better at night than during the day. In a slightly dubious experiment using hidden meat bones, it was found that although Kamala and Amala could smell out the bones at any time, they could locate them more easily in the dark or deep shade. Throughout the month of March the weather became steadily hotter and as the power of the sun grew fiercer day by day they became increasingly susceptible to its blinding rays and would always seek out the darkest and coolest corner of the room or courtyard and stay there until dark, coming out only to look for food. If they were left in the sun for any length of time, as sometimes happened when they were put out in their pen, they were unable to keep their eyes open and started blinking and panting like dogs with their tongues hanging out. According to the Reverend Singh, they never perspired and did not appear to want more to drink in the heat. Nor were they any more amenable to being washed: a bath caused them the greatest displeasure. When thirsty they would go to their bowl or, if they were being taken for a walk, lead towards the stream where they quickly lapped up their fill of brackish water. Kamala would sometimes indicate that she was thirsty by licking her lips as if they were dry, but it could scarcely be regarded as deliberate notification; on the other hand Amala, the younger girl, would utter a sound, approximately 'Bhoo Bhoo', as she approached the water, and very soon came to make the same sound when she wanted a drink but for some reason was unable to get one. By giving her water only on demand and making other experiments, Mrs Singh did her best to foster and exploit what appeared to be a genuine attempt at communication but, beyond repeating her little noise when thirsty, Amala would not cooperate and there for the time being this unquestionably important development rested.

There were other minute indications, however, that the wolf children, though by no means ready to take possession of their human senses, were beginning to adapt themselves to a human environment. Among a number of incidents, often over-eagerly interpreted by the Reverend Singh as signs of improvement, but all sharing this much in common: that they showed Amala taking the initiative and Kamala following her example: one incident in particular revealed a significant change of attitude. It happened one morning that a cow tethered in the courtyard was frightened by something (which Singh, perhaps deliberately, does not specify) and suddenly broke loose, running out through the open gate into the garden and passing very close to a group of orphanage children. Scattering in all directions, they reacted by yelling excitedly at the top of their voices; Kamala and Amala, who had been sitting in their shady corner, not far from the other children, but well out of the path of the stampeding cow, ran on all fours to where Mrs Singh was standing, as if to seek her protection. Although they stopped short of coming up to her, again Amala had led the way and later that same day she came shyly, followed at a little distance and clearly with great reluctance by Kamala, into the room where Mrs Singh was working and waited there for some time, watching her from their corner. At first only Amala could bring herself to look at Mrs Singh, but 'by and by Kamala commenced to look at her, at first stealthily by side looks and then slowly by looking straight and meeting her eyes as she looked'.[4] Mrs Singh was touched by this little show of confidence but, deliberately ignoring their presence, made no attempt to approach them or offer them meat and after a while they went away as hesitantly as they had come. It was the first time they had singled her out for any purpose other than that of getting food or drink and, although their earlier reaction to the cow may have been triggered less by fear – indeed, there is some suggestion that it was their presence in the courtyard that had made the cow stampede – than by seeing the other children run, it was significant that they should have begun to copy them and then gravitated towards her. That they should have come to her a second time was proof that at last her efforts had been rewarded. After four months of being nursed and fed by Mrs Singh alone, not only had they learned to expect food and drink from her, but this knowledge and the regular fulfilment of their expectations had led to some sort of attachment that was growing beyond the limits of its conditions.

But if it was through the agency of food that a measure of progress, however infinitesimal, had been made, their eating habits and diet had not changed significantly. It was Kamala, the elder girl, who led the resistance to breaking with old habits. 'She could smell meat from one end of the garden – a compound of three-and-a-half acres – to the other. All of a sudden she went running very fast. I followed her close behind. She at once came to the place, where meat was being prepared for the table, and fell on it with her mouth down to snatch it away...'[5] But on this occasion, much to Kamala's rage, the cook was too quick for her. 'The pupils of her eyes rolled from side to side, as she moved her jaws opening them out and closing with a sharp chattering noise.'[6] Sometimes the wolf children would get there first and whether it was meat for the table or a dead animal or bird that they had found – they were particularly fond of rotten meat – they did not care to be obstructed. 'It was very difficult to take it out of their mouth. Even if [I] succeeded in snatching it away, they always took a bite in the mouth. The meat was simply taken out by force, but as much as the teeth caught inside the mouth remained inside. They swallowed it without chewing. They took the meat from our hand with a gulp like a dog. They made a peculiar noise while eating and remained quite alert that it was not taken away from them. They always became ferocious at such a time with all the attitude of a wild animal.'[7]

In spite of his new resolution to allow Kamala and Amala more freedom, it was almost impossible for the Reverend Singh not to try to contain this side of their nature. As yet they had not been given the opportunity to develop any latent hunting instincts they might have acquired and so far chance confrontations in the courtyard with guinea fowl, chickens, ducks and goats had provoked no incident; but it was a constant worry, after witnessing their summary dealings with mice and cockroaches, that they would soon kill something larger. In view also of their attacks on Benjamin and Khiroda he was obliged to consider the safety of his orphans. But apart from preventing them stealing the best cuts from the kitchen veranda or picking up carrion in the garden, there was little he could do to discourage them from eating meat, for whether or not it triggered their ferocity, it had remained their staple diet. They still could not be induced to eat rice or vegetables unless they were mixed with blood and raw meat; they rejected cooked meat and fruit and would not touch their food at all if it contained salt; if they picked up the least smell of salt or any spice on a piece of raw meat, before eating it they would rub it along the ground first to remove the offending flavour. Mrs Singh, however, had had more success with doctoring their milk (much preferred by Kamala and Amala to water), into which she had gradually introduced sugar and barley, until they became so accustomed to the taste that they would refuse the milk if it was not sufficiently sweet. And yet they showed little liking for biscuits or Bengali 'sweets' like *rasgulla* and other sticky, milk-based confections, prepared by Preeti Lota Singh and always a favourite with the orphans, perhaps, as Reverend Singh suggests, because they did not understand how to eat them.

Mrs Singh persisted patiently, almost stubbornly, in treating Kamala and Amala as if they had been admitted to the orphanage as year-old babies and were really no different from any of the other children. Using food rewards, she encouraged them to participate, if only as unwilling spectators, in the simple routines and learning games of the kindergarten. In the evenings she would sometimes take a tray of biscuits, fruit and sweets, as well as some small chunks of meat, into the infants' dormitory and ask those among them who were learning to talk to name the different titbits on the tray, and where they failed to do so, supplying and repeating the correct names before distributing them. Kamala and Amala would watch from their corner, indifferent to what was going on, until the food was handed out, when they would come forward to receive their share. Mrs Singh would offer them first the fruit and sweets, but after their usual investigative sniff they showed no interest. She then produced the pieces of meat, holding one out to them and then withdrawing it in an attempt to make them reach out and take the meat in the hand rather than with their mouths. After a long struggle she eventually succeeded; first Amala and soon after Kamala learnt to take meat with their hands and transfer it to their mouths. Amala also learnt to hold a cup of milk and with much spillage could even carry it to her lips, though she was unable to drink from it. In addition to these not inconsiderable achievements in motor behaviour, Amala now showed the first signs of a different order of intelligence.

She and Kamala had taken to following Mrs Singh whenever she went into the infants' dormitory in the hope that food would be given out. As often as not they would be disappointed and Mrs Singh would do nothing more exciting than read aloud to the children, or tell them simple stories from the garishly-coloured religious posters pinned to the dormitory walls, pointing out and making them repeat the names of various objects in the pictures. None of this appealed in the least to the wolf children, sitting on their haunches in the corner with heads bowed. But if Mrs Singh happened to mention the names of the different kinds of food and drink that all summer they had heard repeated by her and the children, then Amala would immediately look up, followed by Kamala, at the nearest of the pictures on the wall. The pink-featured, flaxen-haired Christ woodenly returned their unseeing stare from the authorized landscape of the *Sermon on the Mount*, but Mrs Singh knew that she had witnessed a miracle, or at least received a sign that the way forward now lay open to them, and her husband could do no less than agree with her.

But before this more hopeful stage in their development was reached by about the middle of August, the wolf children had gone through a long period of inactivity in June and July, both of body and mind, which had caused their guardians some concern. By now they had more or less given up trying to run away, except at night when they would still give vent to 'that peculiar shout which took the place of articulation' and would ceaselessly roam the courtyard looking for a way out. They had even begun to tolerate the close proximity of the Singhs and the other orphans, but their attitude seemed acquiescent and morose rather than cooperative. The Reverend Singh suggested, as usual in over-simplified but perspicuous terms, that their behaviour revealed 'a pensive state of mind'. Prematurely anthropomorphic, he saw them as becoming familiar with and gradually learning to accept their new environment while still yearning for their old life with the wolves, and being forced to 'compare and contrast' and finally to choose between the two. Indeed, they were set back in a state of suspension, literally of complete acculturation, and it was far from certain how they would emerge from it, if they emerged at all.

The monsoon broke the first week in June, bringing its cruel mixture of relief from unbearable heat and the slow build-up of tension under a stifling humidity. Throughout the long sticky months, while the orphanage garden grew up a jungle of brilliant green under the battering rain, the mango trees bore fruit and the air was heavy with the scent of jasmine, marigold and night-blooming sewlee (the flower of sadness), Kamala and Amala would sit together day after day in a dry part of the courtyard or facing the wall in a whitewashed room with a dark cloud of mosquitoes hovering over their heads, lost to the world. Their renewed indifference towards everything became as enervating and depressing as the reiterative monotony of the rain. It was difficult sometimes to persuade them even to move from where they sat and they had to be dragged out for their morning and evening walks. But the Singhs persevered. Routines and exercises were not allowed to lapse. While the padre continued with his attempts to make them stand and learn to walk on two legs, holding them up by the hands as if they were dogs and slowly moving away from them, so that they had to advance, step or hop at a time, Mrs Singh had taken to giving them both a massage with mustard oil first thing every morning, talking to them affectionately as she did so. They had always been very sensitive to being touched, but even this now became a matter of indifference to them, though Mrs Singh maintained that the massage was having a soothing and reassuring effect. All the time she went on trying to recapture their interest with food games and again with animals, bringing in dogs and puppies, goats and kids to play with them. Here at last she had some success. They began to pay attention once more to the young animals, watching all their movements and even handling them playfully and licking their faces, though if the old goats or dogs came anywhere near they at once scowled and showed their teeth. But the puppies and kids did the trick. Within a week the crisis had passed. Their mood of entrenched apathy was broken and from there the journey back to the stage of development they had reached earlier, and onwards to Amala's triumphant association of the word and a picture was swift and uninterrupted. As the Reverend Singh put it: 'After this period a difference in their state of mind was noticeable. They tried to do some things even though they had no interest in them. They could not remain passive any longer. They must grow or fall backwards. Their activity in the animal world was forcibly stopped in their changed circumstances and they were placed in a different sphere: they must live and to live means adapting to their new circumstances.'[8]

The reason for the break-through, in his opinion, was that Kamala and Amala had at last learnt to trust those around them. He believed that the affection which had been lavished upon them, especially by Mrs Singh, who had always held that love was the key, as with any child, for getting through to them, had finally won control over the embattled course, the zig-zag path of minute advances and crushing setbacks, which their lives had run since they had been admitted to 'The Home'. In comparing their situation to that of wild animals captured at a time when they were too old, too set in their ways, to be successfully tamed, he realized that the crucial difference with the wolf children lay in their untapped human potential. To reach this potential and develop it required a willingness to change on their part, that was dependent not merely on the breaking down of the conditioned habits and reflexes they had acquired in the wild, but on the dawning recognition, in which trust came before consciousness, that they were among their own kind. 'It is only possible,' Singh wrote, 'if you can create a liking in them for the change so desired. To create a liking means you must make them understand that you are their well-wisher and that you love them sincerely . . . their understanding turns then from aversion to friendliness. As they grow in this knowledge, they grow in that relationship of attachment. This knowledge expels the distrust, which alone stands as a great demon to destroy the incoming awakening of all finer feelings and thus cruelly blocks all doors of learning.'[9]

Notwithstanding the rather pompous note he sometimes sounded in committing his reflections on the wolf children to paper, as if their problem existed chiefly for him in the abstract, there can be no doubt that the Reverend Singh was genuinely concerned for their welfare. Although less intimately involved than his wife in the day-to-day trials of their existence, he was interested in their behaviour and development both as an educationalist and as a priest. More than that, he was deeply affected by their presence at the orphanage. In spite of what he knew of their past, and in spite of seeing them every day in his own house, he experienced a constant frustration of expecting these small wild-eyed creatures scurrying around on all fours in their dirty loin-cloths, so pathetically and sordidly estranged from human life, to behave like ordinary children. In a sense they made him feel inadequate, because he wanted to help them and was powerless to do so. It was partly a question of professional pride: he was a man who had always been particularly successful in his dealings with children. The orphans loved him, they called him 'Papa', they feared and respected him; yet on Kamala and Amala he could have no such rewarding effect. He had even come to believe that in some mysterious way they disliked him, out of resentment for having taken them from the wild, for depriving them of the security they had known and of the affection they had no doubt received from the mother wolf, that 'noble animal' which he had failed to defend against the arrows of the Lodhas. On occasion, seeing their regard for the pet animals of the orphanage and even more their affection for each other, which became evident in any attempt to separate them and in the touching way they would cling together when frightened, he wondered if he had done the right thing in bringing them back from the forest. Then he would tell himself that he had had no choice, that they were human children, possessed of a soul like any others, and that it had been his duty as a man and a missionary to rescue them, and he would feel somewhat reassured; but even as he watched and rejoiced in the slow painful process of their recovery, 124 thanking God in His infinite wisdom for showing them mercy, he felt the presence of a small nagging doubt.

On 4 September 1921, Amala suddenly fell ill. It began, like any number of tropical diseases, with explosive diarrhoea, turning within a couple of days – by then Kamala had also been infected – to mild dysentery, which was a common enough complaint at the orphanage especially at that time of the year, the unhealthy end of the rainy season. At first their condition gave no cause for anxiety, though the business of looking after them was peculiarly difficult. 'They were boisterous and excited at a little thing. They became peevish and irritated at the least thing which was against their wish. They would not allow anyone to go near them, or to do anything for them. At first when they had strength to resist, they behaved in a ferocious manner. They would try to frighten me and even my wife.'[10] Then fever set in and their resistance evaporated. They allowed themselves to be nursed by Mrs Singh and for the first time in their lives could even be kept in bed, albeit in a crouched position with their knees bent up to their chins. But, as they grew steadily weaker with frequent convulsions and palpitations of the heart, it became clear that the illness was more serious than anyone had suspected. On the evening of 11 September the Reverend Singh, now thoroughly alarmed by the girls' condition, which had deteriorated in the last day or two, drove into town to fetch Dr Sarbadhicari, the family physician. A frequent visitor to 'The Home', both on social and medical calls, Sachin Sarbadhicari had already had opportunity to observe and even examine the wolf children; but, knowing him to be an inveterate gossip, the padre had not taken him into his confidence about their background, sticking to his story, in spite of the doctor's provoking scepticism, that he only knew them to be the deprived daughters of a mendicant fakir. Whenever possible he saw to it that Kamala and Amala were not around when he called.

As he mounted the wrought-iron spiral staircase that rose up from the grand colonnaded ante-room of the Sarbadhicari mansion, where the doctor held his surgery open to the noise and dust of Midnapore's busiest thoroughfare, and emerged among the greenery of a cluttered roof garden, the Reverend Singh thought carefully about what he should say to persuade the doctor to come back with him at once without revealing his secret. He wondered, too, if his reluctance to send for him sooner might not have affected Kamala's and Amala's chances of recovery. At the start of their illness he had taken them in the back of the *tom-tom* to visit Dr Sengupta, a general practitioner who lived out at Chirimarshai on the other side of town. After examining the children where they lay in the cart, he had prescribed the ordinary treatment for dysentery without asking any awkward questions; but, as a doctor, Singh had more confidence in Sachin Sarbadhicari. Finding him in bed, for it was already late, he finally said no more than that two of his orphans were seriously ill and needed his help. The doctor agreed to come and the two men set out at once for Tantigoria.

When he had completed his examination of the patients, however, Dr Sarbadhicari insisted on being told the true story of how they were found and what were the conditions of their earlier life, claiming that without that knowledge he would be unable to treat them. A heavy, moustachioed figure, with the bluff gentility of a high-caste, anglicized Indian, the doctor could on occasion be formidably determined. After prevaricating uselessly, the Reverend Singh, who was unaccustomed to stepping down in any confrontation, retired from the sick-room to consult with his wife. Believing that Kamala and Amala now had little hope of recovery, Mrs Singh tearfully urged him to tell the doctor anything he wanted to know, since there was no longer any point in concealing it. They came back into the room together, and with the earnest request that he should respect their confidence, the padre reluctantly recounted the wolf children's tragic history, but in a censored form. Through the sudden fear of exposure that would cast him, a missionary priest of the Christian faith, at a time of Hindu nationalist fervour, in the role of the cruel hunter, who had torn these children of nature from the breast of a dying she-wolf (the blood of which it was a crime to shed), he thought it best to leave out the part that he and his railway friends, Rose and Richards, had played in the affair and attributed the capture of the girls to the Santals. It was an easy and apparently harmless lie, told no doubt on the spur of the moment; yet it was to have serious repercussions, and although Singh would always believe that he was protecting the truth, rather than disguising or distorting it – for in India it is religious truth that matters finally – it would ultimately ensnare him in falsehood.

Apart from this one omission, which he knew could have no bearing· on the present condition of the two girls, he told the doctor all that he knew about their past life and gave an account of what progress they had made since they had been at the orphanage. Dr Sarbadhicari listened with an air of grave interest and, after asking a number of questions with reassuringly professional detachment, concentrating on the details of Kamala and Amala's dietary and excretory habits as furnished by Mrs Singh, announced his intention to worm the children. Ever since their capture they had suffered intermittently from worms, first picked up presumably from the wolves and perhaps fostered by their association with the orphanage dogs. Dr Sarbadhicari thought it might also have to do with an occasional and very peculiar habit, which they could not be persuaded to give up, of swallowing quantities of earth and pebbles usually just after eating or before defecating. The Reverend Singh attempted to explain the phenomenon: one of his hunting companions had told him that leopards, tigers and other carnivores sometimes ate sand

and small stones to help grind up the food in their stomachs, and he presumed that Kamala and Amala had either learnt the trick from the wolves or had happened on it through the need for an aid to digestion. Dr Sarbadhicari saw no reason to disagree, but found it hard to accept that the children's digestive system could have adapted to such an alien regimen, and even more remarkable that they had not succumbed sooner to parasites or disease. He was not at all optimistic about their chances now of survival, but prescribed nonetheless a number of medicines to control the fever and dysentery and recommended dosing with sulphur powder to deal with the worms. As for diet he advised Mrs Singh to continue giving them barley water, which for the moment was all they would take, and urged her to keep them warm. Apart from that there was nothing to be done except wait and trust in God.

Unfortunately no detailed record exists of the medical treatment the wolf children received during their illness, but it would probably reveal that the fairly primitive methods available to an Indian doctor in a small Bengal country town, applied to a uniquely complex and delicate case, did more harm than good. The day following Dr Sarbadhicari's visit, after being dosed with sulphur powder, the children expelled a large number of roundworms, 'six inches long, red in colour, as thick as the little finger of the hand, and almost all of them alive'.[11] It was hardly a sight to inspire optimism, yet it occurred to the Reverend Singh as he watched these monstrous parasites leaving the weak and wasting bodies of their child-hosts, that in some way they carried with them all the foulness of Kamala and Amala's animal natures and that if they recovered it would surely be to begin life anew as human beings. But his hopes were short-lived.

The sulphur had successfully exorcized the worms, but in all probability it had had a harmful side effect on Amala's kidneys, for she was also suffering from nephritis. At the same time the fever and dysentery persisted and, 128 despite the constant attention of Mrs Singh and further visits from the doctor, the children became gradually weaker. 'They were unconscious, cold and motionless, only just breathing a little, to permit us to perceive that they were living. They just opened their mouths when the spoon containing some drink or medicine touched their lips. The doctor could not give us any hope at all. Our only help was prayer, and we had recourse to it constantly and commended them to the Lord Jesus, the Lover of children.'[12]

On 15 September in the early hours of the morning Amala's temperature sank to a dangerously low level and it seemed certain that she was going to die. All day Mrs Singh sat by her bedside, watching the tiny expressionless face, pale now with anaemia, for some sign of revival and every now and then vainly holding a spoonful of barley water to her lips. Beneath the blanket her emaciated body was beginning to swell to the distortions of dropsy caused by the malfunction of her kidneys. A stick of incense to purify the air burned fitfully from a holder by the door, giving off a sweet, cloying scent that mingled horribly with the feculent stench of her sickness. Kamala, whose condition was not yet critical, had been moved to an adjoining room, where the other orphans, teachers and servants were made to visit in small groups and offer prayers for both children's recovery. Later that morning Amala rallied a little, her temperature rose and remained high for the rest of the day, giving some cause for hope, but already by evening it had begun to sink again.

Since morning the oppressive silence that hung over the orphanage had been disturbed from time to time by the distant clamour of crowds turning out at the station to welcome Gandhi on his first visit to Midnapore and later parading their Mahatma through the streets of the town to concerted cries of 'Gandhi-gi jai' and the blowing of conch shells. The mournful sound of these traditional Hindu trumpets was carried on the evening breeze that blew in across the plains from the bay of Bengal and from the centre of town reached the Reverend Singh's ears as he walked the dogs in the darkening field behind the house. In his confusion of sorrow for the dying child and outrage that the District Magistrate and the Municipality should have allowed Gandhi's visit (and, as fate had decreed, on such a day), it seemed to him that he was listening to the funeral orison not only of the wolf girl but of India itself.

Amala held on to life for another five days and then died without regaining consciousness on the morning of Wednesday 21 September. In the last days of her illness, Kamala the elder wolf child, who had more or less recovered and could no longer be kept in bed or separate from Amala, had unconcernedly joined Mrs Singh's vigil at her side. On the morning of Amala's death she did not appear to notice at first that anything was wrong, but later on when left unguarded for a few moments, she was found interfering with the corpse, touching it in a peculiar way, trying to pull it off the bed. 'Finding her meddling with the body in this fashion, we dissuaded her by coaxing her to come to another room. She did not stay there long and came back to Amala. Mrs Singh followed her and kept a strict watch without letting her know. When Kamala found Amala did not get up and did not even move, she left her side and moved away to her own bed. This she repeated the whole day until Amala was removed for burial.'[13] When the time came for the coffin to be taken out to the Reverend Singh's *tom-tom* which was to serve as a hearse, Kamala had to be forcibly separated from it and, although the set of her features betrayed no kind of emotion, the Reverend Singh believed that she was nonetheless deeply affected. He claimed that she shed tears for the first time in her life at her companion's departure, but he may have been allowing his own sensibilities to run away with him when he wrote that 'only two drops of tears fell from Kamala's eyes, and no change of expression was noticeable on the face to make one understand that Kamala was actually weeping'.[14]

The Reverend Singh had baptized Amala shortly before she died by the name meaning 'yellow flower', which his wife had given her on her arrival at the orphanage. In the afternoon of that same day with the rain torrenting down from dark, miry skies, she was buried in an unkempt corner of St John's churchyard under a banyan tree. It was of some comfort to those mourners who were familiar with her story to know that whereas she might have died in the forest as something less than a heathen to be devoured by the hyenas and jackals, she was here being consigned a Christian to consecrated ground. She was to lie in the august company of English officials of the East India Company, whose once elegant memorials, now the crumbling, whitened perches of crows and mynah birds, stood close by her final resting place. Rain had filled Amala's grave – the *mali* had dug it several days too soon on a false alarm – and the small coffin had to be pushed down to displace the red muddy water on which it was in danger of floating. The bedraggled congregation, their sodden *dhotis* clinging transparently to their brown shanks, consisted mostly of the orphanage children and a few old parishioners who lived near the church and came to every service. Together they stood in the downpour and sang out of tune in endlessly practised, misphrased English the perfectly cadenced sentences of the *Twenty-Third Psalm*. As the coffin subsided in the water, the Reverend Singh, with his servant standing behind him holding a large black umbrella over his head, read from the prayer book: 'Man that is born of a woman hath but a short time to live. He cometh up, and is cut down, like a flower; he fleeth as it were a shadow, and never continueth in one stay.'[15] And with this vague, scarcely intended allusion to the reincarnation of the spirit, the body of the wolf child was committed to the ground.

Chapter Six

At the time I must have been eleven or twelve, I suppose. Naturally, when I heard about this girl I wanted to go and see for myself. Everyone was talking about her in the town – it was the week after the younger one had died – and when people first went to see her they wanted to know whether she was literally half-wolf or human like us.

There was quite a host of people there. I remember we stood in the compound of the Reverend Singh's house and the child was kept on the veranda. People were not allowed to touch her or throw food at her, as some tried to do. She went on all fours and crawled on her elbows and knees but could not stand; nor could she speak, though she made strange sounds that were not really like words. She was quite ferocious with darting eyes, and gave off a strong smell like an animal. We heard how she was captured from wolves in the jungle and that the Reverend Singh used to feed her on raw meat as she would not take ordinary food. She seemed frightened by the crowd and tried to hide behind the pillars.

Surendra Mohan Dey, Midnapore, 1975.

On the day after the funeral a crowd gathered outside the gates of the orphanage. Word was sent into the house that they had come to see the surviving wolf child. This time there was no question of turning them away with the story of the mendicant fakir's daughters, or even a flat denial; the Reverend Singh already knew from his own sources that Dr Sarbadhicari had broken his promise; instead, he told the crowd that for the moment Kamala was too ill to receive visitors (which was true enough) and promised he would let them see her as soon as she had recovered. With that assurance reluctantly they dispersed, but the next day and every day following they came back again in even greater numbers. The orphanage now entered a state of siege; the gates were kept permanently closed and pad-locked; children were not allowed in the front part of the garden and servants strictly forbidden from fraternizing with the crowd. As the tension mounted, the Reverend Singh's temper grew shorter: time and again he had to be restrained by his wife either from driving into town and having it out with Dr Sarbadhicari or from venting his anger on the crowd at the gates. She begged him to con-sider how fortunate they had been to keep their secret for as long as they had, and that it was inevitable in a small town like Midnapore that the news would eventually leak out. There were others, after all, besides Dr Sarbadhicari, who had seen the children — servants, parishioners, visiting missionaries, the Brothers of the Poor, his friends and hunting companions from Mr Woodgate to the Rajah of Narajole, and even if they had not been told the story of the rescue (though there may have been exceptions), many had shown enough interest in their peculiar be-haviour to take seriously the rumours about wolf children that circulated the bazaars. Then there was also the possibility that Rose and Richards in Kharagpur had talked. By implication, Mrs Singh suggested that her husband had perhaps been wrong ever to lie about the wolf children, even if it was only to protect them, and that it would be better now to let people see Kamala and tell them the truth. Then in time the novelty would wear off and they would leave her alone. Although he was bound to agree with his wife, in his present state of mind the Reverend Singh could not brook even the most tentative criticism. He refused to capitulate, as he saw it, to the hordes of sensation seekers who were determined to ruin any chance that Kamala had of ever leading a normal life. He even spoke of the blight on her marriage prospects and by extension on the reputation of all the girls in his orphanage. But in the end he calmed down sufficiently to look for the will of God in all that had happened instead of railing against fate and the treachery of Dr Sarbadhicari, and to recognize that there was nothing to be done now but to open their gates to the curious.

On 1 October the crowds were finally admitted. Kamala, who had spent the week since Amala died sitting in her corner in an abject, trance-like state that verged on the catatonic, was led out crawling on hands and knees with a loose frock thrown over her for the sake of modesty through the prayer room and on to the veranda, where she was exposed to the bewildering scrutiny of a hundred pairs of eyes. Her initial reaction was to try to run away, but Mrs Singh held on to her, while the padre told her story and briefly answered questions before asking the audience to have pity and allow her to go back inside. In the circumstances an appeal to compassion was wasted breath and the excited but dissatisfied crowd had to be held back by the orphanage servants as Kamala and her guardians retreated into the house. The Reverend Singh returned immediately and with little concession to politeness invited all to leave the compound, but no sooner had they gone than the *mali* came into the house to report that a second crowd had gathered and were waiting outside the gates, clamouring to see the wolf child. By evening Kamala had been exhibited at least four times. On the next day the crowds were worse and not only were they alarming Kamala – there was always someone who tried to touch her or feed her or even poke her with a stick to make her fierce – but they were tramping all over the garden and disrupting the work and routine of the orphanage. It was too late now to go back, but as a way of reducing the impact the Reverend Singh established regular visiting hours, which though reminiscent of feeding time at the Calcutta Zoo, made it easier to control the invasion which 'The Home' would have to put up with for weeks and even months to come.

As well as the ordinary people of the town who came to see the wolf child at the appointed times, there were those who – whether they counted themselves friends and relatives of the family, or members of the European community, or belonging to the higher echelons of Midnapore society – wished to have a more exclusive view of Kamala. Very often they caused more trouble and inconvenience than the regular visitors, but it would have been very difficult for the padre to refuse their requests; though Kamala herself, as Singh pointed out, could be less than cooperative. 'When any visitors came – we were infested with these curious people – and insisted on seeing Kamala, she would behave in a most peculiar fashion. The visitors were taken to the dormitory. Kamala at their sight would draw herself close into her corner and would not look at any side. She took care at the same time that no one approached her or touched her. Once a lady wanted to come near her but to her great surprise she showed her teeth and made a chattering noise with her teeth. This frightened the lady and she drew back.'[1]

For several weeks after Amala's death Kamala remained morose and unapproachable. When not ensconced in her corner or on show to visitors – eventually they became an accepted feature of life at the orphanage, though the Reverend Singh would always resent their importunity and blame them for Kamala's decline – she wandered about the orphanage quadrangle as if looking for her lost companion, smelling the places where she used to frequent, the dishes that she ate from, the bed where she had lain during her illness. If allowed to, she carried her search into the garden, ceaselessly roaming around under the trees uttering a peculiar repetitive cry, or remaining in one place for hours at a time, often sitting out in the hot sun, which made her pant, and refusing to come inside in spite of Mrs Singh's entreaties. After dark she was constantly on the prowl in and about the courtyard, looking for ways of escape, as wild and restless as she and Amala had been in the earliest days of their captivity. And for the first time since the end of summer the shrill whining notes of her attempted howl were heard again, jarring on the still October nights. Keeping her under close observation, the Singhs began to worry that with the return of her old ferocious nature she would lapse into idiocy. Limited though they were, she had given up all her former interests and associations; when hungry or thirsty, she no longer came to the place where she knew food and drink were kept, and without Amala to lead the way seldom approached Mrs Singh for any reason at all. What little progress she had made since she had been at the orphanage seemed certain to be lost.

The Reverend Singh had already begun to despair of her recovery, when her chances in his view were further damaged by the publication, on 24 October, of 'her story' in the *Medinipur Hitaishi*, the local vernacular newspaper. The article, for which he held Dr Sarbadhicari responsible, was a brief but garbled account of the censored story he had given him at the time of the children's illness. It was full of mistakes, which included making the foster animals tigers, putting the rescue of the children a year earlier than it happened and getting his own name wrong. The only consolation lay in the final paragraph, which offered 'innumerable thanks to Reverend Singh for his kindness. He has thus gathered many orphans and has reared them with affection. Many people respect Christians, particularly missionaries, because of such qualities.'[2] No doubt he was able to recognize in this Kamala's undoubted potential for Christian propaganda, but for the moment he was more concerned with the adverse effects of such publicity. It was what he had feared all along and he expected now a continuous stream of visitors. There was also the possibility of the story being taken up by the national press. Fortunately, owing to the poor standing in the large cities of Indian provincial journalism, it was either overlooked or disregarded; and, although the story spread locally and the crowds kept coming, the situation did not get out of hand. But if the *Hitaishi* article did not expose Kamala to the unbearable level of persecution that the Reverend Singh believed it would, her predicament remained next to hopeless.

When all their old ploys to encourage her to associate with them had failed, the padre had the idea of concentrating on Kamala's daily massage, which she still allowed Mrs Singh to give her and was now the only point of contact between them. The period of massage was lengthened and repeated morning and evening. With a gentle but strong, sure touch Mrs Singh worked over every inch of her body, from under her eyebrows to the soles of her feet, paying special attention to those limbs and muscles which had been affected by her years spent with the wolves. 'Great care was taken to straighten the knee joints, and the ankle joints by constant light rubbing, twisting with the application of mustard oil and gentle jerking. The circulation of the blood in those parts was improved. In the same way the muscles in the arms, thighs and the calves were treated so as to strengthen the nerves gradually.'[3] The session went on for as long as Kamala would put up with it, but the moment she showed any sign of tiring or irritation Mrs Singh would move on to another part of the body or stop altogether. While she was giving the massage she would talk to her all the time, reassuring her with endearments, 'expressed in the most loving terms possible'.

After a week or two it was thought that the treatment was beginning to have some effect. Kamala no longer seemed to resent Mrs Singh approaching her and of her own accord had begun associating once more with some of the orphanage animals. She began crawling to the kids and sitting among them, sometimes holding one and stroking it rather roughly with her hand. She was even heard trying to talk to them, prattling away like a baby – a departure which the Singhs regarded as significant and encouraging. But a problem arose when Kamala became so attached to the kids that she hated to be separated from them. After they had been taken out to pasture in the field she would leave her corner every five minutes throughout the day to see if they had come back. In their absence she tried less successfully to take up with chickens as substitute companions. 'Noticed at twelve o'clock one morning to enter the fowl house and remain there. But fowls raced out through fear and never came in so long as she remained there. Even the fowls who were brooding left their eggs and remained outside the house moving about but not entering at all. The fowls shunned her company. Noticed her following a fowl in the garden from one end of the courtyard to another aimlessly, simply following.'[4] She would stalk a group of hens and as soon as they scattered in an explosion of squawks and wing-flapping she would pick one out and go after it, making no attempt to catch the bird but pursuing it all day in spite of its obvious aversion to her. The orphanage cat, which she also tried to make friends with, was more responsive to her advances and sometimes even played with her, boxing the air with its paws, while Kamala used her hands and scratched up the ground with her fingernails. Her most successful relationship was with a hyena cub, which because of its close resemblance to a wolf-cub the Reverend Singh had bought for her in the bazaar, in the hope of catching her interest. The cub was not allowed to stay with her, only let out from time to time for her amusement. The attachment grew quickly and seemed to be reciprocated: as soon as it was set free, the cub, an ugly scruffy little animal with enormous ears, came running to find Kamala and after the usual ceremony of mouth-licking, pawing and sniffing, they would follow each other about all day. When the hyena cub was shut up in its cage again at night she would come and sit by it for hours at a time and sometimes could only be removed from the spot by force. Again there was a danger of her association with animals becoming too strong, but again also it was providing the physical means of drawing Kamala out of herself. By the end of the year, through a combination of Mrs Singh's massage and constant barrage of affection, as well as the less avid attentions of the orphanage menagerie, she had regained most of the ground lost since Amala died.

It would be some time yet before she acquired the confidence in Mrs Singh which Amala had enjoyed, but despite herself Kamala was beginning to depend on her. Once more she would come to her when hungry and accept food from her hand. She showed now less dislike of being touched, even indicating by gesture, pulling Mrs Singh's hand on to her chest, that she wanted to be massaged. Now, of her own accord, she would approach Mrs Singh when she was looking after the young children and sit near them, watching everything that was going on and occasionally pouncing on a toy that rolled or was thrown her way and running off with it in her mouth to chew it up in her corner. The extended crisis, brought about by her illness and Amala's death, was finally over and Kamala had emerged from it a little closer perhaps to the goals which her guardians had set for her, as if the eruption of disease and the loss of the last connection with her former life had had a cathartic effect. The Reverend Singh's observation on the round worms leaving the wolf children's bodies – that they were taking with them Kamala and Amala's animal natures – had not been so far-fetched.

Kamala's long convalescence and period of readjustment in the closing months of 1921 left her almost exclusively in Mrs Singh's care. During the cold weather her husband's time was taken up by his parish work and missionary enterprise. In November he had made a particularly ambitious tour of the jungle tracts by bullock cart, if only to keep up with the American Baptists who were mounting a fresh attack on the Santals, driving out to the villages in their new Ford motor car (which was always certain to draw a crowd), armed with flutes, auto-harps and a magic lantern for stereopticon illustrated sermons. Their medicine was unquestionably more powerful than his and there was a real danger of their starting a mass movement among the Santals, which would look very bad for the Anglicans. It made the Reverend Singh think of what the principal of Bishop's College had said about the old style of religious address of twenty years ago having no power any more. Nonetheless, he refused to believe that God would allow money and a merely superior technology to prevail over the Word and with his bullock cart and Bible and the deep booming voice that had told the gospel to the darkest corners of the sal forests, he proudly persevered in the simple but true ways of the early missionaries. Although it had been his intention to do so, he did not have time on this trip to revisit the scenes of the capture of the wolf children; he made inquiries here and there in case he might turn up some clue to their early history, but they yielded nothing new and he hurried back to Midnapore having missed two weeks of protest and civil disturbances over the partition of the district, but just in time to help Mr Cook, the magistrate, with the Church side of the town's pre-parations for the coming visit of H.R.H. The Prince of Wales.

After Christmas, in spite of the recent troubles over rent collection in the Rajshahi district, which were known to have been stirred up by outside agitators and regarded by many as a manifestation of the new hostile spirit that had spread through India since the Amritsar Massacre, the Midnapore Zamindari Company held its annual Boxing Day shoot and this year the Reverend Singh saw no reason not to take part, though he took more trouble than usual to be discreet. After the article in the *Medinipur Hitaishi*, which mercifully had not mentioned his hunting activities, he had become slightly obsessed by publicity. 140

Two days before Christmas he had come across a headline in the *Calcutta Statesman*, wedged between a report on the Highland Games at Inverness and an advertisement for Theda Bara in *Cleopatra* at the Chowringhee Picture House, which read: 'Two-year-old girl saved from jackals in Orissa forest.'[5] At first he thought it must refer to his own experience, but it turned out to be a recent incident where a jackal, rather than a wolf, had snatched a child from a village in the jungle, but fortunately had been killed before it could do the girl any harm. It was merely a coincidence.

Although he had made such efforts to keep his story secret and shun publicity, Singh had himself written in his annual missionary report, which he must have known was liable to be published in the *Calcutta Diocesan Record*: 'It is pleasing to note in writing the report, one uncommon instance regarding two inmates of this institution. We might mention it here and trust it will create an interest among our friends, that we have rescued two wolf girls . . . secured from wolf-dens by villagers in the jungle.'[6] His motive for doing so is uncertain. Although it was not published in the *Diocesan Record* until December 1921, it is possible that at the time of writing both girls were still alive, which would date the report earlier than the article in the *Medinipur Hitaishi*, in which case it is unlikely that he included a paragraph on the wolf children simply to set the record straight since the story had not yet been leaked to the press. But perhaps a clue to his real motive lies in the final paragraph on the orphanage: 'In bringing the report of the year to a conclusion we call attention to our urgent financial need in support of such an institution. We are afraid our claims will be overlooked, or passed unnoticed, as a cry in the wilderness, but we feel it our duty to mention it in our report and present the true state of affairs.'[7] Certainly, money was now in shorter supply at 'The Home' than ever before and it seems clear that Singh was making use of the wolf children's story to create an interest, not so much in them as in his orphanage, which would always take first place in his affections. During the summer he had been grateful to receive a visit of several days – in India it is a maxim that the guest confers the favour – from a friend of his, the Reverend P. C. Webber, an itinerant missionary of the American Episcopal Church, whom he had met with Father Brown in his Oxford Mission days. Webber had had a strong formative influence on his vocation and in particular given him every encouragement (including relatively large sums of money) with his work at the orphanage; or as Singh put it, writing at his most elevated: 'This worthy great man . . . this noble and devout person . . . he, with a tremendous spiritual force and by his association and pious advices, actuated me to proceed forward to my Lord's Vineyard to bring in the unbelieving souls to His Fold.'[8] On this last visit Reverend Webber donated the sum of 225 rupees to the orphanage funds. There is some evidence too that Singh may have told him then about the wolf children; but whether the American advised Singh, as others would do in time to come, to make capital out of the girls, both Christian propagandist and financial, can only be guessed at. Even so, the apparent contradiction in Singh's attempts to avoid publicity on the one hand and court it on the other, may not have been so out of character. In his view, there was every difference in the world between the Christian church-goers of Calcutta, who might be persuaded to send donations to the orphanage, and the sensation-seeking crowds of Midnapore; but it would have been very foolish to imagine that once the story was known, it could be kept to a particular circuit. As it turned out it was Dr Sarbadhicari who was responsible for the leak, but unless Singh did in fact write his report after Amala's death, it might just as well have been himself. But whatever did happen – and there are a number of possible explanations – he was careful in his report to give only the briefest account of the wolf children, playing down the more upsetting aspects of their behaviour and keeping his own part in the affair to a minimum.

At the end of December the Reverend Singh arrived in Calcutta on Church business to find the city given over to a round of festivities and celebrations for the Prince of Wales's visit, but taking place against a background of protest, civil disobedience and political unrest. The fervour of the motley crowd on Chowringhee was equalled only by that of the durbaris, who thronged the reception rooms of Government House and 'Belvedere' for the succession of State and 'dignity' balls, where the Viceroy's quadrille was corded off by members of his bodyguard holding silk ropes, and pressed on to the endless drawing rooms, courts and levees, to which everyone who was anyone had been invited and where, in the scramble to be presented, it was sometimes overlooked if an Indian was not wearing patent leather boots of the approved English pattern. Regulations of dress and etiquette, however, were of the strictest. The clergy in full canonicals with silver buckles at their knees and toes and each carrying his black corded silk three-cornered hat were well represented at every function, though only gazetted officers of the Ecclesiastical Department, earning salaries of 300 rupees or more, were invited to durbars, which eliminated ninety-nine per cent of the Indian clergy and by a very long mile the Reverend Singh. Not that he had come to Calcutta to take part in any celebration, but he had always had a weakness for pomp and circumstance and being highly respectful of the authority which conferred such honour upon those of his colleagues who were eligible, he was the more acutely aware of the distinction which barred him from their number. And yet, almost in spite of himself, on such occasions he felt not resentment, but a sort of vicarious pride.

His love of ceremony at least was requited, along with that of countless thousands of Indians, by the opening of

143

the Victoria Memorial. The pageantry, firework displays, illuminations and parades took place on the *maidan* under the protection of additional troops brought in to Calcutta to take part in the celebrations, but also to prevent trouble should it threaten. They were camped outside Fort William on the banks of the Hooghly, watched over in their turn by the city's ever-circling kites, keening from a great height for scraps of food, the least movement of a rat or snake, or the unguarded remains of a funeral pyre down on the *ghats*.

One afternoon the padre walked across the *maidan*, which he had so often heard compared to Hyde Park that although he had only seen pictures of London he felt he knew one as well as the other, making a special detour to inspect the different regiments, particularly the glorious Second Rajputs, with which his family had long been connected. It was at times like these, when he had left behind the sordid penny-pinching worries of the orphanage and all the petty routines of his office, when his efforts to gospelize a corner of the sub-continent seemed insignificant and doomed to failure, that he sometimes regretted not accepting his grandfather's legacy. It would have taken him to his beloved England, where no doubt he would have been educated at Haileybury, Sandhurst, even Oxford and returned to India to be a high-ranking soldier or rise through the lists of the I.C.S. to become a judge, even to reach the High Court and win his 'K'. Brought down to earth by the sight of some sepoys throwing out stale chapattis to a ragged knot of beggar children, he was reminded of his duty, not only to the Church, but to the work in Midnapore, which his grandfather had begun and he had chosen to continue – a duty to his Santals, to his orphans, even to Kamala, his wolf child.

Ever since he had arrived in Calcutta, despite the excitement over the Prince of Wales' visit, he had been pressed by everyone from Bishop Westcott to his sister-in-law for news of the wolf children. At first he had kept his account as terse and unrevealing as his report in the *Diocesan Record*, which many of them had read, though not all wished to believe. Yet they always wanted to know more and while he continued to beg his listeners to be discreet for Kamala's and the orphanage's sake, he began rather to enjoy being the centre of attention. Away from home he soon found it quite easy to be expansive, telling his story with a great deal of sympathy and not a little skill, so that in spite of his best intentions the true account of the rescue sometimes slipped out. However, like many of his countrymen, he was a man whose respect for the truth embraced the whole rather than its parts, and if he gave out a number of slightly different versions of how the wolf children were captured, neither he nor those who heard him were particularly concerned. At least not for the present.

Soon after his return to Midnapore in the early part of the New Year, the padre received a visit from Dr Sarbadhicari, who just happened to be passing, as he put it, on his way to Gope. With half a dozen of his thirteen children in the back of his new motor car, which was always breaking down in the most inconvenient places, he had stopped, this time intentionally, to leave his card and a request for the Reverend Singh to return a book in Bengali called *Aids to Agriculture*, which he had lent him more than a year ago. But he was spotted by the padre and somewhat awkwardly invited in for tiffin. The two men had barely spoken to each other since their row over the publication of the 'wolf children' article in the *Medinipur Hitaishi*, but the frost which had blighted their relationship was quickly dispersed and the doctor, who had been temporarily suspended by Singh, was reinstated as physician to the family and the orphanage. It was a secret relief to both of them, for they enjoyed each other's company. Being of the same political persuasion and sharing a particular interest in farming and horticulture, they liked to indulge

145

in long conversations, which might range from the horo-
scopes of cows to the difficulties of growing an English
lawn but always ended up on the future of India. After
they had discussed recent events in Calcutta and the significance of Marconi's new wireless contact with Britain,
Dr Sarbadhicari tactfully inquired after Kamala, and,
given the opportunity to examine her, declared himself
satisfied with her progress. But he felt unable to recommend any treatment other than that they should continue
to concentrate on weaning her on to a mixed diet and
teaching her how to walk. He did, however, suggest taking
her to see a specialist friend of his in Calcutta, but the
Reverend Singh, for reasons he thought polite not to
mention, declined the offer and expressed confidence in his
wife's and his own ability, under the doctor's supervision,
of course, to bring her gradually back into the human fold.
The doctor was obliged to agree and having made the
household a conciliatory present of some green, loose-
skinned oranges, which he just happened to have with
him, he herded the children back into the automobile and
took his leave. Friendship apart, with competition hotting
up between the Midnapore doctors and with 'homeopathy
gaining ground every day', the orphanage at 2 rupees a
visit was not a negligible part of his practice.

Money had also become a necessary consideration for
the Reverend Singh where the wolf girl was concerned,
and although he would never stoop to charging people to
see her, he did not discourage donations for the orphanage.
On his recent visit to Calcutta he had asked Bishop Westcott to grant a special sickness allowance for Kamala,
whose dietary and medicinal needs he had made out perhaps to be a little more esoteric and costly than they really
were, but to his disappointment he had been refused.
Owing to a policy of belt-tightening among the missionary
societies, an inquiry was getting under way into the working of orphanages, which some felt were taking up more
funds than they were worth in terms of their value as seed-

beds of Christianity. Questions had been raised at diocesan meetings whether orphans above school age were not being retained and supported longer than necessary and whether in some orphanages mentally and otherwise deficient children might not be hindering the development of others. Much of this seemed like a personal insult to the Reverend Singh, who continued to believe and frequently asserted in his report that 'The Home' was 'the central and essential institution of our Missionary Zeal and enterprise'. In a moment of self-pity he had seen the Bishop's refusal to help Kamala as a threat not only to her survival, but to the orphanage's and even his own. Fortunately this rather excessive reaction was short-lived, but Singh was a man who found it easy to build on a grievance, however slight, and in spite of a special mention later that year in the *Diocesan Record*, which suggested that it was 'difficult to overestimate the witness for Christ among non-Christians by such works as the Orphanage at Midnapore',[9] he began to harbour the first rankling of resentment against the ecclesiastical establishment and a feeling of persecution, which would gradually develop until in old age it would almost overwhelm him.

In the meantime Kamala survived without the benefit of a sickness allowance. Whether or not she could be turned into a useful Christian, there was no question of her holding back any of the other twenty-two inmates of 'The Home'. As far as the older children were concerned, she was something to be left alone, except when 'Papa' and 'Mama' Singh were not around, when they would sometimes dare each other to tease and poke her and try to make her angry. More often they would simply imitate her, as many of the children of the town were doing in their homes, by crawling about on all fours and making strange grimaces and unearthly noises. The younger children were more tolerant of her, but all treated her with the same sort of nervous respect they might have shown to an unreliable pony; and Kamala, for her part, ignored them except when there was a chance of food being handed out.

She spent more time than ever alone. Where once the Singhs had favoured her various friendships with animals, they decided now that she was becoming too involved with them and removed the kids to their farmhouse. The hyena cub luckily died shortly afterwards. The orphanage dogs being shut up most of the day did not present a problem, but she had to be actively discouraged from following the chickens. The Reverend Singh played on an aversion he had discovered that she had for pigeons, particularly when they were flying. The sudden fluttering of their wings startled her and seemed to make her afraid. He tried shutting her in a room with one or two pigeons and watching through the netted windows. 'When the pigeon came near Kamala she got annoyed and would drive it away by raising her hand and making other gestures to show that she did not like the pigeon or its company. She looked puzzled and at times astonished when it flew about in the room to get out.'[10] Any expression of dislike showed a growing power of discernment, but finally all that he established was that she did not like pigeons; the chicken following continued whenever she got the chance.

Deprived of her former companions, Kamala reverted to a state of morose aloofness. For a week or so the Singhs could do nothing to relieve her loneliness. They wanted her to turn to them in her own time, but when she showed no signs of doing so they were forced to take the initiative. They started a campaign, beginning again with Mrs Singh's daily massage and building their most determined effort so far to bring her into the social life of the orphanage around the long arduous task of teaching her to stand and, hopefully, to walk on two feet. When Amala was alive, the Reverend Singh had tried various ways of encouraging them to achieve an upright posture, including digging narrow holes in the ground into which they were introduced with great difficulty and left for an hour to two to be

1. The Santal village of Denganalia in Mayur-bhanj, Orissa, where the wolf-children were taken soon after their capture in the forest nearby

2. Typical Bengal countryside with paddy fields

3. J.A.L. Singh with his wife, Rachel, and daughter, Preeti Lota, *c.* 1906, when he first went to Midnapore as a schoolmaster

4. St John's Church, Midnapore

5. Louis-Mani Das, a former inmate of the Singh's orphanage and contemporary of Kamala, the wolf-child, standing in front of the ruined porch of the Home, April 1975

6. The Rev. Singh with some of his orphans

7. A Santal tribesman in Mayurbhanj

8. A tribal hunting party in May, when the jungle dries up leaving little protective cover for the animals

9. The Indian wolf (*Canis lupus pallipes*)

10. An abandoned termitary (roughly eight feet high) similar to the one in which the wolves had made their den, and from which the wolf-children were captured

11. Lasa Marandi, a Santal from the village of Denganalia, who took part as a boy in the capture of the wolf-children

12. The temple and tank below Amarda Road dak bungalow, where the Rev. Singh brought the wolf-children on the night of the capture

13. Kamala and Amala soon after they were
brought to the orphanage

14, 15. A wolf and Kamala running on all fours. At top speed she could hardly be overtaken by a grown man, but it is doubtful whether she could have kept up with a wolf over any distance

16, 17, 18. Kamala's modes of eating and drinking *c.* 1925

19. *Below right* Kamala with chicken entrails on
the *maidan* behind the orphanage

20. Kamala in the front of the orphanage
compound

21. Kamala scratching the ground in imitation of a rooster she befriended

22. Kamala biting at a spinning top

23. Reaching up for a plate of food as part of an exercise for learning to stand

24. Carrying a toy in her mouth

25. Kamala would sit for hours in a corner of the
room, isolated from the world

26. Scratching at the courtyard gate to get out

27. Disappearing into the lantana bushes at the bottom of the garden

28. Playing with the orphanage dogs

29. Running across the courtyard with a dead chicken (or possibly a pigeon) in her mouth

30. Receiving a biscuit from Mrs Singh

31. Kamala rejects a puppy

32. Hanging from the branches of a tree helped to straighten her legs

33. Kamala first stood on 10 June 1923

34. Kamala walking by herself for the first time

35. The Rev. Singh, Kamala and Mrs Singh
pose for the photographer of the Statesman,
November 1926

36. The orphanage group. Kamala is sitting on
the ground between the Singhs

37. Robert M. Zingg in Red Cross uniform

38. Bishop Herbert Pakenham-Walsh

literally moulded into shape. But the nearest he ever came to achieving success was by holding on to their hands and raising them up like dogs to take a few faltering steps as he moved away from them – a trick Kamala was still made to perform for her visitors. Now everything she did, or had done to her, was turned wherever possible into an exercise for standing. The level of her life was gradually raised off the floor so that if she wanted anything, in other words food, she had to reach up for it. There was little hope of teaching her to stand the way one might a two-year-old baby, since all her limbs, muscles and impulses were already adapted to another form of locomotion. But Mrs Singh wanted her to learn with the other children, and where they would try to stand to reach a plate of food held enticingly just above their heads, Kamala, like some of the babies who could only crawl, would rise up on to her knees.

Mrs Singh devised a number of little games to make her stand on her knees as much as possible, and as long as food was the reward (preferably raw meat, though she would also take biscuits) Kamala cooperated. Sometimes in the course of one of these games, when the time came for the food to be handed out, Mrs Singh would make a pretence of having forgotten Kamala, who 'would be eagerly watching and waiting her turn after the babies. All of a sudden Mrs Singh would turn round to find Kamala thus neglected, and with loving expressions excuse herself for not noticing her, and would hasten to raise her on to a stool and give her a quantity of all that she had on her plate.'[11] It was a simple psychological trick, but effective; and if the successive emotions of disappointment, relief and gratification did not show up very clearly on her face, Mrs Singh had no doubt that they had registered in her heart – or at least her stomach.

By the end of February Kamala had no difficulty in standing on her knees whenever she felt inclined. She did it especially well if something was offered to her, when she would immediately rise up with outstretched hand; but also now, if she happened to stop when crawling along or going on all fours, she would as a matter of course go up on to her knees, and could even walk on them for a little way. All the while her relationship with Mrs Singh and the other children was improving. She very rarely showed any sign of active dislike of their company now, but at the same time there was no doubt that her toleration for them depended almost entirely on food. If Mrs Singh came into the room without the babies, for instance, Kamala would immediately begin to look for them and show her displeasure, for she had learnt that when the babies did not come, the plate with the biscuits and scraps of meat did not come either.

It was convenient from the point of view of teaching her by means of food rewards that Kamala had a seemingly unlimited appetite, but at meal-times she often ate so much, bolting her food ravenously, that she made herself sick and all feeding (as well as teaching) had to be stopped. Although her tastes were becoming a little more catholic, she still much preferred uncooked meat to anything else. Once she was found emerging from the lantana bushes with feathers and traces of blood around her lips and cheeks. Someone had seen her not long before running at full speed towards the bushes with a dead chicken in her mouth, but there was some doubt as to whether she had found it already dead or killed it herself. Another time she raided the meat safe, which had been left open by mistake, but only managed to steal a piece of dried salted fish and then dropped it on the way back to her corner. The Reverend Singh, thinking that she had let go of the fish accidentally or perhaps out of fear of being scolded, picked it up and took it to her but she refused even to look at it. Her dislike of salt remained as strong as ever. One marked improvement in her feeding habits was that, whereas before she would only eat from the ground by lowering her head to the dish, she could now stand on her knees 'and eat in that position till the plate was finished, using both her hands freely, raising them to her mouth. To remain in this position she needed some support in front to lean against, otherwise she could not stand on her knees for long, but having received a piece of food, she would go down on one hand.'[12] She was still unable, however, to lift a bowl or glass of milk to her lips and would always try to lap any liquid even if it was placed on a table.

Most of the special games and exercises for Kamala, though organized by Mrs Singh, were thought up by her husband, and some were quite ingenious. They wanted now to help her stretch and straighten her legs and finally stand on her feet. The padre had the idea of making a square of four benches laid out on the floor with a table in the middle like an island, on which a particularly exciting looking plate of titbits was left marooned. In order to reach the treasure the children (and hopefully Kamala) would have to lean up on one of the side benches and, resting their weight partly on their bellies but also on their feet, stretch across the make-believe sea. But the benches had been arranged so that however hard they tried the children would fail simply because they were not tall enough. The first day of the experiment, Kamala watched the antics of children from her corner but made no attempt to take part. As soon as they got tired and lost interest, Mrs Singh rescued the treasure and distributed it among them, but leaving out Kamala. The next day the game was set up as before, only this time Mrs Singh left the room to observe from outside the window. Again the children did their utmost to reach the plate but gave up almost immediately, whereupon Kamala, who had been closely following all their movements, crawled out of her corner and first looking all around as if to make sure there was nobody watching, leant up on the bench and easily reached across to the island, straightening her knees and letting her weight fall back a little on to her feet as she brought the plate back, spilling most of its contents. She then squatted down on the floor and consumed everything that was left, growling and looking fierce at any of the children who tried to come near, but not bothering to chase them away as she usually did. When she had finished she again looked all around her, but this time with an air of satisfaction. As if to crown her achievement, she promptly seized in her mouth a red doll from the children's toy basket – it was thought she preferred red as a colour – and ran off to her corner where she proceeded to worry it like a dog with a bone.

One evening in March, not long after the game with the bench square had become a regular exercise, Kamala was discovered in the garden playing with the cat under the mango grove. Since the purge, she had not been allowed to spend time alone with the cat, the sole survivor among her friends; but instead of interrupting them straight away, the Reverend Singh waited and watched to see what they would get up to. Before long the cat climbed into the tree and Kamala, much to Singh's surprise since he knew she was unable to climb, tried to follow. She raised herself up on a low branch in the way she had learnt to do on the bench square and rested her hips against it while supporting most of her weight on her feet. From that moment the Singhs felt convinced that Kamala would end up by learning how to walk. Her relationship with the cat was once more approved; when it failed in its duty of inducing her to ride the branch, the Reverend Singh would place some meat a little higher in the tree as an alternative bait; or else he would pick up the cat and suspend it by its two front paws from a branch while Kamala watched from a little way off. After some time she learnt to hang from the branch by her hands and even to swing herself to and fro. Always ready to take things a stage further, the padre had a proper swing put up under another tree for Kamala and the orphans, but although the other children learnt to enjoy it, Kamala for some reason refused to have anything to do with it.

In the meantime the Reverend Singh had devised some

more advanced standing exercises, which became progressively harder as the level at which she received her
reward was raised inch by inch. In one of the rooms he
had fixed up an adjustable wall bracket, which Kamala
could use to rest on while she tried to reach a plate of food
suspended tantalizingly just above her head. The plate
was held in a rope sling, which hung from the ceiling and
could be lowered or raised. However, the least touch sent
it sailing away from her, so that it was almost impossible
for her to get at its contents unless she was supporting her
whole body on her feet in a balanced position. The exercises were repeated again and again until eventually she
succeeded. Then the wall bracket, which had helped her
to stand, was removed: 'Kamala had to get the hanging
plate by leaning against the bare wall. She failed to get the
plate. The plate was left there all the time, and Kamala
remained busy the whole day trying to tackle the plate but
failed every time. Sometimes when she missed the plate,
she came down to the ground, dropping on to her hands.'[13]
The exercise was temporarily abandoned, but some time
later Kamala was seen to go out alone to the children's
swing in the garden and examine it, carefully pushing it
so that it would swing to and fro and then trying to catch
it as it went away from her. But she always missed. In
the end she gave up and fell back despondently on her
hunkers, a tiny brown and white figure motionless in the
fetid shade of the mango tope.

It was a particularly hot and unhealthy summer that
year and, although for once the rains came on time, breaking with a sudden violent storm on the evening of 4 June
after a long period of drought, they brought relief only to
frayed hot weather tempers – too late already to make up
for the damage to the desiccated paddy fields. Life,
nonetheless, began to renew itself with all its swarming
enthusiasm. In Midnapore town, as so often happened at
the start of the rains the flood of water that swept through
the open drains and festering street sewers turned a

minor outbreak of cholera into the threat of an epidemic. The District Magistrate called a meeting of the town doctors to discuss emergency measures, which all knew would avail nothing: it was merely a question of procedure. Dr Sarbadhicari came out to the orphanage and advised that routine precautions be taken with food and water, but there they had the advantage of being isolated from the main sources of infection. By the end of June the number of deaths had fallen off and the danger was declared past. The weather, however, continued unhealthy, for now it was the rain rather than the sun that beat remorselessly upon the nerves and through depression, exhaustion or loss of temper, predisposed its victims to disease, as it clattered incessantly through the leaves of the trees and roared against tin roofs, and hammered the spattered earth into a livid green. Between showers, the humidity, mildew, snakes and flying ants were added irritations and made the heat still more unbearable. But while others weltered in perpetual discomfort and poured with sweat, the Reverend Singh noted that the wolf child's body remained as dry and cold to the touch as a stone.

In his office, the Reverend Singh was kept cool by a punkah. Suspended from the ceiling by ropes it consisted of a long pole, almost the width of the room, to which was attached a strip of matting and another rope, which passed through a hole in the lintel of the door and was pulled and let go alternately by the punkah-wallah who sat outside on the veranda. The punkah-wallah, however, like all the Reverend Singh's servants, was really one of the church-bearers – in most parishes it was the expected thing for these Government-paid servants to be taken in to the padre's household – and his church duties were meant to take priority over any other, which gave him a certain bargaining power. As a result the punkah in the Reverend Singh's office frequently stood still, but the system of ropes could also be arranged so that the contraption could be operated from inside the room and sometimes, when it was very hot, the orphanage children were recruited to pull the punkah for short spells. On one of these occasions in early August Kamala happened to be present.

Several children were playing in the office, viz. Benjamin, Pachu, Bhulu and Saila. They were playing in the room and sometimes pulling the punkah rope that was hanging Kamala was sitting in one corner, watching them at times but remaining quite inactive. After some time, the children left the room and Kamala alone remained where she was. All on a sudden I felt the punkah breeze. I looked behind and found Kamala pulling the rope. I did not say anything . . . The clock hung in front of me. It was eight o'clock in the morning. She pulled from eight to eight-fifteen continuously, and then stopped to leave the room. From this date I noticed occasionally that whenever she entered the room she always looked at the punkah and always had a pull whenever she liked. This duty was not imposed on her but she did it herself. This was the only frolic she indulged in.[14]

It was also her first independent achievement, the more remarkable perhaps because she had not yet learnt to walk or even stand properly, but there can be little doubt that the Reverend Singh exaggerated somewhat her prowess at punkah-pulling. As often as not she would simply sit and twist the rope instead of pulling it, and when asked to perform, would inevitably let go of it all together, but the important thing was that she discovered this game for herself and without the hope of a reward. In that sense the padre was justified in describing it as a 'frolic'.

However, when Kamala made progress in any direction, the Singhs had learnt to expect a setback somewhere else. It seemed to them sometimes that she did it almost deliberately, as if she was trying to express a general resentment at being dragged from the animal world into the human, by reverting sharply to the animal. But a more likely explanation was that at times of stress she merely found comfort in the laws and habits of her old existence – the more poignantly because there were signs now in everything she did that she wanted to succeed and that when she slipped back it was always in spite of herself. After her triumph with the punkah, there followed a period when Kamala would no longer eat with her hands, but insisted on taking her plate and putting it down on the ground and eating once again like an animal. Then came a minor success with the garden swing, which she was persuaded to sit on for a short session and which she seemed to enjoy; but two days later there were repercussions.

It happened when the Reverend Singh was taking her for her morning walk on the *maidan* behind the house. They came across the carcass of a cow, surrounded by vultures. Some of the birds had already entered the cow's stomach and were picking greedily at its entrails, while others stood around in an ugly circle, hunch-necked and squabbling among themselves for position. Still others were turning in the air above the carcass, swooping lower and lower then planing down on a steep incline of air to the ground, their stiff primary wing feathers rattling with the velocity of descent as they stretched their wings to the full extent to break their landing. It was a common enough sight in the Bengal countryside, but one which never failed to inspire the Reverend Singh with horror and disgust. Thinking of himself as much as his companion, who was raising her nose to the parallel and sniffing the air in a tentative way, he gave the carcass a wide berth. But too late: 'Although I avoided the path by it, yet I found that Kamala, after coming away for a short distance, all on a sudden made for the carcass on all fours in hot haste. She did not listen to me shouting by her name and calling her back. She disobeyed and quickly landed at the place. She commenced chasing the vultures to clear her path to the carcass and at once caught hold of the bone by her mouth, and began to bite at the meat.'[15] Amazed by her complete lack of fear of the vultures, which stood taller at the shoulder than she did, and by the practised way in which she drove them off, the Reverend Singh ran up to her and tried to separate her from the carcass. 'At first I tried to persuade her to come away but when I found she would not come then I had to drag her by the hand and thus bring her back home with great difficulty. She came with me and occasionally looked back in the same direction where the carcass lay. She had got a bite or two at the meat and came away chewing and munching and wiping her lips with her tongue.'[16]

Some days later one of the children came to the Reverend Singh in his office and reported that Kamala had been seen dragging a huge bone by her mouth through the lantana hedge that separated the garden compound from the field. He went out to investigate and

found her with the same carcass inside the compound under the bushy lycee and mango trees in the garden. She was biting at the meat sticking to the bone. She was at turns rubbing a particular piece of bone to separate the meat from it. When I came near her she paid no heed to my presence, but went on in her own way. I stood for some time and then caught hold of the carcass at the other end and dragged it towards me. She did not like it, gave a peculiar growl and looked at me with all her ferocious attitude. I managed to remove the carcass as soon as she raised her head. She came jumping towards the carcass and me. I showed a stick and bore the attitude of striking her if she came near. She left the place slowly and sat at a little distance.[17]

The carcass was disposed of by the servants. After debating whether he should punish her, the Reverend Singh finally decided against it and the incident was closed. A week later she was found sitting on the rubbish dump eating the remains of a chicken, but again it was impossible to tell from the look that concentrated her small and sometimes almost pretty features whether she was conscious of having done wrong.

Chapter Seven

The compound lay parched and deserted, undisturbed by a breath of wind or any sign of life other than the occasional bright wing-flash of a scarlet minivet leaving the pale tasselled blossoms of a convolvulus creeper trembling where it had dipped back into a pool of shade. It was early afternoon on 17 April 1923. The sun, still holding position directly overhead, a small vivid circle of incandescence in a burning white sky, had driven everyone indoors and the windows of 'The Home' were shuttered for the rest-period to keep out the heat. A faint scent of charcoal and cow-dung smoke from the lunchtime cooking fires hung about the courtyard still. It was obliterated a moment later by a more acrid smell of burning. Fire had broken out in the orphanage kitchens.

It spread quickly by the thatched roofs along the west wing to where Mrs Singh had her quarters next to the girls' dormitory. Fortunately the alarm was given and everyone evacuated in time. The children, including Kamala, were taken into the garden by one of the teachers, while the Reverend Singh and the servants did their best to fight the fire with buckets of water drawn from the well in the courtyard. But their efforts made little difference and the whole of the west wing was razed to the ground in a very short time. Only the heat of the day and complete absence of wind prevented the fire spreading to the main part of the building. Even so the damage was considerable, estimated by Singh in a letter to his bishop at 3000 rupees, which was perhaps on the generous side, but the padre was never one to make light of a disaster, especially where financial considerations were involved. He felt the loss more keenly because he had built the west wing himself and with money from his wife's dowry. But poking over the charred rubble a few days later he allowed himself to take heart from a Bengali saying, which everyone about him was repeating: that after a fire if the bricks turn black the building is doomed, but if they remain red then it may be restored and made pukka again. Most of the masonry underneath its coating of mud daub had been preserved from the flames: and the rest, as his servants anxiously pointed out following the suggestion that one of them might have been careless with a cigarette that day, would come right with a little judicious scraping.

In answer to his letter to the bishop the Reverend Singh received a visit in May from the Reverend Tubbs who, as Secretary of the Diocesan Board of Missions, had come to inspect the damage to the orphanage, offer his consolations and make the official recommendation that the money for repairs be collected from the parish of Midnapore. But as a friend and supporter of Singh's, Mr Tubbs promised to do his best to get him a grant. He had combined his visit with a general survey of the Midnapore and Kharagpur missions and had come away with a good impression of his former pupil's work in unusually difficult circumstances. Apart from the occasional help of the railway chaplain at Kharagpur, Mr Russell Payne, who complained almost as much as his predecessor, Walters, about the living there and would have nothing to do with missionary work, the Reverend Singh had to cover the five thousand square miles and two million people that potentially came within the limits of his parish, with the help of two readers and two catechists. It was, of course, an impossible undertaking and inevitably the hard, time-consuming missionary work – held up that year by a Santal uprising in the South, not far as it happened from where he had rescued the wolf children – came frequently into conflict with the demands of the Midnapore congregation. After meeting some of the leading Church members in the vestry of St John's after service and having visited a number of other Bengali Christian families in their homes, Reverend Tubbs heard for himself of their unwillingness to support financially a mission to the Santals, or for that matter an orphanage devoted mostly to the care of aboriginal children, both of which enterprises took their priest away from them. Some even insinuated that Singh must be a Santal himself – how else to explain his dark complexion and love of the jungle and its carrion-eating peoples? Others, mostly on the Church Committee, grumbled that he was too high-church for their taste, an authoritarian figure who, in the present political climate, would be better advised to try to create a more democratic Church, which might do something to stop the advance of the Baptists. It was all sadly familiar, the squabbles and intrigues, rivalries and petty social distinctions that were the reality of an Indian parish; but it was not so very different from home and Tubbs, who by no means welcomed all the changes that were being thrust upon the Church in India, any more than did Singh, congratulated him on his delicate handling of a complex situation. He also took care to praise his work among the Santals and especially the orphanage, adding that he felt sure the bishop would share in his opinion that it was a most deserving cause. His praise afforded the padre the greatest possible satisfaction.

A more immediate consequence of the orphanage's 'great disaster', as the fire soon came to be known, was that more than half the children had been left without a roof over their heads. As a temporary measure the boys had been made to give up their dormitory in the east wing to the homeless girls, and camp out in the prayer room, which they thoroughly enjoyed. The fire had also destroyed the little hutch-like room, wedged between the girls' dormitory and Mrs Singh's quarters, where Kamala slept and, as there was nowhere suitable for her to go, she was put in with the girls. It was the first time since Amala's

death that she had slept in company. To begin with some
of the other children objected to her being there. Louise
Mani Das, now a woman of sixty-five and still resident in
Midnapore, remembers Kamala as something of a nuis-
ance: 'She was always restless at night. Sometimes she
made strange noises, even in her sleep, howling and
grunting and going "Hoo! Hoo! Hoo!" Then she smelt
very badly – a smell like an animal. After she had washed it
was not so bad, but that smell always came back.'[1] Yet they
soon got used to her, and Kamala, though she had to put
up with more teasing than before, would eventually benefit
from being brought into closer contact with her sister
orphans. There was no immediate response, however, and
the friendship between her and another child, which the
Singhs hoped and prayed for now more than ever, showed
no signs of developing. Instead she formed an attachment,
as if deliberately to thwart their ambition for her, with a
fierce little rooster, which had chased and pecked nearly
everyone in the orphanage, but allowed her to approach
and even pat it in her clumsy manner without offering too
much resistance. The association, like others before, was
discouraged: it could not altogether be prevented. Even
with the help of their two daughters and Daniel, when he
was at home, the Singhs found it impossible to keep watch
over Kamala all the time. As it was she received already a
disproportionate amount of their attention, and the
criticism had been levelled that her progress so far was
hardly a convincing return on the trouble they had taken
with her. Whatever her past had been she was now an
abnormal and retarded child and showed little sign of
ever becoming anything else. Were there not equally
deserving cases in the orphanage with a better chance of
benefiting from their assistance? It was not an easy argument to counter, especially in view of the Bishop's recent
questions about orphanages. They had often thought of
giving up on her, leaving her simply to exist. But if they
had sometimes lost interest and patience, the Singhs had

never abandoned hope. Nor had the padre forgotten his obligation to the children he had reclaimed from the forest.

In retrospect, Kamala's achievement in learning to stand and walk on two feet would lose some of its significance, but at the time everyone recognized the turning point they had been waiting for. It was early June and the start of the rains. All year Mrs Singh had persevered with the old exercises – the tree, the bench-square, the wall-bracket and swing – as well as some new ones, but without noticeable improvement. Then, at a point when Kamala's prospects of ever learning to walk seemed doubtful, the Reverend Singh decided to take over this part of her education himself. He approached the problem using the same methods as before, even going back to the earliest and crudest attempts to make her stand by holding her up by the hands, but bringing to his tuition a slightly different emphasis. He became stricter, more forceful, more domineering and less patient with her than Mrs Singh had ever been, as if he wanted her to know that he could only spare her so much of his valuable time; but in this new relationship with Kamala, which still carried undercurrents of fear and resentment on both sides, he was at last being true to himself. Kamala seemed to sense the difference, or to appreciate at least the strength of his determination to make her succeed.

Her first attitude was that of dislike for me, so much so that she got irritated at once. When I used to catch hold of her hands and made her stand like us in our morning walk, she would open out her teeth frightening me to bite ... To calm her irritation I would bring out the meat at once and show it to her ... this was a piece of raw meat which I always carried in my pocket during such morning walks ... The very sight of the meat would appease her and she would at once be gentler. I never disappointed her because disappointment at an expectation like this would create disbelief. A disbelief like this would never have permitted her to come to some sort of friendship between us.

After she finished a piece of meat I would take out another and show it to her. She would raise her head eagerly to have it. I would hold it high up beyond her reach, just to allure her again to make an effort to reach it . . . I put the meat at a height just six inches above her head, when she stood on her knees. She commenced jerking her body up a little. It was not a jump but she extended her body by raising her hand with a jerk. She could not reach the meat. Then I tried to help her by raising her bodily to reach the meat. She caught it and I slowly placed her on the ground . . . She permitted me to touch her for the sake of the meat. In this manner she gradually allowed me to raise her by the hand to reach the meat. I raised her knees from the ground as she knelt – nearly six inches, leaving her feet touching the ground. In this way by and by I made her rest on her feet. And Kamala could stand up straight, having a bend at her knees. She first stood (unsupported) for five minutes on 10 June 1923.

After this I paid attention to her walking. I repeated my former practice of trying to move with her by holding her hands. I failed completely. The next I tried was to let her stand and hold out a piece of meat in front of her, six inches distant. She could not move her feet. She remained like that. When she failed I gave her the meat every day. Then at last Kamala moved her feet two steps, one each, and could go no further. I at once jumped close to her and gave her the piece of meat and she took it, pleased, and dropped down on her knees and then on her hands.[2]

Although she tired quickly to begin with, like any child learning to walk, as she persevered so her strength and stamina grew and before very long she was able to walk from one end of the compound to the other without once going down on all fours. Her movements when upright were awkward; she staggered and shuffled along like a spastic and for some time to come would continue to feel more at ease on hands and knees or on all fours, but with encouragement she could always be prevailed upon to walk erect. This was interpreted by her tutors as a sign that at last she wanted to conform and be like them and the other children. It was the turning point, no one doubted it, but a more surprising theory, later held by Singh, would propose that the acceleration in Kamala's development stemmed not so much from her success in learning to walk as from her failure to learn to run. On two legs she could never manage more than a shaky trot; and while she continued to be able to run on all fours, as her walking gradually improved and for the first time she began to sleep with outstretched legs, she resorted less frequently to the faster of her old forms of locomotion. It was Singh's belief that if she had been able to run, 'then her progress in habits, taste, and inquisitiveness, like a learner would not have grown at all. This defect in her legs gave her the opportunity to grow slowly as a human child.'[3] A somewhat dubious contention, yet along with the move into the girls' dormitory, the assumption of an upright posture, her attachment to Mrs Singh and a number of other more gradual influences, it may have been a factor in this most heartening stage of her recovery.

Throughout the rest of the year she showed signs of improvement; incidents, small and barely significant in themselves, betrayed when taken together an awakening of the curiosity and intelligence and even some of the emotions of a normal child. When the younger children – there were thirteen of them between the ages of three and five – went for walks along the paths inside the garden, Kamala would follow them now of her own accord. She liked to watch them play under the mango grove, but if the children happened to quarrel and someone began to cry she would come back at once to Mrs Singh and stand by her as if for her protection. Her appetites changed. She developed a strange passion for fried eggs and learnt to sit quietly at the tea table with the children until she received her daily egg. She did not lose her voraciousness, however, and was frequently caught trying to force open the kitchen door, or meddling with the lock of the meat safe. She explored more. Once she was found hanging over the parapet of the well which stood in a corner of the courtyard by the gate, trying to look down into the sky reflected in its waters. She was also beginning to take an interest in the children's games and seemed to enjoy watching the boys' spinning top: sometimes she would put out a hand to stop it and then become frustrated when she could not get it going again: she usually ended up by biting it. Her performance with the punkah did not improve, but as a new activity she could be relied on now to drive the crows and chickens away from pulse spread out on a mat to dry in the sun. There could be no doubt she was coming round at last and would yet confound her critics.

One evening in late September, as if to test the accumulated wisdom of the past months, by which it was felt that Kamala had finally learnt to prefer the company of other children to that of animals, the Reverend Singh purposely left her outside the house and courtyard to roam about the darkened compound with the orphanage guard dogs.

We all hid ourselves so that she came to know that we had all gone in the house and bolted the door. She came at the door and sat there for some time. We have several doors all round the courtyard wall. All these doors are closed at dark. After waiting at that particular door for a quarter of an hour, she got up and went round the wall and stopped at each and every door. Finding all the doors shut she came back to the general entrance from which she was accustomed to go out and come in. She pushed this door to find out whether it was closed. She found it shut. She did not leave the door but sat at it and tried to listen to each and every sound inside . . . When she did not find any sound escaping through the door she got puzzled and did not know what to do. She got restless. She ran from one door to the other constantly. After half an hour or so she heard someone talking inside and she gave a loud shrill cry. She cried once and stopped. After a while another cry and an abrupt push on the door. At last the door was opened and she crawled in quietly.[4]

165

An important battle had been won and victory was confirmed not only by Kamala's continuing fear of being left
out at night, but in a new reluctance to accompany the
Singhs on their evening walks on the *maidan* by the light
of a kerosene lamp or a more primitive rag and bamboo
torch (of the kind the padre always used in the jungle)
which they carried with them. If she could be persuaded
to come, whereas before she had liked to run free and wide,
she now stayed close to their heels whether walking or
crawling and looked nervously from side to side, as if the
shadows that danced outside the ring of torchlight held
new and unknown terrors for her. In the Reverend Singh's
mind here was proof that she had at last been taken back
from the thrall of night which, he believed, God had
leased to the animal world, just as He had set day aside
for men: he saw her new fearfulness after dark, in contrast
to her former unnerving confidence, as a triumph of day
over night, of light over darkness and good over evil.
'She was no longer the same Kamala who had moved with
the wolves in the dark,' he wrote; and observed gratefully
in his diary: 'This is wonderful.'[5]

Of all the advances that Kamala made in the period
following her learning to walk none were so important or
potentially of such interest, where her development is concerned, as the now more rapid evolution of her ability to
understand and use language. Unfortunately, Singh is less
informative on this subject and less consistent with the
information he does offer than on many other not so
critical aspects of her behaviour. As a schoolmaster
polyglot and amateur philosopher, one might have expected
him to take particular interest in Kamala's efforts towards
acquiring language, and indeed the careful logging of her
first attempts at speech indicate that he was interested, but
he lacked both the time and the close relationship that his
wife enjoyed with Kamala to make a detailed study of her
linguistic unfolding, such as it was. However, it emerges
clearly that Kamala did learn to speak and to understand

considerably more than she could express, and that the progress she made with language, as recorded by Singh, follows a pattern which matches the overall picture of her development.

When the wolf children first arrived at the orphanage it appeared that neither Kamala nor Amala could speak or understand any language. They could make certain noises, usually accompanied by a display of seemingly aggressive behaviour, which were variously identified as growls, barks, whimpers, grunts and a peculiar sound – something like 'Hoo! Hoo!' – which had a more recognizably human quality. They would also give vent to a long, drawn-out cry or howl of varying pitch which they usually performed as a duet. The Reverend Singh and others who heard the sound described it as a cry of loneliness or a call to their former companions, but if this could be seen as an attempt at communication, albeit with other animals, none of their other vocalizations were recognized as such. Apart from the howling there is no record of Kamala or Amala ever making noises or signals to each other to express meaning, though it seems reasonable to suppose that they would have done so; and that the Reverend Singh, who was neither a scientist nor a trained observer of animal behaviour, almost certainly missed or ignored the evidence that was available. Which raises the interesting though necessarily academic question of whether Kamala and Amala during their time in the jungle had acquired the language of wolves, comprising, as it does, not only numerous vocalizations but full paradigms of signs and signals which wolves interpret visually as well as by smell. One can assume that some degree of communication must have existed between the children and the wolves, and that the limitations of their own physical make-up – they had little of the right linguistic equipment: neither tails, nor caudal glands, nor ruffs, nor hairy cheeks, nor mobile pointed ears – as much as their social position within the wolf family, determined what form it took. Whether their presumably pidgin Wolf had helped or inhibited them in adjusting to their new linguistic environment, and to what extent, cannot now be calculated. But Kamala's repertoire of human non-verbal expressions, restricted to what she had learned by imitation since she had been at the orphanage, had remained pitifully small.

Their first significant utterance had been made by Amala and later copied by Kamala. When approaching food she would make a 'Bhoo, Bhoo' sound and subsequently, shortly before she died, she would make the same noise to an empty plate or to Mrs Singh indicating that she was hungry or thirsty. From early on Mrs Singh had taken trouble to speak to Kamala and Amala whenever she was with them, as if they were babies learning to talk, but apart from the single incident when Amala was thought to have looked up at the picture of the Sermon on the Mount in response to the mention of a word for food they gave little indication of understanding anything that was said to them. Shortly after Amala's death Kamala was reported in the somewhat inaccurate article in the *Medinipur Hitaishi* as being able to say one word, 'Bhala', meaning 'good' or 'alright' in Bengali, in answer to any question put to her, but it was clear that she understood neither the questions nor her own reply. Others among the visitors who went to see Kamala at that time do not give her credit for even one word, though Capt. M. Guin, the son of Mr K. C. Guin, who ran the Wine and Providence Stores in Barra Bazaar, where the Singhs did much of their shopping, remembers that Kamala as well as growling and looking fierce used to make a repetitive sound, something like 'Bhoo' or 'Bha', while 'opening her mouth as if she was trying to say something. But she couldn't speak.' The Reverend Singh lists 'Bhal' as one of the first words in the vocabulary which she was to develop some two years later, but his remarks on her use of the word seem to suggest that it had a history. 'This became a very peculiar word with her because once she said ''Bhal'' she went on repeating this word for some time. During the repetition of this word, if anyone asked her any other question, the reply invariably was "Bhal".[6] Possibly her common all-purpose utterance of 'Bhoo' or 'Bha' had as early as October 1921 been optimistically taken for a 'word' by Singh, who had an interest by then in presenting the public, now that the secret was out, with a story of charity and faith and of good to miraculous progress by a 'wolf child' in Christian care.

Actual development probably followed a more conventional course – an underlying assumption being that the children were taken by the wolves, or abandoned or whatever happened, before they had acquired language from their human parents. According to Singh, Kamala progressed very slowly from animal noises, howling, growling and suchlike, to a few vaguely phonetic utterances, chattering and prattling to herself or the animals that she befriended, and from there to actual words. A commensurate growth in comprehension developed, as might have been expected, more rapidly and Kamala began to understand words long before she would try to imitate them. 'Once, she was in the drawing room with several children who were dusting books and keeping them back to the shelf. Kamala was there and I was writing a letter in the same room. I found Kamala turning towards them when her name came up in their talk. And when someone said Kamala is sleeping, she turned round at once.'[7] Before she could speak, she learnt to indicate 'yes' or 'no' by nodding or shaking her head, or at least by a shuddering blank-faced refusal or an eager forward movement of greed, for in trying to teach her words the Singhs always used food for their 'object lessons'. They would ask her what she wanted to eat or drink, usually a fairly limited choice, while they pointed out and named what lay before her. When she reacted positively to anything, they would give her the food and repeat the word for it all the time she was eating. 'We wanted to create an interest in the names by finding out what she liked and what she wanted as far as we could understand. We would take a pup or a kid, which interested her much, and place it before her: she would take it up on her lap and we would repeat its name as "Bacha" (= young one) and go on repeating it all the while she kept it on her lap and was interested in it. The moment she left it on the ground and wanted to go we stopped . . . It was noticed that she picked up this name very quickly.'[8]

It was only when she had been at the orphanage for more than three years, already six months after she had learnt to walk, that the break-through finally came. Within the space of two months from December 1923 to February 1924 she was heard to use at least eleven different words. As to the order in which she learnt them, the Reverend Singh appears somewhat vague, giving one word pride of place and then another. Kamala had long recognized the word 'Ma' to designate Mrs Singh and may have used it first – or so the padre would have it: 'Before Kamala could utter anything, the word "Ma" came naturally to her. She would call out "Ma" to Mrs Singh and then hide herself in a corner.'[9] It seems that she was shy about speaking and if anyone happened on her when she was talking to herself she would at once fall silent. She had also more recently learnt to say 'Hoo' (a sound that she had made since early days) for 'Ha', the Bengali word meaning 'yes', in answer to the question whether she wanted more food; and 'na' meaning 'no', from imitating a little boy who had cut his leg and was objecting to having it dressed: a few days later, when Kamala sprained her wrist, she made the same protest during her massage. The new words came in quick succession: Bha(t) (rice), Bhal (alright), Am(i) (I), Khai (eat), Papa (Rev. Singh) and Lal (red). She learnt the names of some of the other children, but could only get out the first syllable or a one-syllable approximation of their names. She would say 'Soo' for Saraju, for instance. Later on, when she began putting two words together, she would run the sounds into each other so that 'Ami Jabo' (I will) became 'Amjab', or 'Toomy' (I am) became 'Toom'. It was hardly an impressive performance, but in the circumstances it was an encouraging start.

And then, as luck would have it, just at the time when Kamala had been making most progress, Mrs Singh was suddenly called away to Calcutta. An aunt of hers had been taken seriously ill. She was away for more than two weeks and in her absence Kamala pined. She gave up all attempts at talking and many of her more established routines and activities. Most of the day she sat alone in her corner with her head bowed between her shoulders, sulking. At mealtimes, or when she was hungry, she would come to the Reverend Singh, who had taken over the supervision of the house, and stand near his chair in the office. But she did so reluctantly.

At first Kamala would not permit anyone to help her with anything or in any way. She would resist and go away in rage. I used to be called in and used to treat her with affection and mildness, so much as I could show any preference to her doings to the other children under the circumstances.

Someone came to me and told me that Kamala was not coming for her food. 'She is obstinate and would not listen to us.' I went in and found Kamala sitting in her corner very much displeased . . . I approached her. I called her name to make her know my presence. But no! She did not move. I went on calling her name as sweetly as I could. After some time Kamala looked up at me. Her expression and the movement of her eyes clearly showed her displeasure, but she did not speak. I placed my hand very affectionately on her and said: 'I know these children are very wicked to trouble Kamala . . .' I changed the topic. I asked her all on a sudden: 'Kamala, where is Mama?' She looked at me again. I understood she was very much anxious. Then again I changed the topic and at last came to the chief point of disagreement for which I was called in. I would request her to take her food . . . She left off eating much after my wife left her. During her absence Kamala became morose and peevish. She became indifferent to her surroundings.[10]

The Reverend Singh was afraid that she might have a serious, even permanent relapse and that all the advances she had made in the past months would be lost, but at the end of January Mrs Singh came back from Calcutta and immediately everything changed. On the day of her return the children came to tell Kamala that 'Mama' was there. As soon as she heard her voice, Kamala ran out on all fours to meet her and rushing up to her side rubbed herself against her leg and turned around and around while Mrs Singh patted her and caught hold of her chin to hug and kiss her. For the rest of the day Kamala refused to leave her side or take notice of the Reverend Singh or anybody else at the orphanage and although she could not laugh or cry or even smile to express emotion, there was no doubt in their minds that perhaps for the first time in her life Kamala was truly happy. Over the next few days she appeared cooperative, biddable and docile as she had never been before; on the Thursday following Mrs Singh's return – Thursday was her bathing day – she even allowed herself to be washed without undue fuss. Her change of heart brought about a renewal of old activities from punkah-pulling to scaring the birds and, more gradually, a return to her stilted assault on language.

At the same time she began to assert herself more. The Reverend Singh would ask himself whether this was the consequence of her learning to speak or its cause, but her assertiveness was of a limited nature and most likely the result of frequent teasing by the other children. Her personality or conception of self, developing through contact with others, as yet was scarcely emergent. She could say 'Am' (I) in a roll-call, and 'Amna' (not I), when unjustly accused of killing a pigeon, and she could recognize her own clothes or at least the red ones. She had what amounted to an obsession with red. If any of the other children picked up some garment or cloth of that colour in her presence she would pounce on it and try to tear it away from them and, if she succeeded, would refuse to let go of it, whether it belonged to her or not. As far as she knew red was hers, and whenever the word 'lal' came up, she would at once turn to the child who had spoken and look long at them, at first with interest and then reproachfully as if she wanted them to know that she had taken possession of the word as well as all that it described.

One morning in December the Reverend Singh returned from walking up snipe in the fields behind the house to find that Kamala had been taken ill during the night. This time Dr Sarbadhicari was called in without delay. Once again she appeared to be suffering from worms, dysentery and fever, and everyone at the orphanage feared the worst. But the attack turned out not to be serious and within a few days Kamala recovered. Her illness, however, left her weak and irritable for some time afterwards; she became more than usually demanding of Mrs Singh, wanting constant attention and refusing to be left alone for a moment. But there was one favourable consequence of her long convalescence; she made noticeable progress with learning to talk and added a number of words to her vocabulary.

When she was well enough, a 'Thank Offering Service' for her recovery was held in the prayer room. Kamala, showing her displeasure by constantly scowling, was made to kneel in line with the other children, while the Reverend Singh stood facing her, hands joined and cupped before him, eyes raised to the incompleted roof in his favourite attitude of prayer.

A few days later, on 1 January 1925, he took Kamala by *tom-tom* to St John's Church where, along with a group of Santal men and women who had come from their villages in the jungle for formal admission into the Church, she was to be baptized. Before the ceremony there was the usual evening service, but Kamala was kept outside in the carriage and only brought in after the Bengali congregation had dispersed. As a practical joke against the padre and the tribal converts, some of the high-caste Christian boys had filled the baptismal font with fish, dissolving into giggles behind the pews as they waited for the inevitable reaction; but they were to be disappointed. The Reverend Singh would not give them the pleasure of seeing him lose his temper. After blessing the water and all that swam in it he proceeded with the baptisms leaving Kamala's till last, both to save her from the eyes of the curious and because she had already been privately baptized in the orphanage at the time of Amala's death and therefore required a different form of service. She could not be baptized or christened again, only received publicly into the congregation. For the Reverend Singh, who was a firm believer in the power of liturgy, confirming her rebirth as a Christian child – 'an heir of everlasting salvation' – seemed a fitting way of celebrating the recent advances she had made towards the recovery of her human faculties.

Unfortunately, in the middle of the service, Kamala, wearing a freshly dhobied white frock, suddenly crouched down on the floor, frightened no doubt by the unfamiliar surroundings, and glanced rapidly from side to side as if looking for a way to escape. But Mrs Singh and one of the girls from the orphanage, who were acting godmothers and reading her responses, stood beside her and hemmed her in until the end of the ceremony, so that the padre, disregarding the mocking laughter of the boys (with whom he would deal severely later on) could say a thanksgiving that was full of genuine gratitude and optimism.

'Seeing now, dearly beloved brethren, that Kamala is regenerate, and drafted into the body of Christ's Church, let us give thanks unto Almighty God for these benefits; and with one accord make our prayers unto Him, that Kamala may lead the rest of her life according to this beginning.'[11]

Chapter Eight

During Gandhi's second visit to Midnapore, in case they should catch sight of him driving in the Narajoles' open Bentley to or from the palace at Gope where he was staying as a guest of the Rajah, the inmates of 'The Home' had been forbidden to stand near the orphanage gates or remain for any length of time in the front part of the compound. Whether Singh thought he was protecting those in his charge from setting eyes on the Mahatma, as if that in itself was enough to inspire devotion to his cause (indeed it often was), or simply did not want his children and servants adding to the crowds that always thronged the streets wherever he went, the padre meant his orders to be carried out. In the last four years, notwithstanding the growing complexity of the political situation, his attitude towards the man, whom he regarded as the greatest threat to the stability of India, had hardened. When Gandhi had gone to prison early in 1922, having wound up his civil disobedience campaign, ostensibly because he was horrified by the violence caused by his own teaching, the Reverend Singh along with many others had not taken too seriously his declared intention of withdrawing from politics and devoting his energies to peaceful 'constructive' work such as spinning, the removal of untouchability, and Hindu/Moslem unity. Although indeed he had been as good as his word since his release from prison in February 1924 and had made no attempt to regain control of the Congress Party, which had passed during his eclipse to the able leadership of C. R. Das, it was, they felt, only because he had no need of a conventional political base. Gandhi's power in India resided in the susceptibility of the Hindu masses to religious leadership. He had come to be regarded by them as an avatar – one of those rare incarnations of God through the ages, a human soul brought to the highest stage of development in order to help establish the reign of truth on earth. His loincloth and stave, emblems of asceticism and fearlessness, and his unassailable aura of saintliness were the perfect props for compelling the attention and obedience of his countrymen. Whether consciously or not he knew how to exploit the mass psychology of the people: to become the undisputed political leader of India, it was more important to extend his reputation as Mahatma, 'the great soul', throughout the country than to try to control the vicissitudes of patriotic and political sentiment in the hearts of the middle classes. What Singh feared for the continuation of British rule was that Gandhi would carry Indian nationalism, until now the concern of the educated few, out to the villages and in the name of spiritual *swaraj* give the ordinary people a real share in political activity, which they had never known before. In that direction, he felt sure, lay the end of the Raj as well as untold danger and misery for India.

But it was as a Christian that Singh felt most keenly the threat of Gandhiism, not only because he could accuse the Mahatma of poaching among the outcasts, untouchables and tribal people, hitherto the chief recruiting reserve of the missionary Church, but because he believed quite simply and with all the force of narrow conviction that Christianity was the true and only path for India, and that accordingly the country was best served by a Christian government. No doubt there was some self-interest in this attitude, since like most Indian Christians, and more than most, he owed his living to his religion; socially isolated from his own countrymen, what privilege and security he enjoyed was entirely dependent on the continued presence of his European masters, even though, as defenders of the 176

Faith, they were not always as zealous as their converts would have liked them to be. But Singh also belonged to the old school of missionary ambition; still living in chronic hope of the mass conversion of the entire sub-continent, he saw the authority of the Church, both temporal and spiritual, as its strongest weapon in the fight against heathenism. Understandably he felt that this authority was being undermined by the more liberal-minded clergy in their desire to create a democratized Indian Church: in particular he resented the lead which his own bishop, the Metropolitan of India and most influential prelate in the land, was giving in this direction.

In September of the previous year he had been surprised to learn that Bishop Westcott had accepted an invitation to attend a Hindu/Moslem Peace Conference convened by Gandhi in Delhi. Reading the Bishop's report on the conference some months later in the *Calcutta Diocesan Record*, he was outraged by the sympathetic, almost reverential tones in which the Bishop described his visit with C. F. Andrews to Gandhi's bedside on the eleventh day of the fast, which the Mahatma had undertaken as an act of penance for the communal strife that was threatening to destroy all hope of unity and progress in the political life of India. Gandhi had asked from his sickbed to hear his favourite Christian hymn, at which the two Christian priests had obligingly struck up with *Lead kindly light amid the encircling gloom*. The Reverend Singh, who believed that Gandhi was responsible for stirring things up between Hindu and Moslem in the first place, had been critical of the visit. But at a recent council meeting, hearing the Metropolitan repeat that it had been altogether a most rewarding and moving experience – the darkened room, the frail figure of the Mahatma reclining on the couch hardly visible in the fading light, the silent, watching crowd outside in the street and the Christian hymn sung by two believers: 'A memorable setting for the sowing of the seed which can never perish'[1] – he had chosen to say nothing.

For the two days that Gandhi was to spend in Midnapore from the evening of 5 to 7 July 1925, the Reverend Singh had not only put the front garden of the orphanage out of bounds but forbidden any of his family or servants to go into town during the Mahatma's visit. Here at least he had the excuse that there was real danger of being caught up and crushed or worse by the throng. As it turned out the procession went off peacefully enough. The bespectacled avatar was driven through the muddied narrow streets in the Rajah's automobile, perched mouse-like on a wide siege of pearl grey upholstery, to be gently pelted by adoring crowds with an auspicious mixture of durba grass, paddy, sandalpaste and yellow and white flower petals, arriving to the discordant sound of a thousand conch shells, kettle drums and cymbals in the grounds of the Collegiate School. It was here that he held the first of two meetings with the declared purpose of raising a memorial fund in honour of Deshbandu C. R. Das. The leader of Congress had died an untimely death only three weeks before, leaving the party split down the middle and in danger of foundering. Although he asked support for Congress, Gandhi made it clear that he would not accept the burden of leadership. He spoke softly and slowly in Hindi, mostly about weaving and self-discipline, leaving his Bengali interpreter to raise his voice in a vain attempt to reach those at the back of the enormous audience. There were no Europeans present and no overt show of police strength, though because of evidence that terrorists were infiltrating Gandhi's supporters and building up to another campaign of violence, a number of observers had been placed in the crowd. It was one of these undercover men, reporting back to the Superintendent of Police, who happened to mention seeing among the ranks of *khadi*-clad Gandhi-ites an incongruous figure in a white European suit, who bore a striking resemblance to Daniel Singh.

178

The following Sunday after church, the S.P., a man called Waterworth, raised the matter with the padre, suggesting jokingly that his son had been caught fraternizing with the enemy. The Reverend Singh was not amused. That evening he confronted Daniel with the story of his exploits and was shocked by the boy's cool, insolent avowal: he had gone to the meeting because he was curious to hear what Gandhi had to say. Knowing Daniel to hold little sympathy for the nationalist cause, he accused him of deliberately flouting paternal authority; his presence there would reflect badly on the orphanage and the Church; he had struck a cruel, ungrateful blow against his father. Daniel was defiant, unrepentant; in his turn he accused the padre of being a tyrant and a bully. The row flared quickly in the hot, airless night and all the long-suppressed hostility between father and son, the detritus of past quarrels and misunderstandings was resurrected. And suddenly the two men began to shout at each other, wild with rage, now in Bengali, now English or sometimes a comic alloyage of both. Irrevocable things were said. The next morning Daniel left the house; he was twenty years old, and his mother, who loved him, was powerless to stop him or bring about a reconciliation. He would stay with friends until he had completed his course in electrical engineering at Midnapore College; and then he would go to work in Kharagpur at the shops of the Bengal–Nagpur Railway. From now on he would need to support himself, for his father had promised to cut him off without a paise.

After the rift with his son Singh fell into one of his black moods and, as was his habit on these occasions, began to fast, taking only tea and sometimes a handful of *muri* or puffed rice at bedtime to keep body and soul together. He spoke to no one for a week and the atmosphere at 'The Home' grew daily more oppressive, for as long as the padre was in low spirits everyone was forced to keep him company. At meal times he would sit in grim silence at the head of the table while his wife and daughter pecked nervously at their food, hardly daring to say a word. Mrs Singh found an excuse to move temporarily to her private quarters at the back of the building near the girls' dormitory; as often as not the padre spent the night on a chair in his office. Servants and children kept out of his way and even Kamala seemed to understand that all was not well and retreated to the safety of her corner whenever she saw him. Then one morning, as suddenly as it had descended, the cloud lifted and everything returned to normal. It usually happened that way: 'Satan has left me,' he would announce meekly to his wife and apologize with somewhat unctuous regret for his bad behaviour, asking forgiveness of each person he thought he might have offended. Only this time Daniel was not included. Nor had Singh's devil altogether left him and the year 1926, which had started unhappily with the death of his own father and the loss of his favourite daughter, Preeti Lota, who had married a missionary doctor from Trinidad and gone to live in Ranchi, continued wretched as the financial position of the orphanage deteriorated sharply, bringing him into debt and conflict with his own parishioners as well as his missionary superiors in Calcutta.

As a result of these and other worries, perhaps, Singh had begun to neglect his study of the wolf child. Entries in his diary for the year are sparse and not very revealing. Also Kamala was making slower progress after the great step forward of the previous year and, a little disappointed no doubt by the fruit of five years' patient effort and inspired hope, the Singhs paid rather less attention to her now than before. It hardly seemed to matter, for Kamala's life in the orphanage was still tragically sufficient unto itself. And yet the signs of a developing personality do here and there stand out from the long blankness of days.

Kamala was able to recognize her plate and refused now to eat from any other: she had also learnt to drink water from a glass (though not without spilling most of it) and insisted on knowing her own glass from those of the other children. Her taste in food began to change, too. She gradually developed a tolerance for salt which before she had always disliked. The Reverend Singh thought it worth noting how she first came round to it. At breakfast one of the orphans had asked for salt with his food. Mrs Singh had duly given him a pinch in her fingers and then asked Kamala, who had been watching her closely, if she would like some too. Kamala said nothing but continued to stare at her in a peculiar fashion, her small black eyes full of imprisoned meaning. Mrs Singh dipped her hand in the salt bowl and pretended to pick some up and sprinkle it on Kamala's plate. Kamala tasted her food and rejected it immediately, looking up again at Mrs Singh, who now understood that she really wanted the salt, not just to receive the same treatment as the other child (though clearly there were some simple imitative elements present) and gave her some. It was a great success and, from then on, having once acquired the taste, Kamala would often refuse her food if it was not sufficiently salted. Possibly her new liking for salt and a corresponding sweet tooth were the result of being weaned off meat on to a mostly vegetable diet, which would generally thin the blood – a condition for which salt and sugar are the best antidotes. Her craving for meat, whether raw or cooked, had not grown any less; and on the rare occasions when it was served (cooked) to the orphans, she instantly forgot what table manners she might have acquired and emptied her plate before the finish of grace, which earned her a sharp reprimand from the padre. If she was able to understand where she had transgressed it was only because food had kept its place at the centre of her existence; it still governed her emotions and still determined the ways and means of her development, providing her both with stimulus and a hazy but utilitarian sense of right and wrong. She was naturally afraid of being scolded.

The following incident, described by the Reverend Singh, illustrates the extension of that fear (instilled no doubt by the numerous tellings-off she had received for stealing meat from the kitchen or devouring carrion she found lying in the orphanage garden) towards, a more generalized guilt:

She used to be given some raw vegetables along with the other children. At first she would not touch any. She did not know how to eat them but gradually learnt. One day a piece of radish was given to her. She ate that and heard the conversation that it grew in the kitchen garden within the compound. Afterwards she went to the garden and took up two of them. One she ate and the other she was caught eating on her way back. She was simply told playfully 'Kamala is becoming a thief'. She somehow understood it and hid herself under the bed. When she came out from there after some time she was given a radish. She would not take it.[2]

She was very upset by what had happened. Mrs Singh took her on to her lap to comfort her with a soothing massage and kind words, eventually persuading her to accept the radish, but she never looked at another all season.

Perhaps the saddest part of the story is that Kamala had to be trained to like the radish in the first place; indeed there must be something upsetting about the apparently necessary corruption of innocence to induce a sense of guilt. But from there, the Reverend Singh was able to reassure himself, stems the growth of moral awareness, and even of human kindness, for there were signs in Kamala's case that her fear of punishment might eventually lead to feeling sympathy for others. 'When one of the children was found guilty and about to be punished' – the punishment was rarely harsh – 'Kamala would leave the spot hurriedly and disappear. If asked to stay, she would not at first, but afterwards obeyed, remaining there in a very timid manner as if she also was going to be punished.'[3]

By the beginning of 1926, at an age of approximately eleven or twelve years, Kamala still had a vocabulary of no more than thirty words, which she made sparing use of, not always answering when spoken to and rarely initiating speech, except to jabber away to herself as she walked under the trees in the garden, or sat in her corner alone. But she understood more than she could express in words and if she was in a mood to communicate, she could do so now by sign language, pointing out objects when she did not know their name or had failed to make herself understood. Whereas before her face had always been mask-like except to register anger or fear, when she talked now it became more or less animated, as did her whole body in the effort and agitation of speech. And although her features would always return to a state of wooden repose, the possibility of communicating with Kamala by expression and gesture on a non-verbal level – it is estimated that as much as eighty per cent of human communication is non-verbal – seemed to offer new access to her personality. The kind of comforting contact which Mrs Singh had so successfully initiated by her skilful massage had developed into that physical language, which sustains the illusion at least of recognition and trust between members of the same species.

Inevitably there was a danger of reading significance into the least sign of animation on Kamala's face, but some of her expressions (a repertoire acquired over the years she had spent at the orphanage) were unmistakably semantic. On hearing, for instance, that Mrs Singh had returned from Ranchi, where she had been spending a few days with her daughter and son-in-law, Kamala's face suddenly brightened and, as the Reverend Singh noted, 'distinctly manifested an expression of joy'. She left the room on all fours and ran out into the garden to meet her, welcoming her with the words: 'Ma Elo' (Mama come). Catching hold of Mrs Singh's hand, she stood up and walked with her very slowly on two feet down the drive, refusing to let any of the other children come near and jabbering excitedly as if trying to recount everything that had happened in her absence; there was no sense in what she said, but the way she said it was charged with meaning.

In January the weather turned colder than usual for the time of year and Kamala, until now impervious to changes of temperature, accepted a blanket at night and allowed herself to be covered in a wrapper like the other children when they went out for their morning and evening walks on the *maidan*. She even took to testing the temperature of her bath water by dipping her hand into the jug to see if it was sufficiently warm before she would allow it to be poured over her. Her fear of water had grown less and, although she refused to go near the tub, she would play with the stuff quite happily in small quantities. She liked to lick the soap off her body until Mrs Singh cured her of the habit by putting quinine in the water; but washing remained an activity she neither understood nor enjoyed. And the same went for hygiene. Except for occasional excursions to the bathroom when the Reverend or Mrs Singh happened to be present, she continued to show a distinct lack of excretory inhibitions. Along with another habit she could not be persuaded to drop – that of rolling in any foul, pungent matter – it might have accounted for the strong smell she gave off at times, for which she was cruelly teased by the girls in her dormitory. An alternative explanation, that she exuded a musty odour 'like an animal', which never completely left her even after repeated washing, appears somewhat far-fetched; yet it is favoured by those who came into close contact with Kamala. Either interpretation could have given rise to the following curious incident.

The Reverend Singh had taken Kamala to his 'Dairy Farm', which consisted of a few cattle kept in a shed on the other side of the *maidan*. Whether she misbehaved herself he does not say, but as soon as they reached the cattle shed 'the cows began to be restive at her presence there and made a noise with their nose which signified their fright at her presence in their midst. The cows would have broken their ropes if I did not remove Kamala from their midst. Kamala remained quiet but at the same time showed signs of fear lest they chased her. The cows could not bear her sight at the Dairy. The calves even ran away to their mothers and jumped about the place. Kamala stood there on her hands and knees.'[4] Singh does not offer to explain, implying that it was the sight of Kamala on all fours which frightened the cows, but it seems more likely that they were reacting to her smell, possibly from having recently rolled in the scent marks of dogs or jackals or, alternatively, from having lived on a diet of raw meat for most of her life. Either way they had recognized danger – if not the wolf in child's clothing, then the child.

For the Reverend Singh, walking her back across the fields, it had been an unwelcome reminder of the savage past and for some time after he feared Kamala might lapse into old habits, but she appeared quite unaffected by the encounter and the incident was soon relegated to insignificance in a year when Kamala's future seemed to hold the expectancy of unlimited advancement. Even when it became clear that the promise of the early months of 1926 was not to be fulfilled, the padre, buoyant again in his eternal optimism, continued to see progress in the least of her ploys. In his diary he documented a number of incidents that show Kamala still doing her best to make herself understood, mostly without the help of language (which apparently did not develop over the period), but in rather more complex situations than before.

She could now be sent on small errands; on one occasion to fetch a rupee from the Reverend Singh's office – she taps on the drawer in his desk where she knows he keeps the collection bag, he opens it and gives her the money which she brings to Mrs Singh; or to tell Khiroda to bring the children's milk from the kitchen, which she does by repeating the Bengali word for milk and pointing at the dining-room door. Success on these missions, reinforced by praise and no doubt by some small reward, seemed to afford Kamala a certain satisfaction which showed clearly in her face, but it is all too reminiscent of a dog wagging its tail after performing an effective trick which has drawn the 'almost human' reaction from a proud owner. Kamala could run to the dining-room (on all fours) when she heard the dinner gong, then back to Mrs Singh if she found no food on the table to pull her by the arm in the direction of the kitchen; she could indicate that her meat was not salt enough, or throw a tantrum if she could not find her clothes – she was now getting used to wearing a frock and pyjamas; she could even point up to the sky and draw Mrs Singh's attention to the moon. Undoubtedly her 'power of understanding and the consequent requirement for action' was gradually evolving into something that bore a closer resemblance to human intelligence, but the attendant forecast, which the Reverend Singh was making again after the disappointments of the previous year, that 'in the near future Kamala was certain to be reclaimed as a human child' would once more turn out to be premature. A different destiny awaited her.

Towards the end of August 1926 an ecumenical band of Christian young men, some sixty strong, arrived in Midnapore and established a summer camp in the old Wesleyan Mission at Kheranitola on the west side of the town. The camp was an annual event – somewhere between a jamboree and a retreat – organized by the S.C.M. to give young college students the opportunity of enjoying a week or so away from home in a wholesome Christian atmosphere. Each year it took place in a different part of the country; the choice of Midnapore for 1926, because of the town's reputation for political unrest, was considered by some to be unwise.

As it happened it had been a long, uneasy summer in the district with trouble brewing from early April and communal strife between Hindus and Moslems finally breaking out in the railway workshops at Kharagpur in mid-May. For a week the District Magistrate, Robert Reid, and the S.P., Mr Waterworth, had worked day and night with a handful of constables in temperatures well over 100° to keep warring mobs armed with improvised weapons (chisels and files lashed to sticks and sharpened on company grindstones) from cutting each other to pieces. As the toll of dead and wounded rose, the D.M. was finally forced to call out the local battalion of A.F.I. (Auxiliary Force, India), made up mostly of Anglo-Indians working on the railways, who took over pickets and posts from the exhausted police constables and, reinforced by a company of Eastern Frontier Rifles from Chinswah, soon brought the violence under control. But it was an uneasy peace and the situation, which some feared would be exploited by the nat onalists, remained tense for most of the summer. Luckily heavy rains in July and August, causing flooding in the southern part of the district, had cooled things off a little and by the time the Christian students arrived from Calcutta (where the rioting had been considerably worse), Midnapore wore a calm and friendly exterior.

The leader of the group was an eccentric, much-loved Irishman, the Right Reverend Herbert Pakenham-Walsh, formerly Bishop of Assam and now since 1923 principal of Bishop's College in Calcutta. Revered as one of the most holy, distinguished but original churchmen in India, he also happened to be an old friend of the Reverend Singh, who had first come under his 'affectionate and considerate influence' more than twenty-five years before at Hazaribagh in Chutanagpore Division. Pakenham-Walsh had been Headmaster of the Dublin University Mission School there and Singh one of the junior masters. Since then the two men had met on a handful of occasions and the Bishop, who had taken an interest in Singh's career in its early stages, had kept a fatherly eye on him over the years and remembered him from time to time in his prayers. It was only natural, therefore, that while in Midnapore he should call to see him. Bringing along a contingent of students, who he felt might learn something from a visit to the orphanage, the Bishop bicycled out to Tantigoria

187

on the afternoon of 30 August to take tiffin with the Reverend Singh and his wife. It was a happy reunion and after a rapid inspection of 'The Home', the visitors were given tea and biscuits in the drawing room. They sat for some time discussing a wide variety of topics, for the Bishop was a great talker, until one of the students rather awkwardly wrenched the conversation round to the subject of wolves. Most of the seven students from Bishop's College, among them Ronald Bryan (who was later to become Bishop of Dornakal and later still to return to Bishop's College, where he now resides as a teacher and archivist), already knew about the wolf children of Midnapore and were very curious to see the surviving child and question Singh about her: it was the reason why many of them had volunteered to come out to the orphanage on such a hot afternoon. On the way they had primed Bishop Pakenham-Walsh, who until then had heard nothing of the story, and persuaded him to raise the matter with Singh. Prompted by the talk of wolves he remembered his promise and put the question squarely to the padre.

At first Singh was reluctant to answer and tried his best to change the subject. The damage caused by the newspaper article five years before had almost mended and now that the orphanage was no longer besieged by crowds of visitors come to see the wolf child, he was anxious not to stimulate any fresh publicity which might bring them back. But he was unable to resist for very long the earnest entreaties of the Bishop or his students. After setting the only condition that they should not talk about what they saw when they left the orphanage, he agreed to let them meet Kamala and to answer their questions. Some of the students, who already knew the story, had heard more than one version of how the wolf children had been found and were anxious to know the actual circumstances of the rescue. While Kamala was being prepared for her audience the padre told them, without in any way apologizing for his part in the affair, what had happened in the Mayurbhanj jungle. By now the Bishop himself had become thoroughly engrossed in the story. He was particularly fascinated by Singh's journal: 'He let me examine the diary he had kept with almost daily entries from the day he rescued her up to that day.'[5] They were also shown various photographs of the wolf children, mostly of Kamala, which the padre explained were taken at different stages in her development despite a certain difficulty arising from her dislike of being photographed and her habit of turning away her face if she saw what was being done. And then the reluctant model appeared before them. Wearing a clean frock and accompanied by Mrs Singh, she walked on two legs with evident difficulty to the edge of the blue flower-patterned carpet, where she stopped and stood with her long arms held awkwardly before her and stared blankly into the ring of curious faces.

'When I looked at Kamala,' Bishop Pakenham-Walsh later recalled, 'I did not notice much difference between her and an ordinary Indian girl of her age. I was not on the look-out for those physical differences of which I read later in Mr Singh's diary,' – unlike Ronald Bryan and some of the other students who asked to see and were duly shown the callouses on her elbows and knees – 'but I noticed that Kamala stood quite still with no expression of any sort on her face, until she was asked to say her name, or until I pointed to an object and asked her what it was; then her face lit up with a sweet smile and she answered quickly and clearly in Bengali . . . But her face would immediately relapse into a state of expressionless immobility and if she were left alone she would prefer to go off to the darkest corner and sit facing the wall motionless for hours . . . She had an affection for Mrs Singh and was most amenable to her directions during the time I saw her.'[6]

After she had been taken away there was a certain amount of discussion about the significance of the wolf children both from a psychological and a religious point of view. The students thought up endless questions, which

Singh did his best to answer: enthusiastic speculations on how the children came to be with the wolves, how they managed to survive and whether or not they had souls, he met with the polite condescension of one who had reached his own conclusions on the subject long ago. The Bishop, struck by the idea of the absence of vice or virtue in the children, suggested it might have an important bearing on 'the consideration of what we mean by "original sin"'. Later on he would blame himself for not realizing at the time how great the scientific interest in Kamala would one day turn out to be and for not insisting even then that she be examined by medical experts. But he praised Singh and his wife for what they had done for Kamala and commended the keeping of the diary as a unique and valuable record which one day he should try to get published. The padre thanked the Bishop for his encouragement and, taking the opportunity to remind him of the awkward financial state in which the orphanage found itself, asked him to put in a good word for his 'life's work' with the D.B.M. in Calcutta. The Bishop promised to do what he could, and with that the party broke up: but not before the padre had once more received the assurance from his visitors that they would not mention what they had just seen or heard to anyone. A few days later the camp dispersed and the Christian students, having enjoyed a trouble-free, if hot and rain-sodden, holiday, returned to their respective colleges.

In October the cold weather came in, a succession of crisp blue days, and life became bearable again. It was the time of year the Reverend Singh liked to spend visiting his Santals in the jungle villages, but this year he sent word that he was unable to come and concentrated instead on gentler outdoor pursuits – he went snipe shooting and worked at his garden. It was there one day that he saw one of the younger children who had been playing near the gate fall and cut her knee. Before he could get to her he noticed Kamala come running back on all fours towards the 190 house, only to appear again moments later bringing Mrs Singh to the scene of the accident and looking rather pleased with herself, as if she knew she had done the right thing. The padre wondered about the incident, whether she had acted out of altruism or for herself. At times it seemed to him that she showed now a genuine affection for the younger children, responding to their childish games and the love that a few of them gave her; but then she would retreat once more into a cavern of isolation and he would be forced to recognize that her relations with the other orphans were as distant as ever. The moment for virtue, which he looked for in her as a vindication of all their efforts to bring her back into human society, had not yet arrived.

The story of the wolf children of Midnapore broke in the West on Friday 22 October 1926. The *Westminster Gazette*, a popular London daily, ran it on the front page under a four-ply heading: 'Two children live in a wolf's lair – Bishop's amazing story – Girl who barked – Ate with mouth in the dish'. Bishop Pakenham-Walsh's 'narrative' then gave a more or less accurate account of how a Reverend J. A. L. Singh had rescued two girls from wolves in the jungle, taken them back to his orphanage at Midnapore and tried to raise them as human children: it created, however, a misleading impression that these events had occurred recently, not six years ago.

Anthropological experts from the laboratory of Professor G. Elliot Smith at University College had been consulted by the *Gazette*, but would not give the story credence beyond admitting that humans can subsist on any form of animal milk. Dr G. M. Vevers, Superintendent of the London Zoo, was equally sceptical and gave his opinion that the wolves would probably have eaten the children. In its follow-up to the story next day, however, the *Gazette* produced more positive statements from Lady Dorothy Mills, 'a noted traveller', who had heard stories of monkey children in West Africa, and from Julian S.

Huxley, Professor of Zoology at King's College, who thought the present case 'just feasible – it might be possible for a mother wolf to adopt human babies if she had just lost her own cubs'.[7]

Instantly there was controversy: the *Gazette* knew how to keep its scoop alive. The story, in its own words,

> was widely quoted in all the leading American papers, where it was given prominence on front news pages and aroused widespread interest and discussion. Throughout Great Britain and the continent also, this remarkable revelation attracted great interest. Over British breakfast tables yesterday morning it was the principal topic of conversation. Some people could not believe the phenomenon possible; others, world travellers among them, related similar stories arising either from their own experience or from their knowledge of native customs. At clubs frequented by big game hunters and explorers it was the chief topic at the lunch table.[8]

Over one lunch table in a 'well-known' London club discussion about the wolf children became so heated that it ended up with two members hauling off and punching each other. Again it was the *Gazette*'s story and once more it went world-wide through Associated Press with the American papers responding enthusiastically to the 'fisticuffs in London club' angle. For the next two or three days, letters poured into the *Gazette*'s offices expressing strongly-held opinions, taking sides in the controversy and giving further instances of animal-reared children. But after printing a number of them and allowing the famous woman explorer, Mrs Rosita Forbes, and Lord Wolseley to air their views on the subject, the *Gazette* quietly buried the story.

In India, however, it had scarcely been born. It was not until 13 November 1926, some three weeks after publication in the West, that the *Statesman* in Calcutta printed the story almost word for word as it had appeared in the *Westminster Gazette*. Bishop Pakenham-Walsh had apparently been interviewed by a *Statesman* representative at

Bishop's College the day before, but had added little to the original 'narrative' other than to confirm that the facts of the case were true. 'It is understood,' the article concluded, 'that the case has strained the belief of certain eminent home scientists, but the circumstances are so reliably vouched for that they can leave no room for doubt.'[9]

Two days later, on the morning of Monday 15 November, the Reverend Singh in Midnapore received a letter from Bishop Walsh explaining and profoundly apologizing for what had happened. The padre, under the impression that he had been betrayed by an old friend, was relieved to learn that he had been over-hasty in his judgement. The Bishop himself was hardly guilty. As he explained in another letter some years later: 'It was an indiscreet relative of mine who was on the *Westminster Gazette* staff in London, who saw a private letter of mine to a close member of my family at home, giving an account of the wolf children and who could not resist the temptation of good "copy", and got the story into the press, which led to its being reproduced in the Calcutta *Statesman*.'[10] But the damage, such as it was, had already been done; and there was worse to come.

That same afternoon the Reverend Singh received a visit from the *Statesman* reporter, accompanied by a staff photographer, who had come out from Calcutta to interview him and take pictures of the wolf child. Still aggrieved, the padre was perhaps not as welcoming to the journalists as he might have been, but after some discussion he complied and reluctantly told his story more or less exactly as he had told it to the Bishop and the students two months before, and as it had appeared in shortened form in newspapers all around the world. After producing Kamala, he answered a number of questions about her upbringing at the orphanage and finally was persuaded to pose with her and his wife for a group photograph in the garden. Before leaving, however, the reporter, who had done his homework, now suddenly confronted him with an earlier version of the story which had appeared in the provincial press shortly after Dr Sarbadhicari first leaked it to the *Medinipur Hitaishi*, and which attributed the rescue of the children not to him but to the people of the jungle. The padre could do no less than deny the insinuation in strong terms and insist angrily that his version was the correct one: 'I assured them that this is the true story and all that they and the other papers wrote and re-wrote before this were not partly true and I was the very person who rescued them by digging out the white ant mound with the help of cultivators from a distant village . . . because all the people in that area were scared about this "Manush Bagha".'[11] He also explained that until then he had not bothered to challenge the various false versions in the local press, because he had wanted to avoid stirring up more publicity. He omitted to explain that it was he himself who had given out the false version in the first place. However reasonable his motive, whether it had been to protect the children or his own reputation, the Reverend Singh was not the man to admit, especially before the press, to having told a lie: it was neither in his character, nor for that matter in the interest of the Christian Church.

The next morning he discovered that the reporter had not been impressed by his asseveration of the truth. The *Statesman* had given the story plenty of space and on the whole the interview had been fairly written up; but, whether out of malice or because he knew better, the reporter had opted for the wrong account of the rescue. He offered no explanation for the discrepancy between this and 'the Bishop's narrative', which the *Statesman* had published two days before, other than to state that 'fuller details regarding the finding of the child' had been obtained from the Reverend Singh. The padre was furious, but he also knew that he had been caught out; trapped by the consequences of his own distortions of the truth, he had no redress against the calumnies of others. He decided against writing a letter to the *Statesman* in protest. Later,

194

when the fuss (which again he had no wish to exacerbate) had died down, he would ask Bishop Walsh to produce a short statement of the facts.

Meanwhile he cut out the article for his files. He also cut out a letter from a woman reader protesting against the shooting of the mother wolf, and in the paper's 'News in Pictures' section, a photograph of Kamala standing by his side in the orphanage garden with Mrs Singh seated near by. It was flanked by two cruelly apposite pictures, one of a blank-looking American soldier who had lost his memory through shellshock during the War, and the other a study of Jackie Coogan, the child star, with a caption which suggested that a hair-cut and long trousers had transformed him into a young man. Nothing so positive could be said for Kamala's appearance; the shaven head, gingham frock and bell-metal bangles only underlined her pathetically unadroit stance and the look of puzzled affliction in her gaze. The Reverend and Mrs Singh no doubt saw her differently.

The divergence between the two rescue stories printed by the *Statesman* did not seem to worry its readers unduly or the editors of the other major newspapers in British India, which ran either one or the other version but not both. There were a few letters from the sceptical, but most of the correspondence published offered accounts of similar cases of wolf, bear and even leopard children dating from the previous century; on the domestic front and more recently there was a story of a pariah dog which had nursed a child in Ceylon. Letters, too, began to pour into the orphanage from all over the world, asking for more information, congratulating or criticizing Singh for rescuing the children from the wolves, offering advice and occasionally financial assistance or simply expressing wonder. At first the padre felt it was his duty to answer them all, giving priority to communications from scientists and academics, but the volume of correspondence was overwhelming and in despair Singh had to ask a friend of his,

Mr Jena, of the *Midnapore City Press*, to run off copies of a standard letter entitled 'A Short Sketch of the Wolf Children Diary', which he sent together with an outline history of the orphanage in reply to the most serious inquiries. The cost of postage, however, soon became prohibitive and many of the letters had to go unanswered. Bishop Pakenham-Walsh, with all the practicality of an Irish churchman, advised him only to answer letters that held out promise of a subscription to the orphanage. Among those that did receive a reply, a letter from Paul C. Squires, Professor of Jurisprudence at the University of California, opened a correspondence which was to have unexpected repercussions.

The wolf children were the talk of Calcutta and, as Singh had anticipated, it was not long before the crowds found their way back to the orphanage and were clamouring at the gate, demanding to see Kamala. As often as not he would oblige them, but sometimes, sickened by the circus atmosphere that had once more invaded his compound, he lost his temper and drove the people away. The more distinguished visitors he nearly always managed to accommodate; for although annoyed by this second round of publicity and the trouble it had caused him, the Reverend Singh was not altogether immune to seeing his own name – the name of 'a humble Indian Missionary' as he sometimes referred to himself – writ so large before the eyes of the world. It had also occurred to him that in the long run the orphanage might benefit from becoming famous. If so, then Kamala would turn out to be the saviour of the institution which had succoured her; and that surely could only be the work of Providence. And who was he, a humble missionary, to oppose the will of God?

19 December 1926. 'It was noticed that Kamala stealthily ate raw meat, somehow managing to enter the kitchen to steal it.'[12]

Chapter Nine

A gentleman from Bombay had written to the Reverend
Singh offering to cure Kamala by Hat Yoga: he suggested
simply hanging her upside down until her human faculties
returned. The padre took him seriously.

Treatment to increase brain power: early in the morning every
day I used to take her into my room and asked one or two grown-
up men to help me. I fixed a peg on the wall and had a noose
from it. We took her up by her legs and put one leg in the noose
and held the other leg, having my left hand free. Placed a soft
cushion on the ground for her head to rest on. I kept my left
hand on her forehead, passing the hand from side to side. I
commenced this process counting for two minutes and gradually
increased the period up to fifteen minutes. This treatment
helped her to grow her brain faculties noticeably.[1]

Encouraged perhaps by the interest and concern being
shown by so many people in Kamala's welfare, Singh's
optimism had once more taken wing. He began to see
progress in all that she did and said; her prattling and
broken speech seemed to him more distinct than before,
her punkah-pulling more adept, even her walking had
somewhat improved; she was discovered trying to take
water from a bucket in a clumsy attempt at washing herself, and her fits of temper were no longer seen as outbursts
of rage from some unknowable frustration but heartening
evidence of human emotion and involvement. She was
becoming a person, even 'a sweet, obedient child'. And no
doubt in many respects the signs were encouraging, yet an
element of fantasy had crept in somewhere – borrowed,
perhaps, from the outside world. A letter had arrived

asking for Kamala's hand in marriage: Ranjan Ghosal, fourth year B.A. student at Serampore College, claimed to have been struck with pity for her after reading of the Singhs' fear that she would never find a husband. The padre, uncertain of whether or not he was being made the victim of a joke, politely declined the offer. Another letter held out the prospect of fame and fortune: Madan Theatres Company of Calcutta had come up with the idea of making a film about the wolf child: after seeing their representative, Singh turned the offer down. Kamala never became a star of the silver screen; but she did meet the Viceroy, or to be exact, a former Viceroy. Lord Lytton, now Governor of Bengal, had sent word through his Aide-de-Camp, Count J. de Salis, that he would be visiting Midnapore on 11 February 1927 and would like to make the acquaintance of the wolf child.[2] The Reverend Singh wrote back at once on her behalf to say that she would be honoured.

As it turned out the visit was deferred until November. By a curious coincidence on 11 February a serious strike erupted in the Kharagpur workshops, and the station, where the Governor had been due to arrive, was taken over by an unruly mob of railway workers. Fortunately Robert Reid, the District Magistrate, happened to be staying in Kharagpur at the time, making the best of a rare opportunity for relaxation – Kharagpur unlike Midnapore was blessed with electricity, amusement facilities and a large population of European officers – when he was called from the cinema to deal with the situation. It took all night and a couple of rounds of police fire before they managed to clear the station premises, and again it was the A.F.I. who came to the rescue, only this time the D.M. did not call them out: an enthusiastic Anglo-Indian officer just happened to be exercising his company that night and hurried straight to the spot at the first sign of trouble. Later the use of the A.F.I. and their alleged brutalities would be the subject of comment in the Legislature and in the nationalist press; in the meantime the A.F.I. had to be kept out for a week until they could be relieved by 200 Eastern Frontier Rifles. The strike spread to a number of places on the Bengal-Nagpur Railway before the Company met some of the workers' demands, but despite delays and upset schedules the trains were kept running. Many believed the strike had been inspired by nationalists, others that there had been a plot to kill the Governor which had mis-fired because of a change of plans.

Closer to home, if not to reality, the Reverend Singh became convinced that Mohammedan railway strikers had stolen his favourite dog, a white mongrel with black patches over its ear and one eye, answering to 'Laddy'. He notified the police, but Laddy was never seen again and the padre, who could be sentimental about animals, mourned him as a casualty of terrorism.

One morning Kamala was heard singing in the garden, a soft atonal drone, scarcely distinguishable from the white background noise of cicadas and the gentle murmuring of doves. She was chanting words and nonsense to herself as she walked under the trees.

Then singing became a habit with her and for a time she was scarcely ever quiet, so much absorbed in her incanta-tions that nothing could distract her and she had to be taken by the hand before she would stop. The Singhs, who were a musical family, welcomed the development and tried to encourage her to join in their Tuesday sessions of hymn and community singing around the harmonium in the drawing room, but Kamala's only contribution was to shout occasionally at the top of her voice on a shrill quaver-ing note. Apart from this dramatic increase in volume she made no response whatsoever to the music, nor showed any interest in the dancing that sometimes accompanied it. As Mrs Singh put it: 'Kamala did never imitate dancing or singing or music after she was given a chance to attend it at the orphanage, nor did she ever inquire or ask any to repeat any of these . . .'[3] And after a time she gave up

199

singing privately too, as if the improvised mantras had lost their charm as well as their power to shut out the rest of the world.

There was some indication, however, that the need to keep and conserve her own company was diminishing and that she was at last beginning to turn away from morbid preoccupation with herself. She was becoming more assertive and at the same time more reactive, though not necessarily amenable, to the will of others: a truculent, almost comic, confidence in her own ability – the certainty that she could do anything and that whatever she did was bound to be perfectly right – made her as difficult but as encouraging to deal with as a rebellious two-and-a-half year old. If she determined on a course of action there was no stopping her and when things went wrong only occasionally would she let herself be helped by anyone but Mrs Singh. The other children, some of whom were quite grown up, treated Kamala more or less as the orphanage pet; kind enough to her in their way (apart from the teasing) and looking after her as much as she would allow them to, they had also learnt when not to interfere. On one occasion when Kamala was attempting to tie the cord of her pyjamas and having very little success with it, none of the children offered to lend a hand. Only when she began to weep with frustration did one of the older girls try to help, but Kamala would not have it and ran off to find Mrs Singh. As it happened she was out and Kamala had to take her problem to the padre. The Reverend Singh discovered her standing behind his desk – she had entered his office without making a sound – holding up her pyjamas with both hands and letting the tears roll silently down her cheeks. He asked her what was the matter, but she refused to answer; then Manica, the girl who had presumed to help her, arrived on the scene and explained what had occurred. The padre reassured Kamala that no one was going to take her pyjamas away from her and asked Manica to tie them up for her in his presence, 200 which seemed at once to satisfy her sense of propriety and to banish the shame of her failure to manage the knot herself, for she now gladly let Manica perform the operation and went off with her afterwards as if nothing had happened.

Kamala had little aptitude for games or playing with toys. 'We persuaded her to play,' Mrs Singh recalled,

and that too, with balls. When we raised the ball before her and explained the way how she should roll the ball, she then could do so. In doing so she used to smile and we could feel that she was smiling in her sleeve. She did not play with blocks herself. When the other children used to teach her how to do it with the blocks, she used to make round figures with them. Sometimes she could do so, sometimes she could not. If she was given a slate with a pencil to write, she used to scratch anything and everything with the pencil. She did not at all like this nor could she do anything else when she was given a slate with Bengali letters to copy.[4]

Although she rarely played by herself, she would watch the other children's games and now and then make an unwelcome contribution. Once when the children were playing a game of arranging their toys, mostly rag dolls and tin soldiers, in a line on the floor, Kamala caused an uproar by collecting all the red ones and quietly removing them to her corner. Mrs Singh was sent for to settle the dispute and at once asked who had taken the red dolls. Kamala said nothing and moved away to her corner where the dolls lay in an untidy heap. The children began to complain and accused her openly, but when Mrs Singh approached her Kamala pointed at the dolls proudly as if she had done something rather magnificent. She was made to give the toys back, but later received from Mrs Singh some red dolls of her own and a wooden box in which to keep them. The present seemed to give her pleasure and after the box had been put away in the *almirah* she ran off on all fours to tell the other children: 'Bak-Poo-Voo' (Baksa-Pootool-Vootara, Bengali for 'Box–Doll–Inside'), repeating the phrase – her first three word sentence – until the children had to ask her to stop.

By the end of March 1927 the steady flow of visitors to the orphanage who came to see Kamala had last begun to fall off. On 6 April, however, the *Pioneer* reported the capture of another wolf child from a cave near Maiwana, some seventy miles from Allahabad. Both the timing (only five months since the publicity over the Midnapore case) and the suspicious circumstances of the discovery indicated that the Maiwana wolf boy was probably a fake, but the Indian press, anxious not to be scooped again by the rest of the world on its own news stories, gave the case full coverage. As well as provoking a month-long correspondence in the letter pages of the London *Times*, which until now had remained aloof from the recent excitement over wolf children, the Maiwana boy kept interest in the topic alive in India and as a result the orphanage at Midnapore continued to be pestered by the curious. Despite his deteriorating financial situation and Bishop Walsh's pragmatic advice, Sihgh still refused to demand money from those who wanted to see Kamala, but he was not above accepting gifts for her or donations to the orphanage if they were offered. He was also sensible enough to take a certain amount of trouble with those visitors who were likely to be generous. In these cases he usually extended an invitation to tea, after which Kamala was brought in to perform her party piece.

Mrs Geeta Mallik, a former resident of Midnapore now living in Calcutta, remembers going to see Kamala at the Singhs' orphanage in April of 1927. She was accompanied by her mother and brother, who also remember the occasion though perhaps not as vividly as Geeta, then a bright and impressionable fourteen year old. As members of one of the foremost families living in Midnapore at that time, they were given the grand treatment by the Singhs, which was plainly resented by the children who were impatient to see Kamala. When they had finished tiffin and she was finally sent for, confrontation between these two girls of similar ages and widely differing backgrounds made a deep impression on one of them:

I shall never forget her. She came in walking rather awkwardly and stood in a corner. She was thin and scraggy with curly, close cropped hair and a very sullen expression. She wore a white dress and silver bangles on her arms. The Reverend Singh told her to say 'Namaskar', the Bengali form of greeting, and she was able to do so, putting her hands together in the correct manner as in prayer, but when he asked her some questions she refused to answer. She just sucked her hand and glared at us. I remember the strange contrast of her neat little frock and bangles, and the wild expression in her eyes. It was very disturbing.

She had a number of sores, rather like 'mango boils', on her arms and legs and the scars of other sores and scratches that had healed up. She licked at the sores the way a dog might until the Reverend Singh told her not to. He explained that both the wolf children had suffered from these sores when he first found them in the jungle, and that although they had managed to clear them up, Kamala still had trouble with them. While we were talking she suddenly went down on all fours but quickly stood up again when the Reverend Singh corrected her. He was kind with her but strict, and she seemed rather afraid of him. He told us he believed she resented him for having captured her. Then she left us at his bidding, walking in an unsteady manner.[5]

According to Mrs Mallik the padre talked much of the progress that Kamala had made since she had been at 'The Home', but did not try to deny the wild side of her nature, still apparent in her general bearing and persistent habits, which he described, of scratching herself, eating sand and pebbles, rolling in the dirt and occasionally making 'animal' noises at night. This does not contradict but is in contrast to the tone of his diary account for the last three years of Kamala's life in which Singh stresses (both for reasons of mild propaganda and because it is what interested him) the more positive aspects of her behaviour.

There are reminders of a bleaker reality, but they are rare and cryptic and if one considers that Singh, and indeed Bishop Walsh, believed Kamala's progress to be due partly at least to the sacrament of her baptism, he had reason now to want to play down, if not suppress, the dark phase of an existence which could usefully be seen to represent the Christian idea of the flesh that struggles with the spirit, of the darkness that brings forth light, and of the grotesque which reaches up to the sublime.

Yet there was something more. Kamala, who had never shown the slightest fear of thunder or lightning – on 28 April a violent storm that turned the sky over Midnapore black with dust and brought the mango fruit crashing from the trees had no more effect on her than hitherto – was badly frightened a week later by the Reverend Singh firing his gun in the orphanage garden. 'As soon as . . . the report was heard, Kamala was seen running on all fours very fast towards the kitchen where Mrs Singh was seated, and tried to hide herself behind her.'[6] Singh does not offer any explanation as to how she came to be afraid of gunfire; no doubt the shot had simply startled her. But was there not a remote possibility that she recognized the sound, that the last time she had heard it at close quarters was seven years before through the mouth of the white-ant mound in the forest of Denganalia, and that the barrage of arrows which brought down her foster-mother had been backed up by a rifle shot? One can only speculate, but the atmosphere of guilt which clouded the padre's relationship with Kamala is far from conjectural and the need to justify her capture from the wolves in terms of a successful re-entry into human society may also have affected the bias of his record.

Kamala is depicted as sloughing off the attributes of her animal past. When she passes by the orphanage dogs now at feeding time not only do they bark at her as they would at any other child, but she takes fright and goes round another way, giving them a wide berth. The ties of their former alliance are broken. Some puppies are given to her to play with but she rejects them angrily. She does not steal meat any more, even when it is left lying all day on the dining-room table. Assumptions about her behaviour are beginning to be proved wrong. One afternoon just before school finishes for the day, she climbs inside the hen-house and closes the door. At four o'clock the bell goes and the children detailed to collect the eggs on that day – a regular orphanage routine, which Kamala had been observing for some time – arrive at the hen-house to find the wolf child in residence. Everyone expects her to have eaten all the eggs, but it turns out that she has merely heaped them in a corner and when Mrs Singh, ignoring a few breakages, praises her for doing a good job, Kamala is delighted with herself and struts about, as the Reverend Singh suggests, 'like a great hero who had gained a big victory'. Over her own nature or the prejudice of others? It hardly matters. A few weeks later a chicken is found dead in the hen-house. The padre does not for a moment entertain the suspicion that Kamala might have killed it, but points out that when offered it to eat she refuses and when the carcass is deliberately put out in an obvious place she makes no attempt to retrieve it. The battle has been won, but one gets the uncomfortable feeling that in the process Kamala has been canonized.

Fortunately Mrs Singh is there to restore the balance with her simple but candid line on Kamala's total ineptitude for housework.

If she was asked to put fuel into an oven, she used to place heaps of fuel into the oven, with the result that the fire was extinguished. She was once given [some utensils to clean] after she was instructed how to do it. She did not only do it, but also besmear her whole body with ashes with which the utensils were to be washed.

She never knew how to sew, once I tried to have it done by her. But it was a vain attempt. She could not learn it at all. She twisted the thread along the piece of cloth she was given to sew. Later on she did not try any further. I realized she was unwilling to do it.[7]

The picture of her unwillingness and inability to cooperate seems somehow solid and reassuring after the padre's eulogizing, but in fact he does no worse than overstate his case. Clearly it is of the greatest importance to him that she should be seen to be saved. And so she will be. Whereas in the past Kamala always had to be forced to come to morning and evening service and would sit by herself away from the other children (who used to tease her and call her 'heathen'), now she came regularly of her own accord and sat or knelt in a line with everyone else. Singh recognized her presence there as the acme of his achievement, a witness to the domitable spirit of the uttermost pagan.

Kamala had begun to identify to a limited extent with the other orphans. She still spent much of her time alone and out of reach, sunk in irredeemable vacuity, but the kindling awareness of her own individuality (as much evident in her ability, for example, to recognize and retrieve her own clothes from a mixed pile of washing as in her dislike of being helped to do so) allowed her to establish herself in relation to the group. She formed no strong ties or friendships, but there were signs now that she wanted to take part, even to conform. On one occasion, when the other children went to market and she was left behind with Mrs Singh, she grew very upset and could only be consoled by the promise that on the next day she would be taken to the market by herself while the other children would have to remain at home. Another time, standing at the dining-room table while it was being laid for tea, she happened to be given a biscuit by Mrs Singh. She ran off and showed it to the other children who immediately came to Mrs Singh and asked for the same treatment, but they were told to go away and wait for the tea-bell. Displaying what the Reverend Singh believed to be a true feeling for fair play, Kamala then replaced her own biscuit on the table and went away until it was time for tea. It seems more likely that she simply misunderstood what was said to the others, thinking Mrs Singh's instructions also included her, but after the bell when the children all rushed into the dining-room and were given two biscuits each, Kamala only took one from Mrs Singh and then picked up the other from the table where she had left it.

The story was told to visitors, who readily accepted the Reverend Singh's interpretation of Kamala's motives and were charmed by the notion of a reformed wolf child with tendencies that were not only Christian but distinctly British in character. Among those who no doubt would have appreciated the anomaly was the Governor of Bengal, who came to Midnapore at last on 22 November and stayed overnight at Circuit House in the middle of the old racecourse. Between holding a durbar, attending a garden party in his honour and inspecting a variety of institutions, Lord Lytton found time to pay a private visit to the S.P.G. orphanage, where for the price of a discussion with the Reverend Singh on the future of India and a good-natured promise to heed his warnings about the threat of terrorism, he had the pleasure of meeting the wolf girl. Although no detailed record of the Governor's visit survives, memory has it that Kamala behaved exceptionally well, as befitted the occasion, and gave the padre good reason to be proud of her.

Early in 1928 the Reverend Singh received confirmation of a rumour that a certain element among the Midnapore Church Committee, which for some time now had withheld full support for their parish priest, had expressed their dissatisfaction with him in a letter to the Secretary of the S.P.G. and the Diocesan Board of Missions in Calcutta. It was by no means their first attempt to undermine him but this time, it seemed, his enemies were making a concerted effort to get rid of him altogether. Normally the petty squabbles and intrigues of Church Committees, the minute jostling for position that was common practice in most of the smaller, more out of the way Indian Christian communities, were paid little heed by the diocesan and missionary authorities. They had learnt to accept it as 'all a part of Indian life' and that it did not necessarily reflect on the competence of the priest-in-charge, though inevitably more trouble occurred where the priest was an Indian rather than a European. But in this case the Secretary of the S.P.G., Arthur Balcombe, happened to be a man who never let a single complaint or hint of indiscipline go by him without a full investigation. To make matters worse, Balcombe and Singh did not like each other.

Indeed, Father Balcombe was not an easy man to like. He belonged to a new breed of European missionaries, deeply committed to the recently created Church of India (the Anglican Communion in India became autonomous, with a general council as its supreme governing body, by the Act of 1927, which took effect in 1930), but like so many who take a new cause to heart, lacking in tolerance towards those who still espouse the old. In the Reverend Singh he saw a horrible caricature of the jingoist mentality which he was committed to stamping out, for he held the radical view that the domination of the western missionary with his hard and fast western vision of Christ and western methods of worship, a religious literature with the exception of the Bible produced wholly by western minds, had prevented the Indian Church from making any real contribution to the interpretation of Christ and the application of His message to the needs of modern India. Balcombe was determined to communicate his ideas to those missionaries who came under his control. 'In those days,' the Right Reverend Ronald Bryan recalls,

missionaries were still more or less a law unto themselves and what they did in their own fields, the methods they used and the ceremonies they adopted or adapted varied considerably. The Missionary Societies were very independent and as a result the Secretaries had a great deal of power since they controlled the money that their clergy received. In this respect a man like Father Balcombe was really a bit of a tyrant. Although he 'went Indian' himself he was very hard on the Indian Clergy. After a few years in the field they did tend to vegetate, but they were so hard up that they had to do other things like keeping a few chickens simply in order to survive, though of course if their work suffered, then Balcombe would come down on them.[8]

A keen reformer full of energy and ambitious plans for the hopeless task of reorganizing the vast mission fields and revitalizing his weary and disaffected workers, Balcombe had little appreciation of the art of the possible and no sense of humour to extenuate inevitable failure and disappointment. His was the sort of temperament which by all rights should not do well in a tropical climate but, unfortunately for those who came under his sway, Father Balcombe seemed to thrive in Bengal. He was a tall, thin man with an ascetic air about him, which was heavily underscored by his affecting the dress of a Sadhu or Hindu holy man; permanently got up in saffron robes, *longhi* and shirt, wearing his hair shoulder-length with a full beard, he went everywhere barefoot, his only concession to the climate being a large *sola topi*, from under which he peered out at the world white-faced and disapproving through a pair of steel-rimmed spectacles. To someone like Padre Singh, whose idea of heaven on earth was a good day's shooting followed by a quiet time in his favourite armchair with his dogs at his feet and perhaps a glass of port wine at his elbow, smoking a pipe and listening to the songs of Harry Lauder on the phonograph, Arthur Balcombe was anathema.

The inevitable clash between the two men came in February 1928, when Father Balcombe visited Midnapore at the request of the rebellious Church Committee and, investigating their complaints, found Singh guilty of neglecting his duties in respect of both his missionary work and his parish. The issues have since become blurred by time, but it seems likely, allowing for personal antagonism, that the accusation was justified in some degree. Whether for reasons of ill-health (he was an incipient diabetic, though his condition had not yet been diagnosed), financial distress or simply mission fatigue, the Reverend Singh had taken things rather more easily in recent years. He had cut down on his long missionary trips into the jungle, which had once been a cause for dissatisfaction among the members of the Church Committee; in itself a sensible enough move for a man of fifty-five, who was already beginning to age under the inexorable toll of the tropics: but he was also losing touch with the more accessible Christian centres and villages in the *moffussil* and many of his former converts were going over to the American Baptists. At home, too, in Midnapore he had allowed the Baptists to gain ground, giving way before the superior technology of their new Chevrolet chapel bus and the indefatigable spirit of their supporters who were always meeting trains with bibles and leaflets or organizing Band of Hope picnics by the river. But he no longer minded so desperately. He was even on fairly good terms with the resident Baptist missionary. A portrait of the Reverend John A. Howard, his wife and children, an unbearably wholesome-looking family, had found a place on his mantelpiece in deference to the good-natured injunction 'hang us up where you can see us' printed on the back of the photograph. Their competitiveness still irked him, but he had lost his resolution for the struggle and was content to reserve his energy for the less demanding tasks of looking after his congregation and carrying on the work of the orphanage. In spite of the alarming debts it was beginning to incur, he continued to regard 'The Home' (largely because it was his own creation and conveniently at the centre of his existence) as the most important part of his job, a lasting contribution to the conversion of Santalia and the crowning achievement of his ministry.

In this as in most things Balcombe did not agree with

him and informed Singh bluntly that he thought it was time he made way for a younger man who could handle what was undeniably a large and onerous parish. He would recommend to the Bishop that he be transferred to Geonkhali, a trading station on the banks of the Hooghly, where there was a small, manageable Christian community of Portuguese origin, which stood in urgent need of a pastor. In the meantime, since he was no longer going out on tour, his travel allowance was to be cut and the orphanage, which after all he had started on his own initiative, would receive no further grants from the S.P.G. or the Local Mission Endowment Fund until his transfer, when it would have to be closed down.

The Reverend Singh had a strong inclination to throw Balcombe, bare feet, saffron togs, pith helmet and all, out into the street, but fortunately he restrained himself. He had no intention, however, of giving up without a fight and immediately set about enlisting the support of his congregation and a number of Midnapore's highly placed non-Christians, men such as Dr Sarbadhicari and the Rajah of Narajole, who agreed to make representations to Father Balcombe, and if need be to the Bishop in Calcutta, in favour of retaining their priest. There can be no doubt that Singh was widely popular among his parishioners; Balcombe returned to Calcutta impressed in spite of himself; but he did not hesitate to report his findings to Bishop Westcott and recommend the proposed transfer to Geonkhali. The Reverend Singh, meanwhile, had asked his friends on the District Board of Missions to put in a good word for him and at the same time had appealed himself to the Metropolitan on numerous grounds including the wild but rather appropriate charge that Balcombe was victimizing him because he was an Indian. The Bishop, a kind and sagaciously fair man, while appreciating Father Balcombe's many qualities, had no illusions about his shortcomings (and the same applied to the Reverend Singh); but he saw no sense in transferring a perfectly adequate priest, even if he was past his best as a missionary, and causing him a great deal of misery when anyway he would be due for retirement in a few years' time. He turned the recommendation down and although he shared many of Balcombe's views on the future of the Church in India he could not resist suggesting to him with gentle irony that perhaps Mr Singh might have done better if he had spent a little longer under the supervision of a European Missionary, when he first went into the field.

In Midnapore the Bishop's verdict was received with feelings of relief and of vindication by Singh; but over the question of the travel allowance and the orphanage grant, Balcombe had won, and the prospect of budgeting for an institution that was already deep in debt on a substantially reduced income filled him with despair. How the orphanage had originally got into financial difficulties is not altogether clear, but there had never been even the remotest prospect of keeping it going on the salary of an Indian missionary, which was scarcely enough to keep two people alive, let alone thirty. The Singhs had started 'The Home' with their own money and survived with the help of a grant from the S.P.G. and charity from the people of Midnapore, depending especially upon the generosity of the European community, which unfortunately had dwindled in recent years to barely a handful of officials. It was most likely the failure of this source as well as the padre's somewhat ambitious building and improvement schemes and an almost aristocratic attitude towards money, which combined to put him in debt. Nor can there be any doubt that although the Singhs lived simply enough according to their needs, they had started out on a quite different scale of expectancy to the families of most Indian clergy. But apart from their grand ideas, the cost of feeding, clothing and schooling twenty or more children over the last fifteen years had insured that now and for the rest of their lives they would be beset by financial worries. And if the Reverend Singh imagined that he could take some comfort at least in the security of his living, he would find out soon enough that his reprieve by the Bishop had been only temporary.

A letter arrived – an invitation from the Psychological Society of New York to bring Kamala to America. The Lecture Bureau wanted Reverend Singh to undertake a tour of the United States at their expense, accompanying 'Kamala, the wolf child', and appear with her before their audiences to tell the story of her life to the American people. If the offer reeked a little of the fair-ground, from which he had tried to protect Kamala for so long, the padre had a vision of the New World – formed by his own experience of the vast wealth of the local Baptists, the unforgotten generosity of his Episcopalian friend from Boston, the Reverend Percy Webber, and heightened perhaps by the fabled visit of Vivekananda, the Bengali poet and philosopher, whose portrait against a back-drop of the New York sky-line, captioned 'The Hindu Monk', was hanging on his drawing-room wall – a vision of bright opportunity that was as yet unclouded by the dangers of exploitation. He saw the lights going up on a new career: the public speaker, once awarded a gold medal for oratory at Calcutta University, fêted again and lionized (with Kamala at his side) across the world: and for a moment he considered the idea seriously, convinced that God was presenting him with a unique chance to restore the fortunes of the orphanage. But the euphoria was short-lived for he knew already, even before consulting Dr Sarbadhicari and Dr Santra, that Kamala's health, which in the last few months had sadly deteriorated, would never permit her to travel. A little regretfully perhaps he wrote back to the Psychological Society declining their offer.

Kamala continued to be unwell for the remaining two years of her life with only occasional remissions from a condition which the doctors were never able to diagnose satisfactorily. Unfortunately the Reverend Singh made no attempt to plot the course and symptoms of her illness or its treatment and any case notes taken by the doctors have long since been lost. Apart from the padre's brief diary account and the records of their deaths in the Register of Burials at St John's Church, Midnapore, all that exists on the wolf children's medical history is a general statement by Dr Sarbadhicari, which gives no more than his opinion that both girls died of kidney failure and that this was probably caused by their inability to get used to a normal diet. The possibility of some anatomic abnormality of the kidneys having developed as a result of their living with wolves which, if not the direct cause of illness might have made them prone to renal infection, seems to have occurred to the doctor, yet he states blandly: 'As a post mortem examination was not made, the structural and pathological state of the kidney and other organs was not ascertained.'[9] And revealing more perhaps of his own limitations than he intended, he continued:

There was great difficulty in feeding the girl (Kamala) with a mixed diet . . . the acquired instinct of taking raw animal food by being reared by a carnivorous animal was retained up to the last though all attempts were made to return to a normal human diet. The progress of education was very slow owing in part to the heredity of the subject (from Aboriginal tribes) and also to nutritional defects, not contributing to the proper hormonal function. In my opinion if the unfortunate wolf girls could have been . . . induced to take a proper mixed diet with properly adjusted vitamins, improvement would have been more marked.[10]

It is interesting to note that in a case which was to become famous as an illustration of the effects of extreme environmental impact on development, Dr Sarbadhicari seems to attach more importance to Kamala's primitive ancestry than to the influence of the wolves (except insofar as they taught her to eat the wrong kind of food), but the Aryan prejudice of Hindus against the original dark-skinned inhabitants of India is as old as their history. The Reverend Singh, like the British, viewed the tribal peoples with affection and a certain respect for their independence, which ironically they owed largely to the Hindu policy of apartheid. In his insistence on the significance of the wolf children's failure to achieve a balanced diet the doctor may have been on safer ground, but any discussion on the subject is limited, in Kamala's case at least, by the lack of exact information about her eating habits during the last few years of her life. Singh implies a slow but steady progression from the days when she would take nothing but milk and raw meat to an acceptance of a mixed diet, giving a few instances of the gradual refinement of her palate, but he does not describe the diet fully at any time, nor does he state finally whether or not raw meat was struck off the menu. A reasonable assumption, supported by the doctor's statement, would be that considerable efforts were made at all stages of her development to suppress her carnivorous habits, but that on the whole they failed and that during the period when she was not allowed meat, Kamala's diet may have been inadequate to her needs. But it is unlikely that it produced the symptoms of her final illness. Whether Kamala and Amala succumbed to disease that stemmed directly (as in the case of parasitic infestation), or indirectly (possibly a lowered resistance to certain infections) from their existence with the wolves, or whether it was purely coincidence that both children died of renal failure, remains unanswerable. There is only the certainty that their deaths were premature and the likelihood that the traumas of rehabilitation to the society of first wolves and then men were in part responsible.

The doctors put Kamala on different diets and prescribed various medicines but they seem to have had little effect. Although the Singhs 'strictly followed the direction of the doctors', Kamala's health did not improve. Yet there were times, as far as can be made out from Singh's summary account of the period, when she was well enough to lead a 'normal' existence – times during which, he suggests, Kamala 'grew in mind and in human character', though Bishop Pakenham-Walsh, on the strength of a short second visit to the orphanage in the summer of 1928, saw little improvement: 'Except that she had learnt a good many more words, I did not notice any mental change.'[11] As a 'human character', too, she begins now to fade from the pages of Singh's diary. Possibly the obscuration is deliberate, because she had become a disappointment to him, or because he felt responsible for her deterioration – a reminder of his failure to give her back her humanity; but most likely, as his own life became more difficult and Kamala's relatively normal, he simply lost interest. He records one incident, however, prior to her terminal illness from which the wolf girl's personality emerges clearly and touchingly; as always, a little less than human but tragically more than animal. It was July of 1928 and Kamala, who no longer liked to go out at night, had been taken for a morning walk.

We took all the children and Kamala to the *maidan* in the morning and heavy rain came on. We all got wet. The children could not run as fast as Kamala on all fours, and we had to lag behind and get wet. Kamala ran in quickly but came out again to meet us; this she repeated several times to find that we could not get in with her and were getting wet. Kamala got irritated to such an extent that when we came in long after Kamala had gotten in, we found her in a corner; and, if any of the children went to her, she waved her hand roughly at them to drive them away.[12]

And there she must remain, bowed and solitary in her favourite corner, until almost exactly a year later on Sunday 7 July 1929, when she is briefly resurrected in a yellowing but sharply defined photograph from the memory of Puno Chandra Ganguly, at the time a ten-year-old boy and son of one of Midnapore's premier Christian families. It shows Kamala attending a service at St John's Church, sitting on the right hand side of the aisle, up in the front pew with all the other children where the Reverend Singh can keep an eye on them. She is wearing a long white   216 frock and sits eccentrically in her seat, her shaven head tilted towards the altar and catching the evening light that leaks in through the tall, shuttered windows. 'I always used to watch her in church because she was different from the other children. I knew her story of course and I tried to sit opposite her so that I could get a good view of her.'[13] The punkah swishes the length of the church. The Reverend Singh, in a white summer cassock, white surplice and a black-ribbed silk tippet, billows like a sail as the draught catches his vestments; white against the dark mahogany altar-facings as he crosses the chancel to read the King's Message from the lectern. The service, a form of thanksgiving for the recovery from a serious illness of H.M. The King Emperor, used a month before in West-minster Abbey, has at last been distributed to the Indian dioceses.[14] After the King's Message, for which the con-gregation rose loyally to its feet, the Reverend Singh asks them to remain standing for the Acts of Thanksgiving.

'Let us give thanks,' he intones in his effective bass, 'for the skill and devotion of the doctors, surgeons and nurses who tended our Sovereign King George during his illness.'

The congregation responds: 'O give thanks unto the Lord for He is gracious and His mercy endureth for ever.'

'Let us give thanks,' he cries again, 'for the patient and diligent research of men and women to whom have been revealed the means for healing sickness and disease.'

And as the congregation begins the antiphon, 'O give thanks unto the Lord . . .', a small indistinct voice stutters out the Bengali word for 'SATAN', followed by 'PIG', and the children sitting next to Kamala, who have taught her the words and prompted her to say them, suddenly crack up with laughter. The Reverend Singh pauses threat-eningly, waiting for the miscreants to be silent, and then continues the service with a brow of thunder.

On 26 September 1929 Kamala fell ill with typhoid fever. The disease appears to have followed its normal course, characterized by a high and continued fever over a period of about three weeks, delirium, diarrhoea, convulsions and other symptoms. In the fourth week the fever abated leaving Kamala weak and emaciated, with a dry, brown tongue and persistent bowel complaints. During the first part of her illness she was treated – treatment for typhoid in those days was entirely symptomatic and supportive – by Dr Santra, a junior doctor who dealt mostly with the town's cholera cases and other infectious diseases, working in close consultation with the family physician, Dr Sarbadhicari. After the fourth week when Kamala showed no signs of recovery she was put on to a course of injections starting on 3 November. Unfortunately, neither the doctors nor the Reverend Singh specified what the injections contained; probably they were aimed at correcting the renal disorder, nephritis, which developed now as a complication of the typhoid infection. As to her diet, the only information comes from the Reverend Singh's daughter, Preeti Lota Jana: 'While she was sick, Dr Sarbadhicari told father to feed her with raw blood, as that would be the only thing that she could digest at that time. A man would be sent to bring a glass of blood from where the goats are cut for meat . . . the blood would dry up and pieces were cut and fed to her . . . she also ate a lot of earth.'[15]

The combination did not appear to do her much good for she grew steadily weaker. But during this latter part of her illness, just as when she was sick once before, she made considerable gains in language. 'She not only could talk,' the Reverend Singh noted, 'but talked with the full sense of the words used by her.'[16] She could recognize the two doctors who looked after her and showed a preference for Dr Sarbadhicari, especially for his gentler technique with the hypodermic. As Mrs Singh recalled: 'During her illness . . . she was given injections daily by the two doctors. Once she said in a low voice in Bengali colloquial terms to me – "Ma Ma chota bulu fullachbe." (Ma, the little one hurts.) She said so when an injection was applied by Dr Santra.'[17] The incident was not isolated. 'She once said to one female attendant – "Palul didi, baile jaba" – i.e. Parul, I will ease myself so take me out of the room. So the female attendant took her out of the room and she satisfied the call of nature . . . While doing so she did not hesitate to eat up pebbles and stones lying on the ground.'[18]

The strain of contradiction between her efforts towards progress and the compulsive reversion to habits acquired in the wild, which characterized Kamala's whole life at the orphanage remained with her until the end. But as her condition deteriorated and she became too weak even to move, the past ceased to exert any influence over the present. Nephritis terminated in uraemia and she fell into a stupor which gradually deepened into coma from which she did not emerge. Kamala died at 4 a.m. on 13 November shortly after the Reverend Singh, in the presence of his wife and daughter, had commended her soul with the appropriate prayer: 'We commit unto Thy loving care this child whom Thou art calling to Thyself. Send Thy holy angel to lead her gently to those heavenly habitations where the souls of them that sleep in Thee have perpetual peace and joy.'[19]

She was buried the following day next to Amala under the banyan tree in St John's cemetery.

On 12 December, a public holiday in British India to celebrate the occasion of the Prince of Wales' visit in 1911, the District Magistrate held his customary durbar on the *maidan* in front of the Collectorate buildings. At the end of the ceremony, when the assembled native populace were expected to salute the Union Jack and sing *God Save the King*, there was an unprecedented hush. Only a few hands were raised in homage. Then as one or two stalwart loyalists standing beside the podium began to sing, the crowd suddenly found its voice; uneasily at first but soon gaining confidence, they drowned the others with a rousing chorus of 'Bandemataram', raising as they sang a vermilion flag with the word 'Swaraj' written on it in Devnagri characters. Significantly, no one tried to stop them and the meeting broke up in stunned silence.

If Kamala had lived in the shadow of a storm, the signs that it was soon to break were unmistakable. The restlessness and discontent that had spread across India in the decade spanned by her life at the Reverend Singh's orphanage were turning now in the vortex of a whirlwind.

Chapter Ten

On the evening of 25 March 1931 in a field behind the station, across the road from the Singhs' orphanage, four Bengali students met under the cover of darkness to plan their second attempt on the life of Mr Peddie, the District Magistrate of Midnapore. Their motive was political. As members of the Bengal Volunteer Party, a revolutionary organization responsible for a number of assassination attempts on the guardians of the British Raj during the last year, they saw themselves striking at the office rather than the man. But in the case of James Peddie they were making an exception. In the words of Bimal Dasgupta, one of the four and a nephew of the Headmaster of Midnapore Collegiate School, Peddie was 'the prime author of all oppressions let loose in the district . . . the chief perpetrator of the diabolical violation of the chastity of our mothers and sisters'.[1] Dasgupta had no doubt that 'the forfeiture of all Peddie's rights to live was what every man and woman of this district did then earnestly desire'.[2] He would take pleasure in executing their wishes, and this time there would be no mistakes.

A month before, Mr Peddie had taken the unusual step of calling together his officials and all the prominent citizens of Midnapore who were loyal to the Government to discuss how the town and district could best deal with the twin problems of Gandhi's Non-Violence Movement and the recent increase in terrorist activity. The meeting took place on 11 February at 10 a.m. – the time had been moved forward from 1 p.m. as originally planned, as a security measure – in the hall of the District Board Offices. Among those present representing the town loyalists, the Reverend Singh, easily distinguished by his great stature and all black costume, sat in a prominent position. The padre, who had every other reason for being there, also counted himself a personal friend of Mr Peddie and, although the latter could have had little time for friendship with Indians or anyone else in the troubled year he had spent at Midnapore, the two men did have a certain amount in common. At least it pleased Singh to think so.

James Peddie, a Scot from Coupar, Fife, was commonly regarded as a star of the I.C.S. A former soldier with an exceptional war record, he had risen through the ranks to be made Lieutenant-Colonel at the age of twenty-six and was twice mentioned in dispatches before resigning his commission in 1919. In India, where promotion could hardly be so rapid, he had enjoyed a corresponding success and when a month before, in January 1931, he had been awarded the C.I.E., it was agreed to be the best-earned on the list. He was a tall man of great physical strength with a heavy black moustache, a sepulchral voice and a great deal of charm. He preferred outdoor work to office routine and spent as much time as possible touring his district. Like Singh he was also a keen *shikari* and held a particular affection for the Santals. It was partly because of his interest and sympathy for the agricultural classes, as well as a talent for working with young people, that he had been sent to Midnapore. But he also had a reputation for being tough minded and something of a disciplinarian, and it was for these qualities that he became best known in a district where the difficulties of enforcing tax collection and maintaining the public peace allowed him little time for the sort of constructive work which really interested him. In the eyes of the Reverend Singh and Peddie's I.C.S. Fellows he was 'the embodiment of the ideal District Officer ... consumed by a veritable passion for justice, [who] could not bear to see the weak oppressed or the helpless defrauded'.[3] The nationalists saw him rather differently: the militarist thug sanctioning and encouraging the brutalities of his police force, the cruel and sadistic despot who ruled the district with an iron swagger stick. He was missing two fingers from his right hand, a legacy of the war: it became the mark of a devil.

Addressing the meeting at the District Board Offices he had briefly outlined the political situation which had developed over the last year, plunging India into a state of turmoil unknown since the mutiny. It had begun in October 1929 with Macdonald's Labour Government in London and the Viceroy, Lord Irwin, inviting the Indian political leaders to take part in a Round Table Conference to achieve 'the greatest possible measure of agreement' in planning the forthcoming Indian Reform Bill. Gandhi had demanded full dominion status as a basis for taking part in any discussions and when this was not conceded he had launched, with the full support of the Congress Party, a new Civil Disobedience Movement, which he inaugurated on 6 April 1930 with the renowned march to Dandi beach on the Bombay coast in defiance of the unpopular monopoly of the Salt Law. This time the idea of *Satyagraha* (Civil Disobedience) really caught hold and before the Government realized that the situation might turn serious, revolutionary disturbances were breaking out over the whole of India, with mobs taking control of towns, clashes occurring between police and pickets over commercial boycotting, agrarian unrest and in the north-east, particularly Bengal, terrorist bomb outrages.

The revolutionaries, as Mr Peddie explained, had been cunning enough to synchronize their campaign with the Civil Disobedience Movement. On Good Friday, 12 April 1930, after a daring raid on the armoury at Chittagong, they had got away with rifles and ammunition and gained a large number of young recruits to their cause. Many believed the time for armed rebellion had come at last. But for the moment the terrorists had made do with the murders of Sir Charles Tegart, the Commissioner of Police in Calcutta, Lowman and Hodson in Dacca, four months later Lowman's successor as Inspector-General, Mr Craig, and many other attempted assassinations, all interspersed with armed robberies for revolutionary funds. The police, who had their hands full trying to cope with the *Satya-grahis*, and the Government, still hoping to persuade Gandhi to come to a conference in London, appeared to do nothing. There followed a clamp-down with provision for 'rule by ordinance' – martial law where necessary, dawn arrests and the outlawing of certain political associations. Unfortunately none of these measures seriously affected the terrorists. And when the Government, as a conciliatory gesture towards Gandhi, had withdrawn the Press Ordinance, the nationalist newspapers immediately launched a campaign to drum up public support for the revolutionary movement.

The attempt at conciliation had provoked an angry reaction from the European community in Calcutta; among the most outspoken were some Anglican Missionaries of the old school and a group of young bloods calling themselves 'The Royalists', who demanded 'firm rule and no nonsense'. In Midnapore, Mr Peddie suggested to his grave and attentive listeners, the problem could only be aggravated by inflammatory talk, even if there was truth in it. He urged rather that all those present, whether or not they were in positions of authority, should use what influence they had to persuade people that the future of the District and of India herself depended on keeping the public peace. This meant in particular not taking part in Gandhi's non-cooperation movement, which encouraged boycotting foreign goods, non-payment of taxes and general lawlessness: for one thing, it wasted the time and resources of the police, for another it provided a suitably confused background from which the terrorists could operate. Garbed in homespun, the Midnapore cell of the Bengal Volunteers were known to have infiltrated the ranks of the Gandhian workers. They had to be exposed: 224

a task that would be made easier if their friends and relatives did not try to conceal them. They were the sons of educated middle-class Hindu families who ought to be susceptible to reasoned argument – some of them might even be present at this meeting.

A stir of protest rippled across the hall. It was followed by questions about police brutality and house to house searches and a few half-hearted objections, but in the end all pledged their support. As an exercise, however, in raising the spirit of civic responsibility, Mr Peddie's address was not an unqualified success, perhaps because in Midnapore as yet the terrorists had not made much impression. Comparing it to the meeting he had attended at the Bayley Hall after the Murder of the Kennedys in Mozufferpore more than twenty years ago, the Reverend Singh noticed a critical difference – the sense of shock and outrage at what had happened and alarm at what might happen was missing.

A little after mid-day the meeting was adjourned and citizens and officials emerged from the gloom of the District Board Offices into the bright sunlight. Mr Peddie, escorted by armed police constables, turned to walk towards his bungalow. No one noticed the two nervous-looking students standing close in to the side of the building. They carried guns concealed in their *dhotis* but, having received no warning that the time of the meeting had been changed, had arrived fractionally too late to use them and be certain of their target. Rather than risk failure and arrest they had decided to wait for a better opportunity.

It presented itself finally on 7 April 1931. As part of his policy to win over the student community by patronizing and encouraging various cultural events, Mr Peddie had organized an exhibition of local arts and crafts to be held at the Midnapore Collegiate School. The exhibition, as it happened, had also been chosen by the students at their clandestine meeting in the field behind the station as a suitable venue for his assassination. Peddie had been expected to open the exhibition on 1 April, but was called away at the last moment to deal with a disturbance in another part of the district. The chance was lost; nor was it certain when another would materialize. The political situation had deteriorated sharply in the month following the signing of the Irwin-Gandhi pact, and the life of every District Officer in Bengal had become as frenetic as it was unpredictable. The pact, which took the form of an agreement between two sovereign parties and appeared to most loyalists as a deep humiliation for the Government, also entailed the release of political prisoners. More trouble seemed inevitable. Sir Robert Reid, a former District Magistrate of Midnapore, now Chief Secretary of Bengal, and incidentally among the most illustrious of Kamala's visitors, had received a letter from James Peddie, whom he regarded as one of the finest officers ever recruited to Bengal, saying that he felt ashamed, after this, to meet the Indian Officials who had stood by him loyally in his efforts to repress sedition in the Midnapore district. Reid himself had made a single comment in his diary: 'The whole show seems to be slipping.'[4]

Bimal Dasgupta along with Jatijiban Ghosh had won by drawing lots the honour of making the final attempt on Peddie's life. On the morning of 7 April they heard that he had returned unexpectedly from the *moffussil*. For the rest of that day – the last of the exhibition – Bimal pestered his uncle, Hiralal Dasgupta, who was Headmaster of the Collegiate School, for news of whether Peddie would visit the school before the exhibition closed. Luckily for Hiralal Babu he did not know, but at about six o'clock word came that the D.M. was on his way to the school. The assistant headmaster immediately sent Musha, the gatekeeper, and Bhaju, the school bearer, to fetch hurricane lanterns to light up the exhibition.

In his father's house Bimal Dasgupta washed quickly and put on clean clothes. He was joined there by Jatijiban and the two boys prayed together at a shrine to the Goddess Kali before arming themselves and setting off, at a deliberately leisurely pace so as not to arouse suspicion, in the direction of the school. Each carried a revolver in the front knot of his *dhoti* and a glass ampule of potassium cyanide in the hollow of his cheek. They had said good-bye before leaving the house; neither of them expected to return from their mission.

Mr Peddie, who was well known for an eccentric habit of going everywhere on foot, chose to walk from the bungalow to the school. He was accompanied by the Deputy S.P., Mr Carret, and the Assistant D.M., Aswini Kumar Maitra. His personal bodyguard for once was not with him. They arrived at the school, where a number of masters, students and officials were waiting for them, and proceeded at once with inspecting the exhibition. The light from the hurricane lamps was poor and Mr Peddie had to bend down to see the detail of the exhibits. He was leaning over to examine a table fan, operated by a treadle, when Bimal and Jati, moving unnoticed through the crowd of people, entered the small room and came up close behind him. Neither of them said a word. They withdrew their weapons and fired at point-blank range three shots into Mr Peddie's back and, as he was spun round by the impact of the bullets, two more into his side.

'We exhausted all our bullets on Mr Peddie,' Bimal would recall later with some satisfaction, 'While making ourselves ready for swallowing the ampules of potassium cyanide, we took our last wishful glance at the world. But we were surprised to see not a single man in the room. It was fully deserted. All heroic attendants of Mr Peddie had made good their escape for fear of life. There was no one to obstruct our way.'[5] In the confusion and darkness, for the room was not only badly lit but full of smoke from the black powder they had used to prime their home-made cartridges, the two students managed to escape. Subodh Chandra Bose, an assistant teacher, who witnessed the attack, confirmed that 'those who were present in the room fled away out of panic. They were almost fifteen or twenty in number. Hiralal Babu, Narayan Babu and other teachers were looking about for Mr Peddie, who in the meanwhile had crossed the sill of the eastern door of the room and entered the adjoining one. Mr Peddie was then found standing, supporting himself against the western wall. He was a man of long stature and equally stout and strong. Narayan Babu inquired anxiously, "Are you hurt, Sir?", to which he could only reply, "Yes."[6]

While a phaeton was being called to carry Peddie to hospital, Bimal and Jati commandeered a bicycle from a passing cyclist and set off on a ten- or twelve-mile ride to Salboni station. Later that night they caught the Up passenger to Purulia and in the early morning the Down train to Calcutta and safety. The police in the meantime took statements from all those who had been present at the exhibition, while Mr Peddie, surrounded by guards, lay in an upper room of the Midnapore hospital, waiting for the arrival of a British doctor from Calcutta.

Major Murray, First Surgeon of the Presidency General Hospital, accompanied by an assistant and a nurse, reached Midnapore by special train at 2.30 a.m. They operated at once and removed a bullet from Peddie's abdomen. His condition deteriorated, but by morning he had rallied sufficiently to be able to speak to some of his colleagues and friends. Peddie was unmarried. He asked to see the Reverend Singh, who had come to the hospital as soon as he had heard news of the shooting and had been standing by all night in case of need. Visitors were strictly vetted and their visits kept brief, but the padre was allowed to spend most of the day with the dying man. At 10 a.m. Dr Murray operated again, but with no more success and as Peddie's life began to fade, the Reverend Singh administered the rites of Extreme Unction and gave him his last communion. The padre was with him when he died at 5.10 that afternoon. He faithfully recorded his friend's last words, a garbled message to be relayed to his mother in Coupar,

Fife and then the suitably emotive cry of 'Home! Home!', which, though he would tell the story often enough, Singh found more deeply affecting than he could adequately express; for in James Peddie's death he had not only seen the certain end of British rule in India but a distorted reflection of his own fate, for Peddie was the man he would have been.

The funeral took place next day on the morning of 9 April at St John's Cemetery. The coffin was carried on the back of a motor lorry from the Civil Hospital, preceded by a body of armed police and followed by a host of I.C.S. and other dignitaries at the head of a large crowd. The cortège, discreetly by-passing the school building, where Peddie had been shot and police constables now stood guard with fixed bayonets, eventually reached St John's. The padre was waiting at the head of a platoon of boy scouts assembled in silence in the church compound. A grave had been dug, on the Reverend Singh's instructions, in a position of unusual prominence directly in front of the church, and there Peddie was duly buried with full military honours. The padre, at the height of his dignity, made a short funeral oration and, when all the obsequies were done, the commissioners of Midnapore Municipality read an emotional statement expressing their 'deep abhorrence of and indignation at the dastardly outrage'.[7]

It was a sentiment that would find wide support all over India, but in Midnapore itself the public face of shame and sorrow concealed a certain satisfaction at Peddie's death that was not confined to the extremists; and, as the efforts of the police to trace the killers were redoubled, resentment and bitterness at their methods of search, arrest and questioning (accompanied, as rumour had it, by torture) crept into many a Hindu household. As a result the European community and the loyalists came under stress and there returned to Midnapore something of that siege mentality, born of the Mutiny, which the British had never really shaken off in the north of India after seventy years of direct rule. Fear, solidarity, love of justice and the courage of protocol still reinforced each other under the colonial presumption of Duty.

In Midnapore it was Indians loyal to the Government who suffered most, but as they stood in doughty aloofness from their own countrymen, so were they rewarded. None was better praised for the help and advice he gave to the administrators and the brave example he set to others than the Reverend Singh. He preached loyalist sermons that put steel in men's hearts, he lent his services as an interpreter and a go-between, and when one morning Peddie's grave was found desecrated, he stood guard the following night with his own servants until police reinforcements could be spared. It was his finest hour, and it did not go unnoticed. At the end of the year the new Collector, Mr Burge, made him an Honorary Magistrate – an unpaid but honourable sinecure, which had been coveted by most Indians as a prestigious distinction until the Congress Party had declared the Honorary Magistracy to be on its black list. The Reverend Singh, however, was nothing daunted by the idea of winning the disapproval of the nationalists. He looked out an old schoolmaster's gown from his teaching days and wore it to court with pride, taking his new duties seriously. It was just as well that he did, for in December 1931 he received a letter from Father Balcombe informing him that he was shortly to be retired from the S.P.G. as a missionary.

The reasons given were his age – he was fifty-eight – his indifferent health and the recent cuts in the S.P.G. grants from home. But Balcombe had been worried for some time about the Midnapore district, where reports of converts stolen by the Romans and the Baptists, of Christians lapsing into Hinduism, suggested in these days of anti-missionary feeling (recently stirred up by Gandhi) that precious ground had been lost for ever. Aside from his personal antipathy towards Singh he had long wanted to see a younger and keener man take over and stop the rot.

On the same principle he had engineered the retirement of the Reverend Russell Payne, who had been vicar at Kharagpur for the past fourteen years and, as the Archdeacon wrote in a letter to his successor, 'allowed things to go to sleep a bit'. Like Godfrey Walters, his predecessor at Kharagpur, he joined the list of casualties to the missionary ideal, men who had been left to grow old and inept at their jobs in a country where the European was never encouraged to outstay his usefulness.

As an Indian, the Reverend Singh fared somewhat better than his colleague; not only did he have redress to his grievance against Father Balcombe and to a whole chronicle of real or imagined persecutions (for everything from his political views to his harbouring the wolf children at the orphanage): but being loved and respected by his parishioners and many non-Christians in the district, he could not be seen to be too shabbily treated. A full-scale row developed nonetheless. Although relieved of his missionary duties, Singh was to be kept on as parish priest of St John's, Midnapore, so long as his health and work remained satisfactory, on a monthly allowance of 35 rupees and an S.P.G. pension for the same amount – in all 70 rupees or roughly £3 sterling. The arrangement was to take effect from July 1932. Wisely perhaps Father Balcombe left it to the Reverend A. C. B. Molony, who was taking over Singh's district from Kharagpur, to explain the details to him. Molony reported back to Bishop Westcott:

I saw Padre Singh yesterday – he is very upset about the smallness of his pension, so I expect you will be getting Volume I of his Life and Works. He was busy on it yesterday, and on the whole it is not uninteresting. But seriously I feel that it would have been wiser to have given him a better pension . . . if it came out that his pension was only 35 rupees, there would be a lot of feeling in Midnapore and Kharagpur, where Singh is popular. I would be looked upon as responsible for the mean ways of the church. I cannot help feeling that Balcombe has tried to make use of me over the whole Singh affair.[8]

With Singh appealing to the Bishop for more money and Balcombe protesting that the S.P.G. grant, growing smaller each year, would soon be entirely swallowed up by pensions and that there would be nothing left for 'the active work', the row was extended by the posting of a third priest to Geonkhali, from where he was to help Molony and Singh with the Midnapore parish. The Reverend Lionel Hewitt, an Eurasian excommunicate of the Catholic Church, had joined the Anglicans some years before and after marrying rather too soon (much to his Bishop's disappointment) had proved himself a keen, if unlucky, missionary. He had been in trouble with the police. Caught hanging around outside a brothel wearing Indian dress, he had been arrested because, it was said, he bore a strong resemblance. to a certain ex-convict wanted in connection with the Elder Murder Case. The Bishop had promptly come to his defence, but according to Hewitt, who was given to self-dramatizing, the police had continued to shadow him for years. He was a simple character, well-meaning, not very worldly-wise, touchy and sometimes given to stints of mild paranoia – a common enough syndrome among Anglo-Indians, but in his case probably as much a consequence of chronic ill-health and recurring bouts of malarial fever as racial insecurity. He fell out almost immediately with Father Balcombe and for a long time was unable to make friends with the Reverend Singh because of the latter's resentment towards him; but in A. C. B. Molony, a big untidy Irishman brought up in the lowlands of Scotland, a confirmed bachelor, able Scoutmaster and eccentric rugger player, he found his hero. The two of them, Hewitt believed, would convert the entire district, and he wrote endless notes and letters to Molony bursting with enthusiasm and full of breathless suggestions for 'thorough missionary visits' to the Santal villages armed with the cross, a communion set and some blazing red vestments – 'just enough to impress them'. But sometimes he went too far: 'I am just suggesting the following for consideration,' he wrote. 'Is it possible to make the Reverend Singh hand over his orphanage to us . . . in a year or so? I do not know how we can secure intensive instruction without some sort of institution like that.'[9] It was an unintended compliment, no doubt, to Singh's work, but Molony, who felt sympathetic towards the padre and knew how much the orphanage meant to him, did not allow the suggestion to go any further. It was Molony's business now, after Balcombe had finally given up interfering in the Midnapore affair, to keep the peace. He worked hard to reconcile Hewitt and Singh. At his suggestion the three of them made several journeys into the jungle during the cold weather of 1932 so that the older man could show them round the district. Singh insisted on travelling only by bullock cart, which Hewitt suspected was simply to bring home to them the vast size of his former territory, but both he and Molony were impressed by the padre's popularity and high-standing among the Santals. And Singh himself, although he took less and less interest in missionary activities, was flattered by his companions' reliance on his knowledge and experience.

In June 1933 he published an article in the *Calcutta Diocesan Record*, a reminiscence of his first missionary voyages into the jungle as a young man in the years before the Great War; undertaken in a spirit of humility, inspired by the majestic beauty of the sal forests, they seemed to him now in retrospect to have been blessed by qualities of purity and innocence, even danger, which appeared sadly lacking in today's exchanges between missionary and heathen. Not that he was either able or anxious to take up the staff again himself, but now that the storm of Balcombe's onslaught on the district had abated and Molony and Hewitt were getting on with their jobs, leaving him more or less to his own devices, he sometimes enjoyed reliving the memories of his own pioneer work in the Lord's Vineyard. It was a way, too, of escaping the political realities of life in Midnapore. Since the death of James

Peddie and the subsequent arrest of his murderer, Bimal Dasgupta, on the steps of the Writers' Building in Calcutta – he was caught in an attempt on the life of Mr Villiers, the President of the European Association – both his successors to the post of District Magistrate in Midnapore had suffered the same fate at the hands of the terrorists. Peddie, Douglas and Burge, the 'Midnapore Martyrs' as they were known in the loyalist press, lay together in St John's cemetery: no one dared to guess how long it would be before there was a fourth grave which needed guarding by night against desecration. For more than a year now Midnapore had been living under what amounted to martial law. There were curfews, a system of coloured identity cards restricting the movements of individual citizens and a company of soldiers permanently stationed near the police lines. For some it had become a time of continual harassment by the police, for others the restrictions were merely inconvenient, but it was no longer safe for Europeans or prominent loyalists to walk alone through the bazaars, where an atmosphere of resentment, suspicion and fear hung over the hot narrow streets like strata of putrid air.

As an Honorary Magistrate the Reverend Singh officially had nothing to do with politics or the administration of the district; he dealt judicially only with infringements of a minor kind; yet during the troubled years in Bengal from 1930 to 1936 there was some danger in having any connection at all with Government, and when the padre reassured his wife that not even the terrorists would think of harming a priest, he did not always sound convinced by his own argument. Out at the orphanage, however, the Singhs enjoyed peace and relative security. At night as many as fifteen guard dogs were allowed to roam the compound and it was a joke among the local *dacoits* that it was best to stay away from 'The Home' because the Padre Sahib was such a fierce man and his dogs were even worse. They were the fiercer no doubt for not getting enough to eat, for the

234

shortage of money in the Singh household was becoming desperate. The padre and his wife even talked now of closing down the orphanage, but neither of them finally could face up to the prospect – particularly Mrs Singh, who in the words of her husband, was 'doggedly desiring that she could not part with the children, whom she had loved and reared from their very infancy and for whom she had spent all her own money'.[10] They were forced to borrow instead a substantial sum to pay off their most pressing debts, putting up the orphanage buildings as surety and doing so on their own responsibility as there was no help forthcoming from the Church, despite intermittent pleading on their behalf by the Reverend Molony and Bishop Pakenham-Walsh.

As standards at the orphanage declined, affecting his own living as much as that of the orphans, Singh grew increasingly resentful. He became morose and irritable, often losing his temper both with his family and the orphans, imposing fasts on himself and others without apparent reason, constantly nagging at his wife and generally helping to make life in 'The Home' a misery. Histrionic tendencies found unfortunate expression in his work. At Kharagpur, where once his sermons were well received by the European and Anglo-Indian congregation of All Saints, his preaching was now regarded as something of a joke. 'Singh is terrible,' the Reverend Molony complained to the Archdeacon. 'He either yells or whispers and I will soon have no congregation left if I have him every time I am out on line.'[11] In Midnapore his own parishioners were less discerning, but it had not escaped notice that their priest was under considerable stress. Many felt sympathy for him and friends offered to help, but donations for the orphanage were few and far between. In every way these were hard times and the Church's popular appeal 'to stand behind Christ to the last rupee' carried little conviction with those who were hungry.

·   ·   ·   ·   ·

Shortly after Kamala's death Bishop Herbert Pakenham-Walsh had begun to urge the Reverend Singh to prepare his diary account of the wolf children's lives at the orphanage for publication. He persuaded him that it was his duty not only to science – for he had already given his word to a number of scientists all over the world that a full account would be made available – but also to his family and to the orphanage. The Bishop believed that there was a fair chance of making money out of the wolf children, and now that the unfortunate girls were both dead he saw no reason why the padre and his wife should not receive some reward for the charity they had shown them. Partly because he felt responsible, after unintentionally leaking Singh's story to the newspapers in 1926, for the unwanted publicity that had been forced upon the padre and his orphanage without doing either much good, and partly because he himself had always been fascinated by the wolf children, Bishop Walsh had taken a continuing close interest in the fortunes of 'The Home' and its inmates. Although he could not offer Singh direct financial assistance or try to interfere in Bishop Westcott's diocesan affairs, he hoped to make amends for any disservice he might have done him in the past by ensuring publication of the wolf children diary. The Reverend Singh, however, took his time about completing what he referred to as 'the second part' of the diary. It seems to have comprised mainly a naive and repetitive philosophical essay, a sort of religious-cum-scientific interpretation of the wolf children and their behaviour, on the strength of some indiscriminate, but avid, reading in the social sciences. No doubt he also rewrote a few passages of his original journal in the light of these speculations, which would be almost entirely cut from the final version, yet at the time clearly meant a great deal to the padre.

In April 1933 he wrote to Dr Arnold Gesell, the famous child psychologist of Yale University, who had corresponded earlier with him, that 'the writing of the Diary is nearing completion. I am delighted to have arrived at a
236

great Truth in Social Biology: with regard to "Heredity and Environment"'.[12] He also asked his advice on getting the diary published, but if Singh was by now enamoured of the idea of being welcomed to the confraternity of science with his *Experimentum Crucis* in rearing wild children, he seemed in no hurry to present his paper. Indeed, it was to be almost five years before the work, which can only have taken a matter of months to produce, finally emerged in manuscript form. Apart from the difficulties and distractions of living in Midnapore during the turbulent years of 1930 to 1934 and the complications of his own life, the chief excuse, according to a recapitulatory letter he wrote to Bishop Pakenham-Walsh, was laziness and blindness to duty. 'You . . . goaded me on to finish the second part (of the diary) as soon as possible, but unfortunately I was slow to see the Divine Will in it and slept over your repeated requests like a slothful man . . .'[13]

His letter to Dr Gesell in 1933, however, suggests that he had at last seen the light and was growing keen on the project, but soon afterwards an incident occurred which was to delay the completion of the diary by another two years. One of Singh's first correspondents after the story of the wolf children reached the West in 1926, Dr Paul C. Squires, a Professor of Jurisprudence at California University, now wrote to him asking to see the diary and offering to take care of its publication. Singh duly sent him the first and most important part of the work and waited for his reaction. Dr Squires, who had published a short note on Kamala and Amala in the *American Journal of Psychology* in 1927, was not particularly impressed by Singh's diary and made no attempt to disguise the fact. The padre felt hurt and insulted by Squires's bluntly expressed scepticism and demands for authentication. He was further outraged to discover that Squires had also written, without telling him, to the District Judge of Midnapore, Mr H. G. Waight, asking for an investigation into the truth of the wolf children story. This Singh regarded as tantamount to being called a liar and he immediately wrote to Dr Squires cancelling his publication rights over the diary and demanding the typescript back. It was not returned. The padre, full of righteous disgust, worked himself into a state over the whole affair and, after threatening dramatically to burn all his records, shelved the project indefinitely.

Despite the Reverend Singh's accusations of almost criminal intent on Squires's part and suggestions that he was 'not a gentleman' it has never been clear exactly what passed between them: the correspondence exchanged by the two men unfortunately has not survived. Dr Robert Zingg, who would later take over the role of Singh's literary agent, had some communication with Dr Squires, who appeared to him to be 'pretty sore about losing publication rights of the diary, and wrote me when I first got it, to discourage me from going on with it'.[14] Which suggests Singh's belief that Squires wanted to exploit him may not have been all that far-fetched. But from Squires' letters to Dr Zingg, which seemed to verge at times on the manic, it is not difficult to see how a misunderstanding might have arisen with a man as touchy and vulnerable as the padre. 'Singh was furious with me,' Squires wrote by way of explanation, 'for having discovered what appear beyond all doubt to be hopeless internal contradictions in his diary ... I am rather surprised you have fallen for this stuff. Singh so disgusted me that I would have nothing to do with helping him get out his diary for publication: it is a hopelessly ignorant piece of drivel by a religious fanatic.'[15] But he ends the letter on what might be construed as a conciliatory note: 'As regards our good friend Singh's diary, that, I much fear, will have to be ruthlessly dissected by me later on. Too bad you did not confer through the mail with me before you stepped into it. Nor am I saying that Singh is a liar, understand that.'[16] His chief objection to the diary appears to have been that its author was a priest and not a scientist. The contradictions, muddled thinking, broken English and poor spelling were immediately apparent to anyone reading the diary, and a need for caution in assessing the scientific value of such a document was not in dispute; but there can be little doubt that Dr Squires had over-reacted. His attitude, however, was by no means unique, though others among American academics were able to view the situation more calmly. W. N. Kellogg, a psychologist at Indiana University, who had also taken an interest in the wolf children from an early stage, proclaiming them 'unquestionably the most striking example of wild children in our time',[17] wrote to Dr Zingg: 'I believe that the chief difficulty is that Singh is not only a layman and a missionary, but a man who is not capable of expressing himself in English with accuracy and precision. No doubt his practical work has kept him so busy that he has had little chance to perfect himself as a man of letters. It is clear that he writes so effusively and emotionally that the facts behind his descriptions are confused or fogged in a great deal of verbiage which often means nothing.'[18] The criticism was valid and true yet it scarcely touched on the wider, more complex difficulties of cultural misunderstanding and failure of communication, which had already arisen on both sides of the ocean and would now accompany the story of the wolf children to its close.

One useful outcome of the altercation between the Reverend Singh and Dr Paul Squires was the request for Harry Waight, the District and Sessions Judge of Midnapore, to look into the facts of the case. Though it is unlikely that his investigations were particularly rigorous – certainly not by scientific standards – they were at least straightforward and honest. And at the end he was able to provide the padre with the following affidavit, dated 4 October 1934 and stamped with the seal of the Judge's Court.

The Reverend J. A. L. Singh has placed before me all the documents and evidence relating to the so-called 'Wolf children' of Midnapore, which I have studied carefully.

I know Mr Singh personally and I am convinced that every

word that he has written regarding the children is true, to his knowledge. I have also spoken to several people who saw the elder of the two girls on several occasions at Mr Singh's orphanage and they have confirmed Mr Singh's accounts of the manner (for example) in which the children walked and behaved.

There is not the least doubt in my mind that Mr Singh's truthfulness is absolutely to be relied on.[19]

Since Mr Waight had not himself seen Kamala and Amala, the affidavit could in no sense be regarded as evidence for or against 'wolf children', but it did help to remove possible doubts about the Reverend Singh's honesty and suspicions that the story might have been a hoax. The padre, however, did not appreciate the suggestion that he was even capable of telling a lie; whether through pride or because he had had his feelings hurt by Dr Squires or because he really did have something to hide, when it came to finding evidence to support his statement that Kamala and Amala had been rescued from wolves – evidence that from now on scientists would try to elicit from him with the greatest possible tact – the Reverend Singh did not appear eager to cooperate. His word, he believed, should have been good enough. As long ago as 1927 a few months after the appearance in the *Statesman* of Calcutta of the two conflicting reports on how the children were found in the jungle, Bishop Pakenham-Walsh had suggested to the padre that in order to clear up that and any future controversy he should obtain and publish statements from Richards and Rose, his two Anglo-Indian hunting companions, who had been with him on the *machan* and witnessed the capture. At the time the orphanage was under daily siege from Kamala's visitors and the padre, who was anxious to avoid further publicity – 'I wanted the news to die out as soon as possible. To contradict, or correct, meant to me reviving the publication freshly, and I hated that from the very inmost core of my heart'[20] – refused to have anything more   240 to do with the *Statesman* or stories being published in the press about the wolf children. He did, however, make some attempt to get in touch with Richards and Rose, but both men and their families had long since moved away from Kharagpur and could not easily be traced. There the Reverend Singh was quite happy to let the matter rest. The transient nature of employment on the Indian Railways, particularly among the 'lower European subordinates' and Eurasian community, meant that they were constantly on the move from one dingy railway town to another, leaving scarce evidence of their passing. Some seven years later Mr Waight, the District Judge, had tried to find them but with little more success. In Singh's words: 'Mr Waight talked with the authorities he knew on the phone, and could get Richards but not Rose, and afterwards inquired from others at Kharagpur and Midnapore (and in the interior) to satisfy himself and was fully satisfied.'[21] Presumably if he had wished to, or thought it necessary, or been asked to do so by someone more polite than Dr Squires, the Reverend Singh himself could have obtained without much difficulty statements from a number of other people (from Chunarem and Bhagobhat Khatua to Dibakar Bhanj Deo, the Maharajah's hunting officer), who were also present at the capture of the wolf children. But this he did not do, and it would be several years yet before any of the scientists interested in the wolf children would get round to asking him for the statement of a supporting witness, by which time the Reverend Singh would be past caring whether or not they had their 'proof' of what he knew to be true.

In the meantime the diary (a carbon copy of the first part, the second was as yet unwritten) gathered dust on the shelves of the office of the orphanage and despite repeated entreaties from Bishop Pakenham-Walsh the padre refused to complete it, still childishly sulking over the treatment he had received at the hands of Dr Squires. In December of 1934 the Bishop's term of residence as

241

principal of Bishop's College in Calcutta came to an end and he set off for England on an extended furlough to gather support for the project to which he was now to devote the rest of his life. At an age when most men look forward to retirement he was proposing to take the vow of poverty and set up an *ashram*, a small religious community, for missionary and 'uplift' work in cooperation with the local Syrian Orthodox Church in a poor district of Coimbatore in southern India. Since he was obliged to spend some time in London he had hoped to take Singh's manuscript with him to show to publishers, but when the time came for him to leave India the diary was not finished; nor was it ready several months later when the Bishop, armed with gifts of money, devotional books, a fifteenth-century communion paten, a Syrian New Testament and papers on Divine Healing, set off again to settle for good in his chosen corner of the sub-continent. Before leaving he wrote to Singh requesting that he send the diary, as soon as it was complete, to his brother in England. Shamed into action, Singh did as he was asked and the manuscript with photographs finally reached the desk of Mr Goffin of the Oxford University Press by the end of 1935.

As a friend of Bishop Walsh, Mr Goffin had promised to do his best to find a publisher for the diary; but his efforts were not rewarded with success. The manuscript was prolix, not very well arranged and written in unattractive English; the photographs, mostly taken by Singh himself, were of poor quality, and since Kamala objected to being photographed in the early (and more interesting) years – she would turn her head away rather than face the camera – there were scarcely any front views or close-ups. British publishers were not impressed. 'The general judgement', Mr Goffin reported back to Bishop Walsh, 'is that the story falls between two stools, it just misses both the scientific and the more popular markets. For the former there is not sufficient technical detail – bodily features, exact tests and results . . . For the popular there is insufficient story.'[22]

It seemed to the Bishop that they had entirely missed the point; as he saw it, the central interest of the diary lay in the psychological, moral and spiritual condition and development of the children and the story, as told, seemed to him most illuminating on these grounds. But Mr Goffin's letter left no room for argument and the manuscript with photographs was recalled to India.

The Reverend Singh reacted predictably to the rejection of his work. He was mortified. Declaring once again that he wished to have nothing more to do with the diary he abdicated all responsibility regarding publication to Bishop Walsh and chose to forget to how many of his friends and acquaintances in Midnapore he had talked proudly of his 'forthcoming book'. As far as he was concerned the wolf children episode was closed. Bishop Walsh, on the other hand, whose belief in the importance of the diary remained as strong as ever, would not give up so easily. Over the next two years, fully occupied as he was with the *ashram*, building houses and a chapel, sinking bore wells and constructing a windmill to pump water, learning Tamil and organizing the work of the Christa Sishya Sangha (Fellowship of the Disciples of Christ), he found time to write a shorter more popular version of the wolf children's story based on the Reverend Singh's diary.

It was accepted by the weekly *Illustrated Times of India* and published as a series of three articles with the best of the photographs in November and December of 1937. Hoping to capitalize on this modest success the Bishop sent off the articles to Mr Goffin in England suggesting that his own work might stand a better chance than Singh's of finding a publisher. There he, too, was to be disappointed; but by coincidence the same mail that delivered Goffin's rejection slip also brought a letter from the U.S.A., addressed to Singh in Midnapore and forwarded on by him. It was from Dr Robert Zingg, an anthropologist at the University of Denver, and expressed in the politest possible terms a desire to help the Reverend Singh find a publisher, if he so wished, for anything he might have written about the wolf children. The letter was full of flattering and somewhat inflated statements that must have sounded sweet to the ears of the padre and, indeed, to Bishop Pakenham-Walsh. 'It has been your privilege,' Dr Zingg wrote, 'to be the guardian and custodian of one of the rarest and most valuable beings – of crucial importance in understanding how much human beings are human because of their experience, education, and contact in the first few years of life ... I would find it a pleasure personally and a contribution to science, if you found it convenient to answer.'[23] This was exactly what the two Churchmen of Christ, laymen of science, had always believed and neither of them doubted that in Dr Zingg's letter 'the finger of God' was showing them the way. Bishop Walsh answered by return of post (three or four days later in the valley of Thadagam) informing Zingg that the diary would be sent on to him in Colorado as soon as possible and that the responsibility for finding a publisher was now entirely his. All profits, he added, were to be sent to the Reverend Singh in Midnapore. The padre, who had just received 226 rupees for the Bishop's articles in the *Times of India*, began once more to take heart: the future of the orphanage no longer seemed quite so bleak.

Chapter Eleven

A son of the West, born and raised in the shadow of the Rocky mountains, Robert M. Zingg was thirty-eight years old in 1938, when he first wrote to the Reverend Singh about the wolf children. He had completed his Ph.D. in anthropology some five years before at the University of Chicago, and since then had produced two academic works on the Indians of Mexico, both of which had been well enough received. Although he sometimes had difficulty in expressing himself clearly in English and enjoyed a reputation for being slightly unconventional in his approach to life both on and off the campus, he was considered nonetheless a useful addition to the Department of Anthropology at the University of Denver. Particularly so since his aunt, Mrs Annie Pfeiffer, a wealthy and philanthropic New York widow, had donated $50,000 to the University on her nephew's acceptance of his first academic post.

Soon after completing his book on the Huichols of Mexico, described as 'a study of primitive culture in relative isolation', Dr Zingg had turned his attention to the more obscure and for an anthropologist not altogether respectable subject of Feral Man, which he believed afforded instances of complete absence of culture in absolute isolation. 'I have been attracted to the study of Feral or "Wild" Man,' he wrote to a colleague in January 1938, 'as [a] subject most significant in revealing to us, how much that [which] makes us human derives from human association in childhood rather than to race, or even brain and nervous structure.'[1] On a sabbatical in Germany the year before, while visiting his wife Christina's relations, he had collected data on a number of cases of European wild or isolated children from earlier centuries; but the available information with one or two notable exceptions (the Wild Boy of Aveyron and Caspar Hauser) was thin and patchy, particularly in those cases where children were said to have been raised by wild animals. However, in Europe historical and mythological animal-reared children (a somewhat tendentious distinction) mostly date from times when men and wild animals lived in closer conjunction to each other, and when scientific reporting – as in the case of the fourteenth-century Hessian wolf boy and the seventeenth-century Lithuanian bear boys – was hardly developed. In making some allowances for the European cases, Dr Zingg found that they corresponded in essential details with the more recent stories of wolf and bear children collected by Colonel Sleeman during the nineteenth century in the jungles of India, where favourable feral conditions still existed. Although charmed and absorbed by the material, which as far as he knew had not been previously collated, Dr Zingg had no serious intention of putting it together in book or article form, until he happened to read in a back number of the *Journal of American Psychology* about the wolf children of Midnapore. Having written to the Reverend Singh, doubtful even of receiving a reply, he suddenly found himself proprietor of all publication rights of a document which could not fail, provided it was genuine, to have some contemporary scientific interest.

As yet Dr Zingg had only seen Bishop Pakenham-Walsh's articles based on the Reverend Singh's diary and published with some of his photographs in the *Illustrated Times of India*, copies of which the Bishop had sent him in reply to his original letter of inquiry; but these had been enough to lift his expectancy, while he patiently awaited the arrival from England of the diary manuscript, to a very high level. He had already shown the articles to psychologists at Denver and sent them to a former colleague and sociologist, Dr Redfield, now Dean of the University of

Chicago, to test their reactions to this preliminary material. They had expressed cautious interest in the story and in seeing the manuscript when it came through, but Dr Zingg, a born enthusiast, felt justified in writing to the Reverend Singh in less equivocal terms. 'From Pakenham-Walsh's article alone, I know I can say "Well done, O good and faithful servent (*sic*)", you have done science a great service. I cannot imagine your ms. [not] finding a publisher in America, though I have not yet seen it. It will surely be some reward for your Christian charity, when I tell you my honest conviction that I address a man whose name will go down in all time as one who has made a fundamental contribution to vitally important human knowledge.'[2]

No doubt Dr Zingg was working on the assumption that it only needed a little flattery and kindness to establish good relations with the Reverend Singh, something he believed essential to the success of their joint enterprise; and indeed after the misunderstanding with Dr Squires this was precisely the right medicine to give the padre. But Zingg's letter nonetheless betrays a certain naiveness, a lack of objectivity perhaps and an over-eagerness to please, which were only partly intended and would continue to set the tone for most of his correspondence about the wolf children. But more importantly the letter established that with all his unbounded, good-natured enthusiasm for the wolf children project, Dr Zingg was not interested in exploiting the diary either for his own financial ends or to enhance his reputation. He proposed merely to write an introduction briefly summarizing other cases of Feral Man for the interest of comparison. Beyond that he appeared to have perfectly understood the Singhs' pressing money problems and the plight of their orphanage: he promised to do what he could to get the Bishop's magazine articles published in the popular press without compromising the scientific value of the diary MS. He even suggested
– apologizing for his own lack of funds – that the padre

should write to his wealthy aunt, Mrs Pfeiffer, whom he had already told about the wolf children, in case she might like to take an interest in the orphanage. From the Reverend Singh's point of view it would have been difficult to have found a more conscientious and obliging agent for his diary; but whether Robert Zingg would serve science as well as he proposed to serve the padre was a different matter. In the short time that he had been acquainted with the story of Kamala and Amala, and that from a second-hand account, he was already very far advanced along the way to believing in it without any supporting evidence other than the word of an Anglican Bishop. Moreover, his enthusiasm for Singh's story was leading him, not without awareness of the pitfalls, towards championing the cause of Feral Man in bringing the subject to scientific status. 'I realize that association with so controversial a matter as Feral Man,' he wrote to Dr Redfield of Chicago, 'may prejudice me [by] association with the mythical and fabulous. But if the document is as honest [as I believe it to be], with as many internal evidences of genuine harmony with the other cases, I am inclined to take the risk . . . in the belief that truth will get a hearing more readily among scientists than other groups, . . . however destructive it may be to current theory.'[3]

It was a jubilant, crusading Dr Zingg, who tore open the promising-looking package from London, England, only to find that Mr Goffin of the O.U.P. had sent him another copy of Bishop Walsh's articles summarizing the diary rather than the diary itself. The MS., it appeared, was still in India. Crestfallen, Zingg wrote to the Bishop the same day explaining what had happened and asking with some trepidation (for he feared now that all along he had misread the situation and that the original had been lost) to see the Reverend Singh's manuscript. Some weeks later he received a letter from the Bishop assuring him that the diary was extant and now at last on its way to Denver. He had assumed in all innocence, though even Bishops are not immune to pride of authorship, that because the Reverend Singh's manuscript had been rejected by publishers in England and his own version had met at least with some success, the latter would be of more interest. He acknowledged, of course, that scientists might view the diary differently, but still felt that there was room for a more popular work ... his own. 'I still think that my account,' he pleaded, knowing, it must be said, that all profits would accrue to the Reverend Singh and his orphanage, 'would make a small book which would have a wide sale among the ordinary public. Already many of my friends in England and in India are asking me when the book is coming out. It could be sold cheap and I feel very sure would sell "like hot cakes".'[4]

While waiting for the diary to turn up, Dr Zingg optimistically set to work on the preliminaries of publication, making early contact with Macmillans through his friends at Chicago and, from a list provided by the Reverend Singh, writing to a number of the most influential scientists who had shown interest in the wolf children when the story first reached the West. He invited among others Dr Raymond Dart, Professor of Anatomy at Witwatersrand University and the celebrated discoverer of *Australopithecus*, Dr Arnold Gesell, the well-known pioneer in child development studies at Yale, and Professor Ruggles Gates, a hereditist of London University, to inspect the manuscript as soon as it arrived and make any prefatory comments they might wish to contribute. He also took a trip north to visit his old university of Chicago and discuss with Dean Redfield the possibility of organizing a symposium of anthropologists, sociologists and psychologists to examine the diary and help prepare it for publication. Whatever his own limitations as an objective investigator of feral truth, Dr Zingg could not be accused of trying to keep his scientific and journalistic scoop to himself. In Chicago Dean Redfield had arranged for him to meet Sydney Hollander, a graduate student in sociology, who happened to be writing his doctoral thesis on Feral Man. Zingg thought him 'very competent and thoroughly scientific' and at once suggested that Hollander, rather than himself, should footnote the Reverend Singh's M S. and, if he wished, publish his thesis as an appendix to the diary, since he had been working on the subject for much longer than he had. He would, of course, put his own researches at Hollander's disposal. It was a characteristically generous offer. Whether through modesty, lack of confidence in his own abilities, or simply because he believed in distributing the load of scientific knowledge and responsibility, he was anxious to bring as many minds to bear on the wolf children project as could be of help. Like the Reverend Singh, he was not above taking simple pleasure in the cachet of corresponding with scientists of the stature of Dart and Gesell, but he had a better idea than the padre of the value of their prestige and what their influence could do to make 'wolf children' respectable if they chose to come down on their side. It would be wrong to insist that Zingg's mind at this stage was already made up in favour of wolf children; touched by the story of Kamala and Amala, sympathetic towards the Reverend Singh and Bishop Walsh, and excited by the romance of working on so outlandish a project, his character predisposed him to believe, but not his training as an anthropologist: he was determined that the facts should be investigated correctly, according to scientific method and principle.

The diary and photographs of the wolf children finally arrived from India towards the end of June 1938. If he had reason to be disappointed in the manuscript, Dr Zingg showed no hesitation in writing back at once to Bishop Pakenham-Walsh: 'I am delighted with it . . . as being far more intelligent, intelligible and complete than I dared hope . . . it is a scientific document of primary importance.'[5] The disparaging criticisms of Paul Squires had prepared him for the worst; he could not help feeling pleased that they appeared on the whole unjustified.

As 'a scientific document', however, the Reverend Singh's diary left something to be desired. For one thing, it was no longer strictly a diary; the chronological entries had been rearranged under topical headings, such as 'Conduct Towards Animals and Men', 'Mode of Eating', 'Intellect – The Power of Understanding', and grouped in chapters; each entry retained a date but some had been rewritten in the past tense to echo the retrospective tone of the philosophical and analytical notes later addended by Singh – in pursuit, no doubt, of his 'great Truth in Social Biology'. For another, the manuscript had been cut and edited by Bishop Pakenham-Walsh, who might have been expected to know better but freely admitted to having corrected Singh's English, removed inconsistencies and repetitions and 'left out certain sections where he indulged in psychological opinions of his own'[6] – though not all. Instead of the original journal account, the two clergymen had produced between them in the interests of science and readability a document which fulfilled the precepts of neither. But, as far as Dr Zingg was concerned, the information contained in the diary was so extraordinary that it mattered little how the facts were presented.

The reactions of the other interested scientists, to whom Zingg duly sent copies of the manuscript, were almost as favourable, particularly so in the case of Dr Gesell at Yale and Professor Ruggles Gates in London; though all were agreed of the necessity – without doubting the fundamental honesty of the document – for checking the Reverend Singh's story by every means available to them. In Chicago the 'Wolf Children Symposium' under the chairmanship of Dr Wilton Krogman, the university's senior anthropologist and Dr Zingg's former teacher, set about examining the diary with a view to preparing a list of pertinent questions to be sent to the Reverend Singh in India. No less anxious than his colleagues to observe scientific propriety Zingg was yet keen to see the diary published as soon as possible. Inevitably, with so many people involved, the checking of the manuscript was a slow business, but the allowable delays were suddenly compounded by the unexpected failure of Mr Sydney Hollander, to whom Dr Zingg had entrusted what he regarded as the key task of preparing the appendix of comparable feral case histories, to produce so much as an index after sitting on the project for nearly six months. Without a word of reproach Dr Zingg resumed work on his own compilation of the data in September 1938 and by January the completed manuscript of the wolf children diary with a 260-page appendix, footnotes and prefaces had arrived at Macmillan's. After an initial display of enthusiasm, however, they were now talking about having to seek financial assistance, because of the unwieldy and academic nature of the book, before they could hope to publish.

In the meantime the Chicago Symposium had produced their list of nineteen questions on the text of the diary, carefully censored to avoid upsetting the padre by any remark that might be thought to impugn his honesty. These were sent off with a covering letter from Dr Zingg, who expressed the opinion that Dr Krogman's questions were too technical, mostly irrelevant and really not worth answering unless the padre had nothing better to do. He was overstating the case, but certainly they were not particularly apt or intelligent questions. The sublime confidence with which the Chicago anthropologists asked of a half-educated Indian missionary whether he had studied the wolf children's feet 'to note opposibility of the big toe' or whether the enlargement of their joints was 'traceable to disuse, or to dietetic imbalance' betrayed as much insensitivity on their side of the cultural divide as Singh and Pakenham-Walsh had shown in their misguided editing of the diary. Dr Zingg assured the padre that they would not hold up publication while waiting for his answers. Despite Macmillan's annoying prevarication he had taken heart from a declaration of interest by the British publishers

Allen and Unwin, to whom Professor Ruggles Gates had shown the manuscript. Also the recent discovery in the South African veld of a wild man, said to have been rescued from a troop of baboons by two Afrikaner policemen, was receiving a great deal of publicity in the world press. At once proclaimed the prototype for Tarzan, the 'Baboon Boy' could do nothing but good, or so Dr Zingg believed, for his own potential Mowglis.

Within a month of the 'Baboon Boy' story, they got their first break: the purchase of serial rights of the wolf children diary by the Hearst Sunday supplement, the *American Weekly*, for $250. The money was wired out to the Reverend Singh in Midnapore, who was more than delighted – a princely sum when translated into rupees, it reduced the orphanage debt by almost a quarter – and wrote back a grateful letter to Dr Zingg, shortly followed by a typescript of his answers to Dr Krogman's nineteen questions and an elaborate apology for the long delay in sending them; he had been seriously ill, but happily was now recovered and 'up again to proclaim the glory of My Father in Heaven'.

The Reverend Singh's answers to their questions, if they provided little in the way of new information, surprised the Chicago scientists by their display of restraint, clarity and good sense. Dr Zingg felt that his faith in the padre had been vindicated and even those, like Dean Redfield, who had believed Singh incapable of answering the questions and favoured an investigation on the spot by a qualified man, were forced to acknowledge that he had not done badly for a layman. Over the more controversial claims of the diary – the phenomenon of Kamala and Amala's eyes giving off a blue glare, the length of their eyeteeth, the formation of their jaw bones – the Reverend Singh had stood his ground and replied to the more or less tactful suggestions of the scientists that such things could not be with a strong affirmation that such things were, and that all he had written was true and that he had exaggerated nothing. His answers left little room for discussion.

Dr Zingg, meanwhile, had begun to investigate the feasibility of human eyes glowing in the dark, which he regarded as 'the most striking feature of the entire account', if only because it had no precedent in other feral cases. Krogman and others insisted it was impossible because the human eye, lacking a tapetum (a special reflecting membrane found in the eyes of many mammals) cannot refract light. With the help of Professor Ruggles Gates in London, however, Zingg managed to collect a respectable amount of evidence to show that the adjustment of the wolf children's vision to the environment of the termite mound and a nocturnal existence was not unique and that despite the absence of a tapetum, night-shining eyes in humans had been recorded from time to time. One account, from a recent correspondence in *Nature*, was given by a speleologist, Mr E. A. Glennie, who reported observing eye-glare among cave-dwellers in North India. Dr Zingg was quick to point out certain similarities to the lives of the wolf children in the forest of Denganalia. Another correspondent, J. Herbert Parsons, explained the phenomenon in terms of the retina and choroid acting as mirror under certain conditions. 'The rareness of "night-shining" in human eyes,' he added, 'is due to the facts that the observed eye must be highly hypermetropic [far sighted] (or still more rarely very highly myopic), the incident light must be bright, and the observing eye must be so placed that some of the reflected rays enter it.'[7] Whether these conditions obtained in the case of Kamala and Amala is not really clear since they were never examined by an ophthalmologist and the Reverend Singh's descriptions of the phenomenon, affected no doubt by his own naïve belief that the glare was not reflected but actually emanated from the children's eyes, are somewhat contradictory. Although the results of Dr Zingg's investigations seemed to suggest that the padre had not necessarily invented eyes-that-glowin-the-dark, Dr Krogman and others at Chicago, when shown the data by Zingg over a macaroni dinner in a Philadelphia restaurant, refused to alter their position. In London Professor Ruggles Gates suggested boldly that anatomists would simply have to restudy the eye and change their minds about it. In Denver Dr Zingg began to divide people into those who were receptive to the idea of Feral Man and those who would not believe in him at any price. His victory in the battle of the night-shining eyes had left him without laurels, but a keener champion than ever of the truth.

Among Zingg's allies in the controversy that now arose over the wolf children, none at this stage was stauncher in his support or carried more weight than Dr Arnold Gesell of Yale University. His pioneer work on the early mental development of human beings at Yale's Clinic of Child Development (founded by him in 1911 originally to work on the backward child) had placed him among the world's leading child psychologists and gave him of all scientists involved in the case the best qualifications for the study of Kamala and Amala. As a pediatrist and clinical psychologist, Gesell had devoted his life to observing the interaction between physical and mental development which, he maintained, takes place in children in definite sequences. His achievement, as well as introducing methods of observing and measuring infant behaviour where none existed before, had been to show that the mental growth of the child reveals itself 'in consistent and characteristic behaviour patterns, governed by laws of growth similar to those which control the development of his body'.[8] Through his writing Gesell's work was already well known and appreciated by a wide public in the United States: *The Mental Growth of the Pre-School Child*, *An Atlas of Infant Behaviour*, and more recently *The First Five Years Of Life*, which were all accessible to the general reader, if largely through the generous use of photographs and film stills (the cine-camera was Gesell's chief research tool), had made him a precursor of Dr Spock as an authority on how to bring up children. But there any similarity ended. Gesell's general sequential theory of development, which attributed certain behaviour patterns in children to genetically conditioned changes in the nervous system rather than social and cultural influences, had established him as a leading hereditist, though his views on the subject were not dogmatic. He regarded the division between heredity and environment as a dichotomy which was becoming increasingly untenable: 'Growth is a unifying concept which resolves the dualism of heredity and environment. Environmental factors support, inflect, and modify, but they do not generate the progressions of development. Growth is an impulsion and as a cycle of morphogenetic events is uniquely a character of the living organism. Neither physical nor cultural environment contains any architectonic arrangements like the mechanism of growth. Culture accumulates; it does not grow. The glove goes on the hand; the hand determines the glove.'[9]

The interest that the story of the wolf children held for Dr Gesell needs little explanation in the light of his life's work, much of which was concerned with establishing norms of infant behaviour through the setting up of simple situations which are culturally generic for the human species and with collecting records of locomotion, manipulation, problem solving, and so on as a basis for comparative study. 'Only by assiduously pursuing this fundamental biological *Urkind*,' he wrote, 'and by mapping the intrinsic neuromotor equipment can we hope to draw a picture of "the natural man" who exists in the world of science, even though we shall never come upon an Emile.'[10] Clearly Gesell did not believe he had found his prototype of natural man in Kamala. Regarding her as a potentially normal child, he was interested in her reactions under the extreme environmental conditions of the wolf's den, providing an almost crucial experiment in the problem of nature versus nurture and one which could be seen to support his own views. 'From the standpoint of genetic and of clinical psychology,' he would point out, 'the most significant phenomenon in the life career of Kamala is the slow but orderly and sequential recovery of obstructed mental growth.'[11]

Gesell found in Kamala's story affirmation of the immense stamina of human nature and potentialities of human growth, which he had always believed in as a child psychologist. His approach to the subject, however, was not exclusively scientific. A convinced anti-technologist, deeply sceptical of man-made Utopias, he admitted to having always been fascinated by stories of wild children, whether as myth, fact or an idealized conception of man at one with nature, which predisposed him perhaps to regard the wolf children of Midnapore in a more romantic light. It is difficult otherwise to explain his growing obsession with Kamala – an obsession that would not be satisfied by contributing a preface to the Reverend Singh's diary or risking his own considerable reputation as a scientist in identifying with so controversial a topic. Without informing Dr Zingg or any of the others involved in the diary project, Gesell was planning to write a 'Philosophical Essay' based on the life story of Kamala. While the inconsistencies and enormities of the diary were being carefully checked and pondered over by the Chicago Symposium, Gesell was busy in the Yale libraries researching local colour and background material to brighten and authenticate his own projected work, finding out about bullock carts, Hindu customs and the Bengal climate and even taking the trouble to read up on the Indian Wolf.

By a curious omission no ethologist or wolf-expert had as yet been consulted over the story of the wolf children. On a visit to Washington D.C. in December 1939, therefore, Dr Gesell took the opportunity to visit the Smithsonian National Zoo and have a closer look at the chief protagonists of his feral drama. Making use of his name and contacts, Gesell persuaded the keeper to allow him into the cages, where he was able to meet some Canadian timber wolves and cubs face to face, and by crawling around on hands and knees re-experience, in the imagination at least, something of Kamala's unique set of four-footed relationships. There was little danger involved and when he had had his fill of wolf company he emerged from the cage relieved but unscathed. As luck would have it, though, on his way back across the park, while still musing on the great mysteries of nature, Dr Gesell met up with a small Washington dog out for a walk with its owner, Mr J. H. Hechtman. The dog, it seemed, took strong exception to the wolves' scent with which his clothes had become impregnated and immediately set upon him, bringing the dreaming scientist back to reality with a painful bite. A subsequent rabies check fortunately proved negative.

Efforts to find a publisher for the Reverend Singh's diary had so far met with little success. Macmillan's had finally pulled out of the project altogether, leaving Allen and Unwin on the other side of the Atlantic still interested but insisting on financial support from an American publisher before they would commit themselves. There was a possibility that backing might be provided by Vanguard, though the outbreak of war in Europe had made all publishing ventures more uncertain than ever, and even Dr Zingg was momentarily discouraged. From India Bishop Pakenham-Walsh, whose articles on the wolf children Zingg had rather embarrassingly been unable to place, took an irritatingly pessimistic view: 'Of course if a European war comes,' he had written to Zingg some months earlier, 'all prospects of the book selling will be gone. I had a book of public school daily sermons ready just when the Great War started, and it killed it!'[12] And yet, as Dr Zingg would insist, interest in the wolf children was still very much alive in America: witness a picture story in the *New-Haven Journal Courier*, 5 December 1939. Entitled *Wild Women*, it showed two photographs, one a faded snapshot of Kamala, the wolf child, scratching about in the Reverend Singh's orphanage compound, the other a glamorous pin-up of Maureen O'Sullivan, dressed for the part of Jane in a Tarzan movie. If the story appeared in bad taste it was a very effective way of showing the discrepancy between myth and reality; though whether the scientists, who had fed the picture of Kamala to the *Journal-Courier* to stir up publicity in the hope of catching a publisher, saw in that telling juxtaposition a warning to themselves is quite another matter.

As Dr Zingg well understood and others would come to realize, the story of Kamala and Amala was in practice only preserved from the realm of myth by a single fact: that of all accounts of feral children it was the only one written by an eyewitness, who himself was present at the capture of a human child from an animal den and from the close company of animals. The Reverend Singh's testimony on this point, although in itself not allowable as scientific evidence without the support of at least one other independent witness, was clearly fundamental to any attempt to raise 'wolf children' to scientific status. It might seem strange, therefore, that the Chicago scientists, who could concern themselves with such minute details as the 'opposibility' of Kamala's big toe, did not make more effort to check this pivotal aspect of the whole story. Many of them were victims, no doubt, of their own specialized interests; but there were other considerations, not least the practical difficulties of carrying out an investigation over the vast distances, both geographical and cultural, that separated Midnapore and Chicago, the fear of offending the Reverend Singh by appearing to doubt his word and the seemingly hopeless task of tracking down the two Anglo-Indians, Richards and Rose, whose evidence alone could at once have clinched the matter. In his diary account of the rescue, the Reverend Singh, for reasons known only to himself, had mentioned none of the other participants in the hunt except for Chunarem, who had told him about the 'manush-baghas' in the first place and his two servants,

259

Karan Hansda and Janu Tudu. Dr Zingg knew nothing, for instance, of the involvement of the catechist, Bhagobhat Khatua, or the Maharajah of Mayurbhanj's hunting officer, Dibakar Bhanj Deo; perhaps if he had, he would have made some attempt to get statements from them, as he had tried to do so feebly and unsuccessfully with Rose and Richards, for instead of insisting upon the need for supporting evidence, he had written to the padre and the Bishop early in 1938 that additional testimony was desirable but would only 'gild the lily of Reverend Singh's thoroughly competent account'.

In January 1940 Professor J. H. Hutton, a social anthropologist at Cambridge University and an authority on the tribal peoples of British India, sent Professor Ruggles Gates a cutting from the *Calcutta Statesman* of 16 November 1926, which gave a different account, yet ostensibly in the Reverend Singh's own words, of how the wolf children were found. On a missionary tour through a remote district of Mayurbhanj the padre, it seems, had been approached by a poor cultivator of the Todha tribe, who had taken him to his hut in the jungle and shown him two wild-looking children lying at the bottom of a cage, sick, dirty, covered in sores and evidently close to death. The cultivator refused to explain how the children came to be there, but implored the padre to take them away with him. The Reverend Singh took pity on the creatures and brought them back to the orphanage at Midnapore, where with the help of his wife he had nursed them back to health. It soon became clear, however, from their peculiar habits, their inability to walk or speak and their refusal to eat any food other than raw meat that these were not ordinary children. Curious about their origins, on a return trip to the jungle he asked the cultivator to tell him how he had come upon them. Very reluctantly, for he was afraid the padre would make him take the children back, the man recounted a story of how the two girls had been found in the jungle near by, living with wolves in an old termite mound. They had later been captured by some Santals and he had foolishly volunteered to look after them. The Reverend Singh persuaded the man to take him to the spot where the children had been found and after seeing the termite mound and the den, which bore signs of recent excavation, accepted his story.

Interestingly, this account, printed in the *Statesman* three days after the appearance of Bishop Pakenham-Walsh's story, gave many of the same details (on the behaviour and death of the mother wolf, for instance) that are found in the Reverend Singh's diary, though which was the original and true version now seemed equivocal. After informing his colleagues in America of what had happened, Professor Ruggles Gates wrote a letter to the Reverend Singh that was characteristically British in its directness and offered no concession to the padre's finer feelings. Gates demanded the truth, but making it plain that he was already inclined to believe the cultivator's story: 'In scientific matters, the precise facts are absolutely essential and I want to obtain from you, instead of the statement given in your diary, the statement direct from the cultivator who made the rescue. If this cannot be done, it may interfere seriously with the whole publication.'[13] The ultimatum was intended chiefly to provoke a showdown with the Reverend Singh, but both Gates and Hutton still considered the diary itself to be a true and valuable account, which ought not to be dismissed entirely even if it turned out that Singh had not rescued the wolf children himself.

In America, too, attitudes were defiantly buoyant, though recent news from South Africa that 'the Baboon Boy' had turned out to be a fake inclined Dr Zingg to exercise rather more caution. He wrote to Bishop Walsh asking him to find out from Singh what had really happened and expressing his own view that, native Indians being 'rather childish', the padre had probably given rein to his imagination and made himself the hero of his story without realizing that inaccuracy could jeopardize its value. Other hopes were dashed when the Vanguard Press finally turned down the manuscript of the diary, not because of Hutton's evidence, but on the basis of a report from an unnamed anthropologist, which was not only extraordinarily critical of inconsistencies, omissions and exaggerations in the text, but accused the Reverend Singh of deliberately manufacturing the wolf children to make money, and put the scientific value of the document at precisely nil. Dr Zingg acknowledged Vanguard's rejection with some relief; new evidence had turned up, he explained, which would anyway delay publication for a while.

In March and April of 1940 two long and detailed letters arrived from Reverend Singh in answer to Professor Ruggles Gates' queries, giving a full history of Indian press reports on the wolf children and defending his position. Beginning with Dr Sarbadhicari's indiscretion in the *Medinipur Hitaishi*, Singh explained, without intimating that he himself had once given out several different accounts, how numerous versions of the rescue story had been printed by the provincial press:

Some paper said that I had gone on a shoot and captured them in the jungle, and others that the Cultivators found them and handed them over to me, and others that I with the help of others dug them out of the wolves' den, and so on. I got so much annoyed at this time at the publication and the way the public was carrying the rescue story with false addition and alteration in the Press, that I did not like to interfere with their statements, expecting simply all this noise to die out and grant us respite.

So I avoided to correct or contradict the Press simply to allow the news to die out soon, as I had no intention of ever publishing the Story of the Rescue or my Study of Children in the Orphanage. My simple aim was purely humanitarian and Christian. I wanted to see them human beings again. It was not a study for Science and its progress. I had no such idea in the least and did not think of it, till the Bishop Walsh persuasively opened my eyes after [the publications] of 1926.[14]

When the reporter from the *Statesman* came to see him on 15 November 1926 after the Bishop had unintentionally leaked the story to the press, Singh claimed that he had told him 'that this is the true story and all that . . . the other papers wrote and rewrote before this were not partly true and I was the very person who rescued them . . .',[15] but nonetheless, the *Statesman* representative had gone away and written up the Cultivator's story as if it came from the padre himself and without any explanation of the discrepancies with Bishop Walsh's account. In retrospect it seemed clear to the Reverend Singh that he had been the victim both of unscrupulous journalistic practice and – introducing a political note – jealousy on the part of the reporter, who resented the accrediting of anything worthwhile to a humble Indian missionary. 'He came to me with a preconceived plan to vilify my statement knowing fully that I never contradicted before any publication in the Press, and he was quite safe with me.'[16] And indeed he was, for once again Singh had remained silent.

The letters to Professor Ruggles Gates, though often repetitive, full of childish argument and in places bright with indignation, were otherwise well-reasoned documents. They contained the statements of various people including the typist of the diary and Dr Sarbadhicari's son, who had seen Kamala at the orphanage and heard from the Reverend Singh the story of how he personally had rescued the wolf children from the jungle. But perhaps the best argument put forward by the padre in his defence was that in August 1926 he had told the original story of the rescue to Bishop Walsh on his visit to Midnapore and shown him the diary where the same story was written down, presumably under the appropriate dates. 'How could it be possible,' he now asked, 'to give another rescue story . . . on 15 November 1926, in the same year? It means this, that the Bishop when he would see the Representative's statement, would naturally think me to be a liar. Was it praiseworthy for me? And what could I gain by it? Rather, on the other hand, I would lose my estimation before the public as a first-hand rescuer, would become a liar. Was this desirable at all, like a sane man?'[17] The same point was made by Bishop Walsh himself in a letter to Dr Zingg suggesting that the order in which the stories appeared in the *Statesman* precluded the possibility that Singh had tried to embellish his account by making himself out to be the rescuer. 'I have not the least doubt,' the Bishop wrote, and he was a man who found it hard to think ill of others, 'knowing as I do the exact care of Reverend J. A. L. Singh in all his statements, and his very high standards of truthfulness, that the story, as he has always given it, is true'.[18]

Dr Zingg was pleased enough with Singh and the Bishop's answers to write back at once to congratulate him. Although some of the Chicago scientists wanted to delay publication of the diary until the story had been rigorously checked – there appeared to be a possibility now of Zingg himself being sent out to India as feral investigator – it was the feeling of Gesell, Gates and others, as well as his own, that since the Midnapore case was so strong, they should press ahead with the difficult task of finding a publisher. Nothing daunted, Dr Zingg's enthusiasm was once more gaining momentum, yet while expressing full confidence in the Reverend Singh and all his works, he let the padre understand for the first time that he was putting a great deal of faith in his word. 'The revelation of any inaccuracies in your account,' he wrote, exerting a little moral pressure, 'would do great harm not only to yourself and to the record of the wolf children, but also to me and my career.'[19] In an especially unctuous reply the Reverend Singh assured him that neither of them had anything to fear from the truth; he felt perfectly clear in his conscience and was looking forward very much to receiving his 'benevolent friend' in Midnapore, where they would have the opportunity of verifying all that he had written about the wolf children. There was nothing ambiguous about the letter and yet Singh's endearing pomposity, his dreadful homilist style and painfully fractured English covered a perplexity of character and confusion of motives, drawn both from ancient and more recent history, that were entirely lost on Robert Zingg.

Dr Gesell was not inclined to regard the Singh diary as a hoax. Its very naivety, omissions, minor contradictions, the paucity of the record for the last two years of Kamala's life, and particularly the photographic documentation – which he was better qualified than anyone to judge – seemed to him to provide adequate internal evidence of Singh's honesty and the document's worth. 'Caution as well as credulity may overreach itself . . .' he suggested to Zingg, 'it would be unfortunate, if not unfair, if the recent scepticism gains too much ground.'[20] Unfortunate and unfair, if only because Gesell had by now written his 'Philosophical Essay' on Kamala's life and wanted to see it published. He had as yet mentioned this work to Zingg only in rather vague terms, but assured him that it could not possibly interfere with the placing of the diary. In fact, just the opposite: 'I should think that the publication of the Essay would have only a favourable effect on the publication and ultimate circulation of your own study and the diary.'[21] At Zingg's request he interceded with his own publishers, Harper's, on behalf of the diary, but with only qualified success: Harper's were definitely interested, but only if the cost of production were underwritten by some university or foundation. Meanwhile they were looking with rather more enthusiasm at Dr Gesell's more popular 'Philosophical Essay' which as the work of one of their authors they had naturally insisted on seeing too.

In view of Dr Zingg's proprietorial rights to the wolf children diary, Harper's alacritous decision to publish *Biography of a Wolf Child* as a slender volume of nine chapters might have proved a source of embarrassment to its author. But in asking Zingg's permission to go ahead with publication – a request that would be extended to the

Reverend Singh and Bishop Walsh – Dr Gesell offered an explanation of his own motivation that all concerned would find irresistible: 'I wrote this exposition from an insistent inner compulsion,' he confessed, 'I was so haunted by Kamala and Amala that I could not exorcize them until I had written out a story which would satisfy my own questionings. In so doing I hope I have also written something which will help others, particularly lay readers, for there is a profound, unfathomed resistance to the acceptance of Feral Man. And I should be pleased if my step by step interpretation will break down prejudices of antipathy and scepticism.'[22] No less moved by the psychologist's avowal of an obsession he also shared, than by his offer to donate half the royalties on his book to the Midnapore orphanage, Dr Zingg agreed with his usual generosity to all of Gesell's demands, including a request to use the best of the wolf-children photographs as illustrations. If it ever occurred to him that he was being scooped, that his fire was being stolen by a fellow scientist, Dr Zingg was much too pleased by the cachet of Arnold Gesell's name being attached to his project and the imminent prospect of Feral Man achieving scientific respectability, to mind. After reading a proof copy of the 'Essay' he felt inspired to write to its author: 'Your brilliant, moving, but succinct summary as a slender and inexpensive volume should have a favourable result on the eventual publication of the complete work ... it is a splendid job, popular and yet reflecting many insights into the (feral) problem, due to your expertness on the child.'[23]

The problem was yet far from being resolved. In January 1941, two months prior to publication of Gesell's book, an article appeared in the *American Journal of Psychology*, attacking the very concept of Feral Man. Wayne Dennis, a child psychologist at the University of Virginia, taking a recent article by Dr Zingg in the same *Journal* as the basis of his critique, rejected the available evidence that a human child had ever been raised by wild animals as unconvincing, and put forward a well-reasoned argument that feral children were probably mental defectives, whose condition had been 'explained' and exploited by an interested discoverer or family. Citing Zingg's own exposé of the 'Baboon Boy' story, he suggested that in view of the uncertainty which surrounded all such stories, they should not be used to support certain social and psychological theories of human nature: namely, that deprivation of social contact in the early years tends to prevent the later socialization of the individual, that the formation of early habits has a relatively permanent effect on the individual and more crudely that 'environmental conditioning' can in some circumstances be total.

Wayne Dennis was perhaps justified in this last point, for Drs Zingg and Gesell were already receiving inquiries about the wolf children from sociologists and psychologists who wanted to include the story of Kamala and Amala in their textbooks to illustrate these very theories. But his general critique of Feral Man, as Dr Zingg pointed out in a rejoinder article, did not take into account the crucial significance of the Midnapore case with its eyewitness description of the capture of children from animals (no longer, it seemed, in any doubt) and the supporting evidence for their truly feral behaviour – indeed, could not, until all the facts were made available. Repudiating the suggestion that he was attempting to prove a thesis, Zingg confidently assured Professor Dennis that when the diary was published the full account of the Midnapore case would do much to clarify the problems he had raised.

Dr Gesell's book, retitled *Wolf Child and Human Child*, came out in America in March 1941 to a modest fanfare of publicity. Wolf children were instantly taken up as 'an issue' by *Time* magazine, clearly concerned to be first in putting a political perspective on the subject. Laying responsibility for the French and American Revolutions squarely on the feral shoulders of the Hessian wolf boy, the model for Jean-Jacques Rousseau's theories about 'natural man',

267

Time announced glibly that subsequent 'stories of wild children became suspect as radical political propaganda'. There was nothing subversive, however, about Dr Gesell's book. Seizing upon a rhetorical question raised by the author, 'CAN WOLF WAYS BE HUMANIZED?', the editors of *Time* put environmentalists in their place with an authoritative 'no': 'A wolf or even an ape reared in the Reverend Singh's orphanage would not attain a human personality.'[24]

In the more serious and academic press, where there was less concern for its political significance, the book received a mixed reception. A good review by the anthropologist, Margaret Mead, was offset, for instance, by 'a hair curler' in the *New Republic*, which suggested with cruel but incisive wit that Dr Gesell had made a complete fool of himself in producing an embarrassingly written and quite unconvincing narrative, from which he drew conclusions that happened to confirm his own pet theories on the heredity/environment debate. Dr Zingg, who unwisely protested against the irresponsibility of the review, was dismissed as a man who did not understand the nature of evidence. The reviewer, however, a professional sceptic by name of Bergen Evans, was not as impartial as his Professorship in English at Northwestern University suggested. He had evidently taken the feral question very much to heart, for in January 1941, when a summary article on the wolf children had been published in *Harpers Magazine*, he had written to 'anyone ... with one speck of honesty or decency connected with the editorial staff of *Harpers Magazine*' an outraged letter, concluding: 'Dr Gesell is probably senile, possibly dishonest, and certainly illiterate. That Yale employs him is, to a college teacher, humiliating. And that *Harpers* prints his maunderings is disgraceful.'[25] He had also written in a similarly abusive vein to Gesell himself, though whether his crankish spleen had been provoked by the psychologist or by the wolf children remains unclear.

Apart from Bergen Evans's review, which though devastating enough, was more literary in character than scientific, and not informed by close knowledge of the Reverend Singh's diary, *Wolf Child and Human Child* escaped serious criticism until the appearance of an article by a social anthropologist, David G. Mandelbaum, in the July issue of the *Journal of Social Psychology*. Here Mandelbaum raised two important points: one, that the acceptance or rejection of the story 'as an historical event involving wolves as foster parents' depended entirely on the testimony of one man, the Reverend Singh: the other that even if the story be accepted as true, the diary itself was so jumbled, vague and contradictory that it could never have any real scientific value. Comparing other accounts of wolf children with that of Reverend Singh, he came to the conclusion that the close similarity between them indicated either the standard behaviour of Feral Man, or (which seemed to him more likely) 'the familiar occurrence of parallel elements in a wide-spread folk tale '.[26]Dr Gesell had merely increased its circulation and rekindled a controversy centuries old.

In Midnapore *Wolf Child and Human Child* was less equivocally received. The Reverend Singh declared himself struck dumb with admiration for the book: 'Great Scientist as you are,' he wrote with difficulty, for he had been suffering from conjunctivitis for the past three months, 'it is simply impossible for me to express my appreciation of it on the same line of your knowledge and experience'[27]; but he went on nonetheless to deliver a panegyric, which gradually transferred from Gesell's to his own contribution to 'human knowledge', developing like so many of his letters now into a self-congratulatory prayer, that was also a reproach for all his trials, persecutions and pressing debts. Yet the padre would soon have good reason to rejoice, for not long after receiving another $250 from the sale of Gesell's article in *Harpers Magazine*, which further reduced the orphanage debt to about

2000 rupees, he heard from Dr Zingg that his own work, *The Diary of the Wolf Children of Midnapore* was going to be published by Harper's. Mrs Pfeiffer, Robert Zingg's wealthy aunt, whose estate had been tied up since the death of her husband, could now afford to underwrite the cost of production.

Dr Zingg generously attributed the final impetus towards publication of the diary to the success of Dr Gesell's book, but the determination he had shown over the last four years in getting Kamala and Amala's story into print and trying to raise it to scientific status revealed a closer involvement in a subject, with which Gesell (as he would soon be anxious to point out) had enjoyed only a mild infatuation. 'Perhaps the problem which really deserves attention,' David Mandelbaum concluded, 'is an attempt to ascertain why this tale has been so uniformly attractive to men of various times and places ... When men of science accept evidence as tenuous as this, we may well wonder about the pervasive appeal of the ancient motif.'[28]

Chapter Twelve

The confident lettering on the gateposts had worn faint; the once pukka gates, long since fallen into disrepair, had been reconstituted with bundles of rattan and bamboo and were scarcely distinguishable now from the brushwood fence that surrounded the compound; the impression from the road was of a neurotic and ineffectual stockade. The white lime-wash and green shutter paint on the front of the house, faded, stained and blistering, no longer gleamed so impressively through the trees. A pile of building materials by the veranda, set aside twenty years ago for the day when there would be enough money to put a roof on the prayer room, lay undisturbed, silted over with earth and weeds. The unfinished aspect of the orphanage buildings had been given a kind of permanence; they wore that air of hopeless defiance which sooner or later overtakes most buildings in India and somehow sustains them, lending dignity to their resigned stand against the implacable climate. In the deterioration of 'The Home' there was the added poignancy of relinquished pretensions, of failure to keep up the standards of orderliness that distinguished the British way from the native. Only the Reverend Singh's compound had remained true to its distant conception of a garden somewhere in Surrey. The paths and tubs were kept as neatly as ever; the fruit trees and vegetable garden still provided an important supplement to the orphanage's meagre diet. Still the lush oasis in the surrounding waste-land of Gope, it was his place of perennial sanctuary in a changing and increasingly hostile world.

The orphanage had fallen on hard times. There were

fewer children now; necessity had restricted new admissions in recent years and nearly all of Kamala and Amala's contemporaries had gone out into the world. Some of the orphans, mostly former child-widows, or otherwise unmarriageable girls, had stayed on into adulthood and contributed what they could – though it was hardly in proportion to what they consumed – to the upkeep of the institution that had become their permanent home. The orphanage teaching staff had been disbanded and those children who were still of school age attended the Mission High School run by the American Baptists as free day-scholars. To the Reverend Singh it was a humiliating state of affairs, but he had no choice. The three house servants paid for by the government (his entitlement as pastor of St John's Church) remained with the family, but they were getting old and slow at their work, their uniforms hung in tatters and three extra mouths to feed sometimes seemed too much to pay for their fidelity. As the price of rice rose inexorably against the padre's fixed and pitifully small pension and other strictures and pressures were brought to bear by the war economy, life at 'The Home' was reduced to a struggle for survival that threatened the very principles on which it was founded.

The Reverend Singh's support for the Allies and India's war effort, however, was scarcely affected by personal considerations. His loyalty to the Government remained as staunch as ever, while his contempt for the nationalists and Gandhi's vacillating intellectual anarchism now knew no bounds. The Mahatma's advocation of non-violence in response to fascist aggression and his remarkable advice to the British people that they should lay down their arms and their lives before the Nazi storm-troopers to show their moral superiority by passive resistance, had left the padre bitterly indignant. He had little more sympathy for the inconsistencies of Congress, whose attitude towards non-violence shifted through the various phases of the war according to its expedience as a political weapon.

Having resigned its provincial ministries in 1939 over the automatic inclusion of India in the war, 'without the consent of the Indian people', Congress was approached by the Government in August 1940 in an attempt at reconciliation, which included the offer of dominion status for India as soon as the war ended, provided the various political parties could agree on a constitution, and in return for wartime cooperation; while hostilities lasted, the granting of independence was held by the Viceroy to be impracticable. The Government's offer was rejected by the leading Hindu and Moslem parties and after Gandhi had been refused the right to preach pacifism to soldiers and munition workers, Congress backed him in a limited civil disobedience campaign. Although it failed largely through lack of popular support, in Midnapore and other 'political' towns the disturbances accompanied by wholesale arrests of Congress *satyagrahis* continued through the summer of 1941. By the end of the year more than 20,000 people would be sent to gaol; but the fire and passion of the previous decade were somehow lacking; the war had produced a political stalemate. In spite of their protest, the majority of nationalists, now that freedom was within their grasp, were willing to wait.

Although no one could guess that within six years the British would quit India altogether, the inevitability of change foreshadowed the country's future. Change meant the progressive Indianization of government and the prospect of knowing India governed by Indians filled the Reverend Singh with despair. In Midnapore he had already had a foretaste of what was to come. Since the departure in 1937 of Percival Griffiths, who had been sent to restore order after the murder of the three previous magistrates, the chief administrative posts in the district had been filled by Indians. The special relationship which the padre had enjoyed in the past with British officials did not survive this limited transference of power. If anything, his former position of privilege counted against him with his new masters. In June 1941 Singh suffered the rare indignity of losing his Honorary Magistracy, traditionally the safest of sinecures. A personal row with a local barrister had provoked him into losing his temper in court and making an unedifying scene, at which the District Judge had asked him to hand back his gown and resign from the bench. Singh complied but not without bitterness or recrimination. Humiliated by what had happened and resentful of the Judge's order – the more so because he had always prided himself on being a conscientious and scrupulously honest magistrate – he recognized that once more he had been made the victim of cruel persecution. Withdrawing from public life to the safety of the orphanage, older than his years at sixty-eight and suffering from depression˙and bad health, he resigned himself to a self-imposed martyrdom.

When the rains came that summer illness prevented him from conducting services at St John's, but he was too proud to make excuses. His old enemies on the Church Committee did not hesitate to report the matter to the Bishop and even encouraged a rumour that he had lost his faith: for some time now, they claimed, the Reverend Singh had stopped visiting his parishioners and had become lax about fulfilling the basic duties of a priest. Only Reverend Molony in Kharagpur, though under no illusions about the padre's usefulness, came to his defence because he felt sorry for him. Singh no longer had any allies in Calcutta; contact with his superiors had been reduced to squabbling with Father Balcombe over tiny sums of money and taking opposing sides in any local scandal or intrigue. Balcombe's attitude towards Singh had hardened since hearing from the Anglo-Indian Missionary, Lionel Hewitt, that the padre had recently received 10,000 rupees from America in payment for his diary of the wolf children and was spending the money on decorating his house in lavish style. There was little truth in the allegation: Arnold Gesell's book had yet to bring in any royalties   274 and his own work was not even published; the orphanage debt still stood at 2000 rupees, apparently irredeemable. Yet Singh himself was partly to blame for Hewitt's invention, for he liked to talk about America and to boast of his correspondence with the world's leading scientists and of their gratitude and respect for his own contribution to 'social biology'. He assured Hewitt and others who would listen that the financial rewards were bound to be considerable, and with vulgar insistence pointed out that considering all that he and his wife had expended on the wolf children it would be no more than a just return for their charitable labours. He lived in hope of money from America and would die still hoping, but his ambitious plans to spend it all on rebuilding the orphanage and leave a lasting monument to his family name acted upon the reality of his impoverished circumstances only as an incitement to doting avarice.

There were moments of relief from the oppressive atmosphere of poverty. The incongruous strains of Harry Lauder, the Mayfair Orchestra and snatches of ragtime were often heard now drifting across the veranda, where the Reverend Singh liked to lie back in his favourite long-chair and listen to the gramophone, operated and assiduously wound by one of the orphans. He spent long hours listening to music, asking always to hear again his two favourite tunes, *Abide with me* and *Home, sweet Home*. He read as much as his eyesight would permit; he gardened and pottered about the compound; at times he seemed almost contented. But even at his most affable, when the cares of orphanage and Empire had been temporarily banished by some resonance of a happier past, his moods remained treacherous and he would suddenly fly into a rage or sink into brooding melancholy without apparent provocation.

Relations with his family, always precariously balanced, had deteriorated. Still refusing to relent against Daniel – ten years before he had attended his son's wedding, but the two men had hardly seen or spoken to each other since – he now proceeded to fall out with his daughters. The eldest, Preeti Lota, whose husband had died in 1935, wished to marry again someone the padre considered unsuitable; while Buona Lota he had discovered in unfortunate circumstances to be living with a man, who was not only married but a Mohammedan. What hurt him most perhaps was that both women had subsequently ignored his injunctions and, while continuing to profess their love and respect for him as their father, had defiantly refused to give up their men. The unquestioning obedience he had once demanded and received from his family, his orphans and even his parishioners, was given no longer; the vested authority, upon which his whole life depended for its meaning and his character for its plausibility, had been cruelly undermined. Even the town children, whom he had always inspired with mild terror, regarded him now as a figure of fun and taunted him quite openly, daring each other to steal the orphanage guinea fowl from under his nose and laughing at his enraged threats to set his dogs after them. Only his wife kept faith with him, defended his dignity and protected him from the reality of his own diminishment. Submitting meekly to unreasonable demands, calmly bearing the strain of uncertain moods and violent outbursts of temper, she indulged his tyranny as a mother indulges an exceptional child of whom she is a little afraid. Out of fear, loyalty and affection for her husband, Mrs Singh made herself a compliant scapegoat; but the effectiveness of her sacrificial role depended on the perverse condition of her remaining in his eyes utterly beyond moral reproach. Her fall from grace was to send him into a fit of depression from which he never recovered.

On discovering that one of his orphanage girls had been subjected to the unwelcome attentions of the son of a local rice merchant, the litigious padre determined to file a suit against the boy for 'eve-teasing'. Mrs Singh did her utmost to persuade her husband not to take the matter to court, but he was adamant – the reputation of the orphanage was at stake. In despair Mrs Singh confessed then what she had known for some time. The young couple were in love, they had been seeing each other in secret and had exchanged letters, which, if produced in court by the boy's defence, would show that the girl was hardly an innocent victim. The padre, who had already made his intentions known to the Judge's Court, was appalled. He realized that he did not have a case. It was for him the culminating humiliation. The orphanage, his beloved 'Home', his life's work, had been reduced to little better than a brothel – and with his wife's connivance. He could not understand that she had not condoned the couple's behaviour so much as tried to protect them from his anger. He saw only that she had betrayed him.

He spent that night in his chair on the veranda refusing to come inside, or eat anything or talk to anyone. The next day he developed a chill which turned overnight into an attack of influenza. He allowed himself to be put to bed, but for days continued his fast in wilful silence; ignoring his wife's entreaties, he even rejected the medicines prescribed for him by Dr Sarbadhicari. He seemed determined not to recover, as if he wanted to punish her with the responsibility for his death.

The infection did not kill him, but it had aggravated his diabetes and left him seriously weakened. Unable now as well as unwilling to eat, he lost weight with alarming rapidity and gradually lapsed into a coma. There were moments of recruitment and lucidity when he would ask repeatedly for news from America, and Mrs Singh, in the hope of giving him cause to live, would reassure him with improvised bulletins from Dr Zingg announcing the imminent publication of his diary. But his appetite did not improve. She was forced to recognize that her husband was dying.

277   Towards the end he rallied sufficiently to receive friends

and members of his family come to take their leave of him. They were shocked by what they found: the old man who stared up at them from the pillows, grey-faced, gaunt-framed and afraid, was no longer recognizable as the robust and proud missionary they had known and loved. In a low whisper, so that they had to bend close to hear, catching the sweet scent of his diabetic's breath, he begged their forgiveness. With the exception of Daniel, whom he persistently refused to see, he begged the forgiveness of all who came, whether or not there was anything to forgive, repeating himself until his supplications took on the babbling continuance of litany.

Attributed by his family with a number of prophetic but suitably ambiguous last words, the relevance of which has since been forgotten, in his ultimate delirium the Reverend Singh is supposed to have cursed the doctor who had come to give him an injection – his deathbed fear of the needle oddly reminiscent of Kamala's – and shouted out at the last 'Asha!', the Bengali word for hope. This was interpreted by some of his friends as an expression of joy at the imminent prospect of being reunited with His Father in heaven, while others maintained that at the point of death, the padre clung with a sudden fierceness to life.

He died of heart failure at 11.50 on the morning of 27 September 1941. The next day he was buried in an outsize coffin that had to be specially made for him, alongside his father and grandfather in St John's cemetery. The Reverend Molony conducted the funeral service attended by a large mixed congregation. The mourners were not exclusively Christian and, ranging from the Rajahs of Narajole and Jhagram to a contingent of Santals, covered a wide social spectrum, for in spite of his decline in latter years, throughout the territories of his former parish and mission field he had been a well-known and popular figure. Although he died several months before his diary was finally published, the Reverend Singh had already achieved lasting fame. 'Outside the diocese,' his obituary in the *Calcutta Diocesan Record* predicted, 'his name will long be remembered because of the two Wolf Children whom he discovered and looked after for some years till they died.'[1] In all fairness, however, it mattered more to him that in taking Kamala and Amala from the jungle and trying to raise them as human beings he had, as he believed, served God and consequently science to the best of his abilities.

In Denver, the news of the Reverend Singh's death came as a sad shock; for although plans for the publication of the wolf-children diary had been temporarily held up, owing to Mrs Pfeiffer having fallen out with her nephew over the break-up of his marriage, Dr Zingg had been looking forward to sharing with the padre the pleasure of seeing their book in print. He had also hoped, when the war ended, to visit Singh in India and check all the evidence with him at first hand to remove once and for all any residual doubts about the authenticity of his story. Not that he himself needed convincing, but it would have silenced the sceptical.

In January 1942 Dr Zingg heard that his aunt, swayed by a personal visit from the august Dr Gesell, had finally been convinced of the importance of her nephew's work and relented on the subject of his marriage, agreeing once more to provide the financial backing for their project. She insisted only that the diary be published under the auspices of a university. The obvious choice was the University of Denver, though Dr Zingg made it known that he would have preferred somewhere else, for he had recently been given notice at Denver that due to a wartime fall in enrolment he was shortly to be made redundant. 'This is despite the fact that my salary here,' he wrote indignantly to Dr Gesell, 'is paid by Mrs Pfeiffer who had the good faith to give them fifty thousand dollars in six per cent preferred stock in her company.'[2] Mrs Pfeiffer, however, decided that a further donation might help save her nephew's career and duly sent Denver a cheque for 1500 dollars to subsidize Harpers' publication. The future of the diary, if not the professorship of Dr Zingg, was now at long last assured.

There were, no doubt, other reasons why Zingg lost his place at Denver. His amiable eccentricity had never endeared him to the authorities, and despite their avowed sympathy, his marital problems had become an embarrassment to the university – a suicide attempt by his German-born wife causing consternation on the campus; but more significantly, Zingg's work on the wolf children was regarded by many as too controversial and by some even as a subversive influence. By August 1942 he was looking for another job, but personal worries were soon forgotten in his excitement over the publication of the Diary. If there was a sense of anticlimax in the culmination of four years' work, he preferred to dwell on the triumph of their perseverance. In a letter to Dr Gesell he thanked him for his long-standing and decisively influential support, which he believed had 'swung the trick' with his aunt as well as at Harpers. 'In closing,' he wrote, 'it occurs to me that getting this problem of wolf children into scientific status has been almost as hard as Mrs Singh's devoted efforts to get the wolf children to human status in the first place.'[3] If neither operation had been a complete success, it was not a point to dwell upon. Dr Zingg ended his letter on a more reassuring note: 'And so, as Tiny Tim observed, "God bless us one and all", and what a pity that Reverend Singh did not live to see this day.'[4]

In reply Dr Gesell capped this last sentiment with a warm 'amen', yet his letter betrayed a certain coolnesss at Zingg's enthusiasm and gratitude over his own involvement in the wolf-children affair. 'I wonder whether you could not conveniently send me a carbon of those portions of the M S. which definitely refer to my connection and participation,'[5] he wrote with studied ease. It was the beginning of a tactical withdrawal.

When it finally appeared in print *Wolf-Children and Feral Man* did not make the impact with which its authors had hoped to stun the world. While the popular press had largely expended its curiosity in the subject on Dr Gesell's book, academic reviewers remained on the whole unconvinced by Zingg's argument and Singh's 'proof' that children had been reared by wolves. Some notices, particularly by anthropologists, were harshly critical. Of these the best tempered and yet the most successful in its demolition of the Zingg–Singh book came from the physical anthropologist, Ashley Montague, who, allowing that the padre's account of Kamala and Amala despite certain difficulties had the ring of authenticity, could not accept the story as true because it relied on the unsupported testimony of one man. 'Now, however much,' he pleaded,

and however sympathetically we might be inclined to put our trust in Mr Singh's word, no scientist can accept as true any statement ... until it has been independently confirmed by others. Such confirmation is altogether wanting in the present case, and, that being so, with all the good will in the world, and in spite of all the forewords and prefaces in the world by learned professors, bishops and magistrates, we cannot accept the story of discovery of the wolf children and their presumed rearing by wolves as true ... Even if the statement were fully corroborated that the children were found together with the wolves in their den, that in itself, would not constitute evidence that they were brought there by wolves, nor that they had been suckled and reared by them.[6]

His argument was uncompromising and rigorously scientific and in that same spirit he took Dr Zingg to task for lack of impartiality in his examination of the evidence, though he sympathized with him in his enthusiasm for a subject with which unfortunately he had allowed himself to get carried away.

A year before, shortly after Dr Gesell's article on the wolf children appeared in *Harpers Magazine*, Professor

Montague had written privately to Gesell that he personally found his article 'entirely credible', and even now after a critical reading of the diary he declared himself emotionally in favour of Kamala and Amala's story, though as a scientist he felt bound to reject it. His attitude was significant because so many others, illustrious scientists among them, had failed to recognize the necessity of making that distinction between what they wanted to believe and what might have been revealed by a dispassionate assessment of the available evidence. It was a question of recognizing, too, the essential power of the story and the archetypal appeal of the myth which lay behind it. Dr Gesell had long understood that the issues of the wolf-children story went deep, but he was still more concerned with explaining unfathomed resistance to the feral idea than precipitate acceptance. More than any other he had been subjected to the reactions of those anti-Darwinians, whose beliefs in human 'instincts' and inflexible inherited tendencies, as well as an exclusively human 'soul', seemed threatened by the very notion of a wolf child. In his review of the Zingg-Singh book Gesell wrote: 'Profound prejudices are stirred if not awakened. We shun instinctively too close identification with *lupus* or even *canis familiaris*. Nevertheless, in these days of inhuman warfare, we may have reason to temper with a trace of humility, our sense of superiority over the wolf species.'[7] But he was on the defensive now, having been made painfully aware that he had gone too far the other way and that as a scientist his position was untenable. Without altogether renouncing the wolf children, he began backsliding.

After the war, with Dr Zingg still engaged in a rearguard action against critics of the diary, Gesell would announce that he no longer wanted his name mixed up in it. Zingg wrote to him, scarcely hiding his disappointment: 'It has been stated that you have also stopped defending the basic claims made in the book with regard to the children being reared in the wolf den.'[8] But Gesell reassured his colleague that this was not the case. With others he could be rather less specific, claiming that although he had helped to ensure publication of the diary, he had never regarded himself as its sponsor, nor accepted it uncritically in all its detail, but that he believed it to be 'a body of valid material which deals with a remarkable case of isolation which needs constructive interpretation, such as I have attempted in my small book'.[9] In the meantime he was somewhat glad of a slackening of interest in the whole sorry business; the rearing of children by wolves having neither been proved nor disproved, it soon fizzled out into inconclusive controversy.

Unable to find another academic post, for reasons of the war as much as any other, Robert Zingg, armed with a character reference from Dr Gesell, took a temporary job with a government agency in the north and then returned to Denver in January 1943 to be an instructor in photography at Lowry Field Air Corps Technical School. Subsequently his former colleagues were not altogether surprised and perhaps a little relieved to hear nothing more of him. Over the four years they had worked together on the wolf-children project, Dr Zingg had been a voluminous and regular correspondent, but absences and silences were becoming commonplace during the war and now that little remained to be said on the subject that had once brought them together, there was no real reason for keeping in touch.

However, in the late summer of 1944 Dr Gesell and Professor Ruggles Gates each received a letter from Robert Zingg, written on American Red Cross paper and postmarked – of all places – India. It began, with his usual disregard for the English language: 'Life is full coincidents; but my work with the wolf children study much more so.'[10]

The letter went on to explain that having joined the Red Cross for overseas service in April that year, after spending only two weeks in Washington, he had been sent to join the American troops in Assam, which by another coincidence, he pointed out, was Bishop Pakenham-Walsh's old diocese. After a pleasant voyage out by troop-ship they had landed somewhere on the west coast of India and travelled across the country by train to Calcutta. During the ten days he was stationed there getting acclimatized and waiting for transport to Assam, Zingg decided to visit Mrs Singh in Midnapore. He sent a telegram to the orphanage informing her of his arrival, not knowing whether she was still living there, or even still alive.

When I heard that she was there for sure, I left Calcutta on the Madras Mail on which I travelled for only sixty miles, getting off at the first stop outside Calcutta. Here I was lucky enough to catch a branch train on which I travelled for fifteen miles to get off at the (to us) historic place of Midnapore. I took a picture of the characteristic RR platform station sign, this one bearing the name MIDNAPUR. I wasn't too sure that this was Midnapore as I hadn't been in India for a week. But it turned out to be.

I got a babu at the station to direct the horse-drawn vehicle I had hired to the orphanage. But in typical Indian fashion it took me somewhere else. The horses were about as big as jackrabbits and I pitied them as they pulled me through the mud of Midnapore at the beginning of the monsoon rains. I was also burned up as the time was passing, the sun was going down and I wanted to take pictures before it got too dark.

The vehicle wandered round through the scattered Indian villages of Midnapore, and finally ended up a few blocks where I had started from, the historic Midnapore Orphanage. The compound is walled and this grown with bamboo and trees. The gate in slight disrepair bears a sign Midnapur Orphanage, Reverend J. A. L. Singh, Deceased.

At last I had arrived. I got out and an English-speaking young man of the orphanage, came running out and took my canteen, rations and GI knapsack. I followed him in and at the door met the dear fine Indian woman who brought up the wolf children with such intelligence and patience, Mrs Singh. We shook hands cordially, with a deep feeling of emotion on both parts I am sure. She invited me into the habitable part of the large building much of which was unroofed by a hurricane . . . [the cyclone of 1942, which had devasted a large part of rural Bengal and was particularly severe in the south of the Midnapore district, contributing to the cause of a terrible famine the following year.] As I went in my eye was struck by the scene of Reverend Singh's reclining chair in a place where he used to sit, reclining even during his last illness. This reclining chair, kept fresh and with its coverings frequently laundered was roped off so no uninitiated person would sit in it. It was covered with fresh flowers, and has been since his death, an offering of his grateful widow and the orphans, several of whom are still living there.

Reverend Singh's study, his pictures, his writing papers etc. are all there. It is a room reserved to his memory, and used by the group only for the family altar, where prayers are made in Episcopalian fashion.

Mrs Singh and the children, most of whom are now well grown, and one of whom is married and has a child, live in other parts of the large house . . . They get along with the salary of an educated daughter, who is a medical employee in Calcutta, the royalties of the wolf-children book, their garden etc. They used to have cows and sell milk but have none now . . .

I had brought along K rations, which they warmed for me after they had prepared my bath. That night they brought an Indian bed into the room of Reverend Singh and strung up my GI mosquito net. I slept beautifully in that place and room . . . almost in the presence of our colleague, the Reverend Singh, in his study, surrounded by his things and in front of his flower-bedecked chair which has not been moved since his death.

In the morning I ate a Breakfast K ration with tea prepared for me by them. Mrs Singh is not well and is suffering from elephantiasis in one leg which handicaps her walking, yet she was everywhere in a slow and quiet way. She is a dear, sweet person. She speaks English very well: but most of the talking was done by Reverend Singh's ancient elder sister, a retired school teacher. She is a bit on the shrewd side, and not altogether truthful. Thank heaven for my own conscience that

Mrs Singh ... was the opposite. She could not have been otherwise after all the letters we have exchanged.[11]

They talked mostly about money, the royalty cheques from America that never arrived, the Church's shameful failure to pay Mrs Singh a widow's pension and the orphanage debt which still stood at 1000 rupees and which they despaired of ever paying off. Dr Zingg gave them some money he had brought with him and promised to do what he could to help them on his return to Calcutta. If he was a little taken aback by their avidity, he had not been in India long enough to understand that laundered clothes, genteel ways and gracious hospitality could conceal starvation more effectively than the *bustees* of Howrah. After breakfast he took photographs of the orphanage and its inhabitants and examined various places frequented by the wolf children, photographing from the same angles the settings of Reverend Singh's famous pictures.

Politely ignoring her sister-in-law's attempts to dominate the conversation, he plied Mrs Singh with questions about Kamala and Amala, welcoming her offer to look out the negatives of the original photographs as well as some of the clothes and toys used by the elder girl, but there was little enough time before his train back to Calcutta and the search for memorabilia had to be postponed until a later visit. On his way to the station, accompanied by the entire Singh household, Dr Zingg made a special pilgrimage to St John's cemetery.

In the churchyard, I stood beside the Reverend Singh's grave and took photographs. It is as yet unmarked. Then I had them show me the grave of Kamala, the elder wolf child. Before I leave India, if I live (which I have every hope of doing) I am going to have these graves marked with suitable markers, that future visitors to Midnapore may find the graves of Reverend Singh (and in the not too distant future, alas, that of Mrs Singh) as well as that of Kamala. Even now Mrs Singh has forgotten just where Amala was buried.

You can imagine I was deeply moved to stand in these spots and to photograph them.

From the church they took me to the train which started there at Midnapore and thus left on time. It was quite an entourage that took me to the station. Already it was so warm that I put on the fan in the First Class waiting room and sat under it until the train came. I was travelling first class on reverse lease-lend, theoretically on a Red Cross publicity trip. The little branch train started and I waved goodbye to Mrs Singh and the children; we passed the Maharajah's palace and a big U.S. Air Corps flying field and I was soon transferring to the main line . . . I was back in Calcutta by noon, only twenty-four hours for the entire trip. And wasn't that an extraordinary way to spend a day for me?[19]

It is uncertain whether Dr Zingg ever got the chance to return to Midnapore after joining his unit in Assam. He was, however, as good as his word about helping Mrs Singh. During the few days that he remained in Calcutta he visited Bishop's House to plead her case with the Metropolitan. Bishop Westcott was away at the time – his residence had been turned into a club for British servicemen – but his chaplain promised that Mrs Singh's pension claim would be looked into, though evidently Dr Zingg's interference was not altogether welcome. Subsequent investigation revealed little more than the unhappy plight of the Midnapore Church, which as the Reverend Singh predicted, had fallen on increasingly difficult times since the withdrawal of European officials from the district and the democratic handing over of St John's to the care of the parish. After the padre's death his job had been taken on by Lionel Hewitt, the Anglo-Indian missionary, once so keen to evangelize the heathen, but who had long since lost his missionary zeal. As vicar he had fared no better than his predecessor at the hands of the troublesome Midnapore Church Committee. Accused of everything from pasturing his cows in the cemetery to stealing the communion wine, he had allowed himself to be drawn into the petty squabbles and intrigues of parish politics, with the result that his standing and authority as a priest were gradually undermined. A frail and neurotic man, he had been reduced to a state of chronic hysteria, which the inquiry into Mrs Singh's pension did nothing to alleviate.

Hewitt claimed that he was so fiercely resented by Mrs Singh and her husband's sister, that they refused even to come to Church on Sundays, but instead would gather with the orphans in the cemetery and deliberately disrupt his services by singing hymns over the Reverend Singh's grave. Miss Singh, particularly antagonistic towards Hewitt, accused him of keeping Mrs Singh's pension for himself; in his turn Hewitt called her a liar and denied that a pension had ever been allocated. The Bishop intervened with the suggestion that Mrs Singh should sell 'The Home' and go to live with her son Daniel in Kharagpur. This she stubbornly refused to do. The situation appeared to be deadlocked until at length it was decided that, since no one could force her to move, Mrs Singh would have to stay on in Midnapore. But whether she ever received a pension Dr Zingg was unable to discover. A sad and arbitrary outcome of the whole affair was that the orphanage was at last declared officially closed, an event which Zingg reported back to Dr Gesell at Yale with solemn regret.

Although he failed to produce results for Mrs Singh over her pension, Dr Zingg succeeded at least in clearing up the problem of her royalty cheques, even if these turned out to be fewer and smaller than they had both hoped. He did his best to help in other ways: sending her food parcels from Assam (for he knew now the real cause of her ill-health), his own ration of orange juice each month, and at Christmas presents for the children; he even tried to find a job with the Red Cross for one of her orphans. At the same time he began to raise money to put up gravestones for Kamala and the Reverend Singh – a project Dr Gesell proved more than willing to contribute towards, though he vetoed the rather curious suggestion that his own name   288 along with Zingg's should appear on the markers. Zingg had also had the idea that the markers should be of the same type and no less imposing than those erected in memory of the assassinated British magistrates, Peddie, Burge and Douglas, 'the Midnapore Martyrs', with whom he knew the padre, though perhaps not Kamala, to have been in close sympathy. But it was not an easy operation to organize by letter from Assam and eventually he decided to abandon it until after the war.

He had difficulty, too, in carrying out his private research programme. Not only were his movements severely restricted, but inquiries were hampered by Indian resistance, particularly among the educated and political classes, to the very idea of wolf children, which many resented as a reflection on the backwardness of their country. Dr Zingg tried to reassure them that even America had its feral problem, and was delighted to quote the recent case of a dog-girl found living in the middle of New York City; but somehow he was unable to convince them. After an unsuccessful attempt at tracing Rose and Richards, he paid a visit to the offices of the *Statesman* in Calcutta, in the hope of finding out the name of the reporter who had given the alternative version of the rescue story, but again with little success. He managed only to track down a Canadian journalist who had worked for the paper at the time of the discovery and who offered a bland endorsement of his own views. 'Reverend Singh's word may be accepted without hesitation. What I knew of his reputation when I was out in Calcutta precludes any possibility of doubt where his testimony is concerned.'[13] It was encouraging, but it hardly constituted evidence. With any luck, Zingg believed, there would be time at the end of the war for a more thorough investigation.

In April 1945, however, Mrs Singh received a letter from Dr Zingg, postmarked Bombay, informing her that he had fallen ill and was being shipped back to the U.S. forthwith. Whether or not this was the real reason for his leaving

Assam so suddenly – a story persists that his sudden departure had more to do with a potential diplomatic incident involving the wife of a British admiral – Dr Zingg came home without having been able to take full advantage of the coincidence which had brought him to India. Had he been allowed to stay out longer, his researches would doubtless have led him into the jungles of Mayurbhanj, where he felt certain he would have found the necessary evidence to confound Kamala and Amala's critics and salvage his own academic career. But it was not to be.

He returned in America to a succession of jobs that had little to do with either wolf children or anthropology. After working for some time in the education department of the *Encyclopedia Britannica*, he indulged a lifelong love of trains by becoming a railway conductor with the Pullman Company. A romantic at heart, he was to end his days more prosaically selling canned meat in El Paso. However, Dr Zingg never quite lost his fascination for his old subject and continued to keep in touch with Mrs Singh, if only out of charity, as long as she remained alive. In answer to her increasingly pathetic begging-letters, which always contained a hopeful reference to her husband and Kamala's gravestones, he sent her what money he could, until in December 1950 he heard from the Reverend Hewitt that she had died the previous October of starvation. India, by then, had been independent for more than two years and Mrs Singh, never much interested in politics, was said to have been glad only that her husband had not lived to see the day. She was buried beside the Reverend Singh in St John's cemetery; where to this day, their graves, and those of Kamala and Amala, remain unmarked.

Epilogue

Like any journey into the unknown, my quest for the wolf children was undertaken in a spirit of anxious determination. Misgivings about the wisdom of chasing what might turn out to be unknowable chimera across two very substantial continents were firmly suppressed in favour of the brighter prospect of arriving at my destination. I travelled with a compulsively simple and definite purpose: to find out whether the Reverend Singh's diary account of discovering Kamala and Amala living with wolves in the jungle was true.

Although I understood well enough that if the capture of the two girls from the white ant mound could be verified by independent witnesses whose statements corroborated Singh's, this in itself would not constitute scientific proof that they had been suckled or reared by wolves, I felt that it would go a long way towards convincing me that this is what actually happened. Equally if I could show that Singh's story was untrue, that Kamala and Amala were not in fact wolf children, although this would not prove that a wolf had *never* suckled or reared a human child, I would regard it as highly probable that animal nurses belonged to the realms of myth and folklore. The child psychologist, Bruno Bettelheim, who has argued persuasively against the existence of wolf children, suggests that the strength and persistence of the feral myth depends on an archetypal longing to revive the lost connection with our animal ancestors, or if one prefers, with the rest of creation, reflecting a widespread desire 'to believe in a benign nature that in some fashion looks after all of its children'.

But his main concern is with the use of this particular myth to cover the behaviour of children, who would otherwise have to be recognized as feeble-minded or autistic. Unafraid to declare his interest in forcing the world to face up to the problem of infantile autism, Dr Bettelheim rejects the feral idea as an adult invention to explain why such children exist. His belief that Kamala and Amala were autistic is based on similarities he observed in the behaviour of American autistic children in his care and the Reverend Singh's descriptions of the wolf children. The diagnosis, based on available evidence, supposes that the Reverend Singh invented whatever connection the children may have had with wolves and consequently disregards his wolf-flavoured specifications. It would not be impertinent to suggest that Dr Bettelheim might otherwise have been at a loss to explain away their more distinctly feral symptoms.

Beyond the inherent interest and appeal of the motif, the raising of a human child by a wolf is not in itself of much scientific significance, but the observable behaviour and personality of a child captured from wolves undoubtedly is, and under ideal conditions would no doubt reveal much about the formation and development of personality, the origins of language, the interrelation of culture and biology and a host of other imponderables. Even under less than ideal conditions, it seems, untrained, incomplete and unauthenticated observation of feral children can also provide insight into these problems, especially for those more pliable branches of science that support and are indeed dependent on the theory that man is the product of society, formed by the conditioning of his surroundings and his circumstances; though, as Dr Gesell and others have demonstrated, the wolf children could also be used to good effect in support of the opposing point of view. From the start of my investigations I had neither particular interest nor qualification to join in the nurture-nature debate; nor have I felt tempted or better able to do so at any time since; but in concentrating my efforts on more immediate, less tendentious areas of research, by attempting simply to establish the authenticity of Singh's story and place it within its correct historical context, I have been nonetheless committed to the truth.

The character and motivation of the Reverend Singh are of central interest and importance in any attempt at appraising the phenomenon of the wolf children. Clearly if Singh lied about the capture of the children from wolves, it must affect the validity of his account of their lives at the orphanage, which would not only remove the basis for a scientific assessment of Kamala and Amala's behaviour and personality in terms of environmental and other influences, but change radically my own lay account of their story. Elsewhere I gave my reasons for telling this story in narrative form rather than presenting it as a report of a long and complex investigation. I felt that the obligation to list and evaluate each piece of evidence before the reader's eyes would make dull and laborious reading, which could hardly be justified by the conclusions that might be drawn from it. As a result I have omitted so far to give my reasons for accepting the Reverend Singh's story more or less as fact. A brief summary of the last stages of my researches in India would seem now to be appropriate.

Before leaving England I discovered two pieces of evidence which changed the direction of my research and inclined me to believe that the Singh diary was at least partly a work of the imagination. In the London archives of the Church Missionary Society I came across that brief mention of the wolf children in the *Calcutta Diocesan Record*, where Singh, in a report to his mission superiors, had stated that the two girls had been captured from wolves in the jungle by villagers and subsequently handed over to him. In other words he had not rescued them himself or seen them cohabiting with wolves as stated in the diary. In due course I found a second and longer account in an open letter from Father Brown of the Oxford Mission, published in July 1922, on the children's page of the Mission magazine, which again attributed the rescue to the villagers. As his former tutor, Father Brown, it seems, had received the information directly from Singh himself. Somewhat reluctantly then I had to come to terms with the idea that Singh was a liar. His motive seemed clear enough and understandable: he wanted to make his story more dramatic and present himself in a starring role; but it meant that the diary was now of little value, for if Singh had invented the rescue story, why not the rest of his account? In India I hoped to find more evidence to expose the truth. Although I had not altogether dismissed the possibility that the children had indeed been rescued by the villagers from wolves, or renounced my intention of following up that side of things, my chief interest now lay in the Reverend Singh's story, in discovering how he had 'created' the wolf children – their existence at the orphanage had never been in doubt – and succeeded almost in getting away with the world's best feral hoax.

I arrived in Calcutta at the end of February 1975 to find myself in unexpectedly familiar surroundings, the city in its crumbling magnificence being a sort of tropical parody of London. I set up base there in a boarding house on Russell Street that had changed little since the days of the Raj. After making contact with the university, where I was given every help by the department of anthropology, I discovered that the wolf children of Midnapore had been investigated as recently as 1952 by the American sociologist, William Ogburn, and a well-known Indian anthropologist, Nirmal K. Bose. Both men had since died, but not before producing a paper on the subject for a scientific journal. After reading their sixty-page report, *On the trail of the wolf children*, I felt singularly disheartened. Although the article provided some useful information, a list of names and a few promising leads, the verdict on the wolf children reached by Ogburn and Bose was both inconclusive and at the same time weighted heavily against the Reverend Singh. The investigators appeared to have covered the ground thoroughly and more or less exactly as I was proposing to do nearly twenty-five years later.

They had concentrated on trying to find: (a) Godamuri, the village in the jungle near where Singh claimed to have recovered the children (b) witnesses to the capture of the children from the wolves and (c) witnesses in Midnapore and elsewhere, who saw the children at the orphanage after their capture and could say something about their behaviour. Rather depressingly, Obgurn and Bose had completely failed to locate the village or any witness to the rescue of the children from wolves. They had come up with some wild and conflicting stories and tracked down a number of people who claimed to have seen the wolf children at the orphanage, but among these – apart from the close members of Reverend Singh's family, whose testimony was assumed to be biased and therefore inadmissible – not one had actually observed Kamala and Amala go on all fours, eat raw meat, howl or behave in any of the wolf-like ways described in the diary. In conclusion the investigators could do no more than confirm that the two girls had indeed lived for a time at the orphanage and that they had been unusual children in that they spoke very little and did not like to mix with other children. As regards the wolf-children story, they could not disprove it, but suggested that Singh had probably exploited a popular myth to make money for his orphanage.

If I had known about Ogburn and Bose at an earlier stage in my investigation, no doubt I would have abandoned the project before coming to India, but somehow, fortuitously perhaps, I had managed to overlook the reference. Now I had no alternative but to carry on the search for the wolf children where they had left off. Although a quarter of a century had elapsed since Ogburn and Bose were in the field, I felt that I had certain advantages over them: specifically, in having access to the Zingg collection of correspondence in America and generally, in my unspecialized, non-scientific approach to research, which allowed me to consider the motivation of the Reverend Singh and the background to the story as important factors in any attempt at establishing what happened. Singh's character was by now beginning to intrigue me and the accumulated evidence (after numberless days under slow wheeling fans in the dusty Calcutta libraries) still suggested to me that despite all the contradictions and exaggerations there remained a substratum of truth to the wolf-children story. Circumstances were, nonetheless, ridiculously unfavourable and I remember thinking as much as I sat marooned on a rickshaw in the middle of Midnapore, newly arrived, stupid with sunstroke and dysentery, assaulted by the stench of open drains, incense and buffalo dung, by the din of scooter horns and processional drums, by flies, beggars and a mad-looking dog, trying to explain to an astonished crowd with three words of Bengali that I had come from England to find out about the Reverend Singh and two wolf girls, who once lived in this delightful town.

I persuaded myself that things could only get better. With the enthusiastic help of Mr Haripada Mondhal, the Headmaster of the Collegiate School, who acted as my instructor, interpreter and a poetic guide through the confusions of Midnapore's bazaars, quoting Dryden, Shelley and Longfellow at every opportunity, I set about tracking down anyone who had known Reverend Singh or seen the wolf children at the orphanage during the 1920s. In all we interviewed more than forty elderly people from every sort of background of whom just under two-thirds claimed to have seen the wolf children. Because of a recognized tendency among Indians to confuse assumptions with evidence, to tell you what they imagine you want to hear rather than what they know, we were scrupulously careful in vetting witnesses, in cross-questioning them and   296 in checking their statements by every possible means, but to my initial surprise they all confirmed with allowable variations that Kamala and Amala *had* behaved in the wolf-like ways described by Singh in his diary and some were able to provide additional information besides. Not one witness, even those who had shown some disapproval or hostility towards Singh, would agree that the wolf children might have been fakes or, as far as they were able to tell, mental defectives.

During the course of these inquiries I found very little trace of Ogburn and Bose's earlier investigation. Nobody much seemed to remember them in Midnapore and the few who had been interviewed by them were now telling a different story. Other anomalies increased my suspicions and on returning to Calcutta I determined to find out more about the circumstances of their research programme through the University. Dr Jyotimoya Sarma, a lady sociologist, who had previously studied under Professor Ogburn in Chicago, told me that he had come to India in 1951 to work on an important project, but because of his interest in the wolf children since the publication of Zingg's book, had asked her if she would help him to look into the story. She had agreed, only to discover that he was unable to give the matter as much time as he had hoped. Professor Ogburn was by then an old man and found the strain of journeying to Midnapore in the hot weather, running around and conducting interviews in difficult conditions too much for him. He was disappointed not to be able to clear up the mystery right away. 'He wanted so much to believe in these wolf children,' Dr Sarma recalled, 'he was really a statistician and the slightest discrepancy in evidence sent him into the deepest gloom. When he could not find positive truth in the story, he was very got down.' In Calcutta, Ogburn found it very difficult to get the scientific community to take the wolf children seriously, but just before returning to America he successfully persuaded Nirmal K. Bose to take over his research. 'Professor Bose at that time was very well known in India and worshipped by many as a former close associate of Gandhi and a freedom fighter against the British. He was not particularly interested in the wolf children, but he knew Midnapore district well and, because he was such a big name, liked to put his stamp on everything – without always doing much himself.'[1] Dr Sarma doubted that Bose had carried out a thorough investigation of the case and suggested that after Ogburn left the work was mostly done by students and later written up by the authors. I could not help making the observation that Professor Bose's former political association also might have affected his attitude towards Singh.

Although I was assured that it had existed, I never found Singh's original diary of the wolf children. One of his daughters, Preeti Lota, who was still living in Ranchi, showed me a portion of manuscript – the rest had been devoured by white ants – which contained a good deal of information not included in the published version. Besides this she let me see letters and photographs, some of considerable interest, and along with her sister-in-law, Daniel's wife, who lives in Kharagpur, provided most of the detailed information on Singh's life. But the essential part of my research was yet to come.

With maps, provisions, mosquito nets, interpreters, police escort and a jeep – the latter kindly provided by the Government of Bengal – I set off into the jungle areas to look for the lost village of Godamuri. I had in my pocket a letter from Reverend Singh to Bishop Pakenham-Walsh (part of the Zingg collection discovered in the attic of the Gesell Institute in New Haven), which gave directions, including a rough sketch-map, on how to get there. These were too vague to be of much use and after several days of discouraging search, during which we encountered no one who had even heard of such a thing as wolf children – 298 though wolves, I had taken care to find out, had once been quite common in the area – a piece of luck finally came our way. We were spending the night at the police station in Nayagaram, discussing whether or not to abandon the search, when a message came through that a friend of the interpreter's from the last village we visited had some important information for us. He was already on his way, bicycling through the jungle – his village was twenty-six miles away – and would be with us by morning. That night I hardly slept in anticipation, not least because a snake had been discovered wrapped round the handlebars of a bicycle on the police station veranda a few feet from where I lay. The messenger arrived in the early hours, but his news, once the excitement over his dramatic night ride had died down, was a little disappointing. A village elder, who had been frightened to come forward at the time of our visit because of the police escort, remembered hearing the story of the wolf children when he was a young man but could not remember where it had happened. He had never heard of Godamuri and could only suggest the names of a number of villages further south into Orissa, where they might know more. There was not much to go on, but it was our only lead.

Acting on the old man's advice and with the trail getting warmer as we moved on from village to village, we eventually succeeded in finding Godamuri, which had changed its name – as Indian villages sometimes do – to Ghorabandha. Unfortunately, there was no one in the village old enough to remember the incident of the wolf children. However, the inhabitants confirmed that Chunarem, who first told Singh about the 'ghosts' in the forest, had indeed lived there, but died 'mad' a few years back. From Ghorabandha we then drove south-east for six or seven miles (in accordance with Singh's sketch map) to the Santal village of Denganalia, where the older people well remembered how the wolf children were captured in the forest near by a long time ago. One old man, Lasa Marandi, had actually taken part in the hunt as a boy of sixteen and testified that the Reverend Singh, whom he was able to describe quite clearly, along with two Europeans (possibly Rose and Richards) and Dibakar Bhanj Deo had been present on the *machan* at the time of the rescue.

After we had drunk to the success of our mission in Santal rice beer and decked the jeep out with scarlet palas blossoms, we drove on in triumph to Amarda Road bungalow, where the interpreter, the driver and I spent the night. Later we discovered, as we sat on the veranda in long planters' chairs, looking out over the silver waters of the tank to the thin green line of jungle beyond, waiting for the *chowkidar* to bring us morning tea, that it was here, to this same bungalow, that the Reverend Singh had brought the wolf children on the day of their capture, 17 October 1920.

I was never able to resolve satisfactorily the discrepancy between the statements of the Santals in the jungle, who claimed that Singh was present at the capture of the wolf children, and some of his own and other statements which averred that he was not. In this book I have attempted to show what the Reverend Singh's motives might have been for lying about the rescue story. That he did not want his mission superiors to know about his part in the rescue because it portrayed him in the role of the hunter, was suggested to me by a number of people who knew him well. Others said that he gave out several different and deliberately misleading statements to those who went to the orphanage to see Kamala, mostly out of irritation at being bothered by so many visitors and their endless questions. Undoubtedly, he was an irascible, arrogant and complicated man and his motives are not altogether clear, probably because they were mixed. There may even have been a simple explanation for his behaviour, which has not yet come to light and perhaps never will. But the fact remains that an article in the Midnapore local paper, a   300 mission report written by Singh himself, a letter from Father Brown and the story in the *Statesman* all indicate that he did not take part in the rescue as he later claimed in his diary. On the other hand, I have no reason to disbelieve Lasa Marandi and the Santals of Denganalia, the *chowkidar* at Amarda Road bungalow, the son of Dibakar Bhanj Deo, Jageswar Khatua (the son of Bhagobhat), Mr Umakanta Pattanaik and others who said that he did. The Santals in that area are known even today for their truthfulness; they appeared uninterested in the information they passed on; there was no question of their having read about the wolf children; and the story was far from being a widespread folk tale in the jungle areas we visited. Most significantly the villages named or indicated by Singh as the places where these events had taken place, not only existed, but were confirmed as such, somewhat reluctantly, by their inhabitants.

The choice finally lay not so much in accepting one set of proofs and rejecting the other, or in evaluating the comparative worth of written and oral evidence, but in weighing the Reverend Singh's capacity for self-deception, measuring his need to feel important against what I believe to be his fundamental integrity. He was a man wholly if unhappily loyal to his Church and to the Britannic ideal, both of which let him down. Like so many educated Indians of his time he had identified too closely with a culture not his own, and with the rebirth of Indian nationalism, betrayed by the Church and the Raj, which were busily discarding past shibboleths in order to survive, he found himself trapped and isolated. There is a parallel with the more extreme fate of the wolf children, isolated through being forced to obey an alien set of cultural imperatives and then being squeezed back into a mould, the shape of which had been erased from their memory. Both were victims of circumstance, but if the choice in this matter lay also between myth, which is the wishful thinking that remodels the universe to our dominant desire, and reality, which returns it to the bleak tragedy of existence, I am inclined to believe, and have written this book in the belief, that the Reverend Singh's diary account of what happened in the forest is true, though perhaps not the whole truth.

Glossary

ahimsa	non-violence
Anglo-Indian	originally the British in India; post-1900, specifically those of mixed blood (Eurasian)
ashram	monastery or religious centre
babu	native clerk who writes English (also derogatory)
banyan	Indian fig-tree (*Ficus bengalensis*, L.)
bhut	ghost
bonga	spirit (Santal)
bustee	native quarter, slum-dwelling
chagal	water-bucket
chatiar	initiation ceremony (Santal)
chowkidar	caretaker, watchman
dacoit	robber, bandit
dak-bungalow	government staging house
dewan	steward
dhoti	loose loincloth worn by caste Hindus
district	one of 250 units of administration in British India
D.M.	District Magistrate, executive head of district, also known as Collector or District Officer
durbar	court, levee
gamchas	tribal loincloth
gariwallah	drayman, cart-driver
gelap	wrapper, cloth
ghats	river embankment
giragath	knotted string used by Santals for passing information from village to village
godown	store-room, warehouse
I.C.S.	Indian Civil Service
jheel	pond, mere (remnant inundation)
khadi	homespun cloth
kharom	wooden slippers

khas	long grass
kudi	primitive spade
kutcha	crude, rough, raw
lantana	dense tropical shrub (*Lantana Indica* Roxb.)
machan	shooting platform
maidan	common, public land
mali	gardener
mantra	prayer, incantation
moffussil	the countryside, rural part of district
mondhal	headman (Santal)
murrum	laterite, red residual soil in humid tropical regions
nagra	type of drum (Santal)
naeke	priest (Santal)
nullah	watercourse
paddy	rice, rice field
paise	small coin
pipal	poplar-leaved fig-tree (*Ficus religiosa*, L.)
pukka	proper, substantial
puja	Hindu prayer or act of worship
punkah	fan suspended from ceiling
Raj	(kingdom), British Rule in India from 1858–1947
rasgulla	sweet, milk-based confection
rupee	standard Indian coinage, worth roughly 1s 6d.
sahib	'Lord', term of address for all Europeans in India; also attached to office (i.e. padre-sahib, or Colonel-sahib)
sais	groom
sakwa	hunting horn (Santal)
sardar	landowner
satyagraha	Civil Disobedience
shikar	sport (shooting, hunting)
sola topi	pith helmet
Swaraj	Home Rule
tank	reservoir, artificial pond or lake
tom-tom	dog-cart
zamindar	landowner

Select Bibliography

Historical India

Allen, C.   *Plain Tales from the Raj*, London, 1975

Bose, N. K.   *My Days with Gandhi*, Calcutta, 1953

Bose, N. S.   *The Indian Awakening and Bengal*, Calcutta, 1960

Bose, S. C.   *The Indian Struggle 1920–34*, London, 1935

Brown, H.   *The Sahibs*, London, 1948

Buckland, C. T.   *Sketches of Social Life in India*, London, 1884

Carthill, A.   *Madampur*, Edinburgh, 1931

Chaudhuri, Nirad C.   *The Continent of Circe*, London, 1965

Das, N. N.   *History of Midnapore*, vols 1–3, Midnapore, 1956

Das, N. N.   *Midnapore 1905–19*, Midnapore, 1956

Dunbar, Sir G.   *A History of India*, vol. 2, London, 1943

Gandhi, M. K.   *My Experiments with Truth*, London, 1949

Gordon, L. A.   *Bengal: The Nationalist Movement 1876–1940*, New York, 1974

Griffiths, Sir P.   *Modern India*, London, 1957

Horniman, B. G.   *Amritsar and Our Duty to India*, London, 1920

Keay, J.   *Into India*, London, 1973

Kipling, R.   *Many Inventions*, London, 1925

Koestler, A.   'Mahatma Gandhi – Yogi and Commissar', *Sunday Times*, 5 October 1969

Macleod, R. D.	*Impressions of an Indian Civil Servant*, London, 1938
Moorhouse, G.	*Calcutta*, London, 1971
Moraes, F.	*Witness to an Era*, London, 1973
Naipaul, V. S.	*Area of Darkness*, London, 1964
O'Malley, L. S. S.	*Bengal, Bihar and Orissa, Sikkim*, Cambridge, 1917
O'Malley, L. S. S.	*Midnapore (Bengal District Gazeteers)*, Calcutta, 1911
Reid, Sir R. N.	*Years of Change in Bengal and Assam*, London, 1966
Webster, J. C. B.	*History and Contemporary India*, London, 1971
Winslow, J. C. and Elwin, V.	*The Dawn of Indian Freedom*, London, 1932
Woodruff, P.	*The Founders*, London, 1952
Woodruff, P.	*The Guardians*, London, 1954

Tribal India

Archer, W. G.	*The Hill of Flutes*, London, 1974
Archer, W. G.	'The Illegitimate Child in Santal Society', *Man in India*, September 1944
Bhowmick, P. K.	*The Lodhas of West Bengal*, Calcutta, 1963
Bodding, P. O.	*Santal Folktales*, Oslo, 1925–9
Bompas, C. H.	*Folktales of Bengal, Journal of the Asiatic Society of Bengal*, Vol. 25
Bompas, C. H.	*Folklore of the Santal Parganas*, London, 1909
Campbell, A.	*Santal Folk Tales*, London, 1892
Das, A. K.	'The Koras and some little known communities of W. Bengal', *Bulletin of Cultural Research Institute – Special Series*, no. 5, Calcutta, 1964
Das, T. C.	'Primitive culture on the borders of Bengal', *Calcutta Review*, vol. 139, pp. 35–40

Datta-Majundar, N.	*The Santal*, Calcutta, 1956
Elwin, V.	*Myths of Middle India*, New York, 1949
Elwin, V.	*Tribal Myths of Orissa*, New York, 1953
Führer-Heimendorf, C.	*An Anthropological Bibliography of South Asia*
Haldar, S.	'Ho Folklore' (Animal Nurses), *Journal of Bihar and Orissa Research Society* – vol. 1, pp. 255–73; vol. 2, pp. 283–303; vol. 4, pp. 322–43
Kochar, V.	*Social Organization among the Santal*, Calcutta, 1970
Mohapatra, K.	'Christianity in a Tribal Village', *Anthropology on the March*, L. K. Bala Ratnam (ed.), Madras, 1963
Molony, A. C. B.	*Santals in Bengal*, S.P.G. World Wide Series, no. 7
Mukherjea, C.	*The Santals*, Calcutta, 1962
Mukhiya, P. K.	'The Primitive People of Orissa', *Vanyajati*, vol. 8, 1960
Mukhopadhyay, A.	'Infanticide in Bengal and its Suppression', *Bengal Past and Present*, vol. 75, 1956
Neogi, D. N.	*Tales Sacred and Secular (Child Exposure in Bengal)* Calcutta, 1912
Orans, M.	*The Santal*, Detroit, 1965
Raha, M. K.	'The Forest in Tribal Life', *Bulletin of Cultural Research Institute*, vol. 2, no. 1, Calcutta, 1963
Saha, N. K.	'The Santal's Supernatural World', *Vanyajati*, vol. 18, no. 4
Sen, R. S. D.	*Folk Literature of Bengal*, Calcutta, 1920
West Bengal, Government of	*Handbook on Scheduled Castes and Scheduled Tribes in West Bengal*, Calcutta, 1966

Alexander, R. D. T. and Martin-Leake, A.	*Some Signposts to Shikar*, Calcutta, 1932
Ball, V.	*Jungle Life in India*, London, 1880
Beddard, F. E.	*Mammalia*, London, 1902
Behura, B. K.	'Studies on wild mammals of Orissa', *Proceedings of the 46th Indian Scientific Congress*, Part 3, 1959
Best, J. W.	*Forest Life in India*, London, 1935
Blanford	'The Indian Wolf', *Mammalia of British India*, pp. 135–7
Blyth	'*Canis lupus pallipes*', Journal of the Asiatic Society of Bengal, vol. 14, p. 345, Calcutta, 1845
Burton, R. G.	*Sport and Wildlife in the Deccan*, London, 1928
Champion, F. W.	*The Jungle in Sunlight and Shadow*, London, 1933
Chaudhuri, K. N.	*Sport in Jheel and Jungle*, Calcutta, 1918
Crisler, L.	*Arctic Wild*, New York, 1958
Eardley-Wilmot, Sir S.	*Forest Life and Sport in India*, London, 1910
Eardley-Wilmot, Sir S.	*Leaves from Indian Forests*, London 1930
Fiennes, R.	*The Order of Wolves*, London, 1976
Fox, M. W.	*Behaviour of Wolves, Dogs and Related Canids*, London, 1971
Glasfurd, Col. A. I. R.	*Musings of an Old Shikari*, London, 1928
Hewett, Sir J.	*Jungle Trails in North India*, London, 1938
Jerdon, J. C.	*The Mammals of India*, London, 1874
Lorenz, K. Z.	*Man meets Dog*, London, 1955
Mech, L. D.	*The Wolf*, New York, 1970
Mervyn-Smith, A.	*Sport and Adventure in the Indian Jungle*, London, 1904

Mowat, F.	*Never Cry Wolf*, New York, 1963
Prater, S. H.	*The Book of Indian Animals*, Bombay Natural History Society, 1965
Puri, G. S.	*Indian Forest Ecology*, New Delhi, 1960
Rao, V. S.	'Status of Wildlife in the S.W. Districts of Bengal', *Journal of the Bengal Natural History Society*, 1958, vol. 30, p. 132
St Quentin, T.	*Chances of Sport of Sorts*, London, 1912
Savory, I.	*A Sportswoman in India*, London, 1900
Stewart, Col. A. E.	*Tiger and Other Game*, London, 1928
Stockley, C. H.	*Shikar*, London, 1928
Stockley, C. H.	*Big Game Shooting in the Indian Empire*, London, 1928
Strachan, A. W.	*Mauled by a Tiger*, Edinburgh & London, 1933
Sykes	'*Canis lupus pallipes*', *Proceedings of the Zoological Society*, London, 1831
Wood, H. S.	*Shikar Memories*, London, 1934
Young, S. P. and Goldman, E. A.	*The Wolves of North America*, Washington, 1944

Feral Man

Allen, A. and Morton, A.	*This is Your Child*, London, 1961
Altrocchi, R.	*Sleuthing in the Stacks*, Cambridge, Mass., 1944
Armen, J.-C.	*Gazelle-Boy*, London, 1974
Bettelheim, B.	*The Empty Fortress*, New York, 1967
Chapple, E. P. and Coon, C. S.	*Principles of Anthropology*, New York, 1942

Dennis, W.	'The Significance of Feral Man', *American Journal of Psychology*, No. 54, 1941
Dunn, C. W.	*The Foundling and the Werewolf*, Toronto, 1960
Eckels, R. P.	*Greek Wolf-Lore*, Philadelphia, 1937
Eisler, R. O.	*Man into Wolf*, London, 1951
Evans, B.	*Natural History of Nonsense*, New York, 1961
Evans, B.	'Wolf, Wolf?', *New Republic*, 26 May 1940
Feuerbach, P. J. A.	*Caspar Hauser*, H. G. Linberg (trs.), London, 1834
Friedrich, H.	*Man and Animal*, London, 1971
Gesell, A.	*Wolf-Child and Human Child*, New York, 1941
Gesell, A.	'The Biography of a Wolf-Child', *Harper's Magazine*, January, 1941
Hutton, J. H.	'Wolf-Children', vol. 1, *Folk-Lore*, pp. 9–31, 1940
Kellog, W. N.	'More about the wolf-children of India', *American Journal of Psychology*, no. 43, 1931
Kellog, W. N.	'A further note on the Wolf-children of India', *American Journal of Psychology*, no. 46, 1934
Kellog, W. N. and L.A.	*The Ape and the Child*, New York, 1933
Kipling, R.	*All the Mowgli Stories*, London, 1933
Klineberg, D.	*Social Psychology*, New York, 1954
Kroeber, T.	*Ishi*, Berkeley, 1961
Lane, H.	*The Wild Boy of Aveyron*, Harvard, 1976
Levi-Strauss, C.	*Les Structures Élementaires de la Parenté*, Paris, 1949
McCartney, E. S.	'Greek and Roman Lore of Animal Nursed Infants', *Papers of the*

	Michigan Academy of Science, Arts and Letters, vol. 4, part 1, 1924, pp. 15–42
Malson, L.	*Les Enfants Sauvages*, Paris, 1964
Mandelbaum, D. G.	'Wolf Child Histories from India', *Journal of Social Psychology*, 1941
Mead, M.	'Wolf-children', *Parents' Magazine*, December 1941; *Natural History*, 1941; *Science News Letter*, 22 March 1941 and 26 April 1941
Ogburn, W. F.	'The Wolf Boy of Agra', *American Journal of Sociology*, no. 64, 1959, pp. 449–54
Ogburn, W. F. and Bose, N. K.	'On the trail of the wolf-children', *Genetic Psychology Monographs*, no. 60, 1959, pp. 117–93
Prasad, K.	'Ramu: The "Wolf-Boy" of Lucknow', *Illustrated London News*, 27 February 1954
Rousseau, J.-J.	*Discours sur l'origine de l'inégalité parmi les hommes*, Paris, 1962
Sandstrom, C. I.	*The Psychology of Childhood and Adolescence*, London, 1966
Singh, J. A. L. and Zingg, R. M.	*Wolf-Children and Feral Man*, New York, 1942
Sleeman, Col. W. H.	*An Account of Wolves Nurturing Children in their Dens*, Plymouth, 1852
Squires, P. C.	'Wolf-children of India', *American Journal of Psychology*, no. 38, 1927
Stuart-Baker, E. C.	'The Power of Scent in Wild Animals', *Journal of the Bombay Natural History Society*, no. 27, 1920
Summers, M.	*The Werewolf*, London, 1933
Thompson, S.	*Motif-Index of Folk-Literature*, Helsinki, 1932
Young, K.	*Sociology*, New York, 1942

Zingg, R. M. 'Feral Man and Extreme Cases of Isolation', *American Journal of Psychology*, no. 53, 1940

Zingg, R. M. 'India's Wolf-Children: Two Human Infants Reared by Wolves', *Scientific American*, March 1941

Newspaper Reports of the Wolf Children of Midnapore

1921 24 October, *Medinipur Hitaishi*
1921 December, *Calcutta Diocesan Record*, vol. 10, no. 9
1922 July, *Oxford Mission Quarterly Paper*
1923 October, *Calcutta Diocesan Record*, vol. 12, no. 10
1926 22, 23, 25 and 26 October, *Westminster Gazette*
1926 22 and 23 October, *New York Times*
1926 1 November, *Time*
1926 13 and 16 November, the *Statesman* (Calcutta)
1926 16 November, *Forward*
1926 26 December, *New York Times*
1927 30 January, *New York Times*
1927 January, *Oxford Mission Quarterly Paper*
1927 6 April, *New York Times*
1927 7–22 April, *The Times* (London) – Correspondence
1927 2 May, *New York Times*
1937 28 November, 5 and 12 December, *Illustrated Weekly of India*
1941 3 March, *Time*

Notes

The two most important unpublished sources on the wolf children of Midnapore are the Arnold Gesell Papers in the Manuscript Division of the Library of Congress, Washington, D.C. and the Zingg Collection, which is at present in the keeping of the Gesell Institute of Child Development in New Haven. There are also some of Robert Zingg's papers at the Centennial Museum of El Paso and others with his widow, Emma Zingg, but few of these are of much interest and relatively a low proportion deal with 'feral' affairs.

On the Reverend Singh's life and times the records and minutes of the United Society for Propagating the Gospel in London provided some useful information, but my chief sources were the archives of Bishop's College and the library at Bishop's House in Calcutta. Mrs P. L. Jana, the Reverend Singh's daughter, who lives in Ranchi, Bihar has in her possession letters and mementoes belonging to her father as well as the original prints and negatives of the wolf children photographs and a portion of manuscript, handwritten in green ink, which is probably the first draft of the wolf-children diary as later published by Harpers, but before it was edited by Bishop Pakenham-Walsh. Singh's original, contemporary diaries appear either to have been lost or destroyed and consequently I have had to rely heavily on the published 'Diary of the Wolf-Children of Midnapore'.

In Midnapore I found another though limited source in the diaries of Dr Sachin Sarbadhicari, who was the Singhs' family physician. I also consulted the Registers of Baptism and Burial for St John's, Midnapore and All Saints, Kharagpur, which are kept at the vicarage in Kharagpur. For much of the information in this book I have drawn from numerous interviews conducted in the course of my researches. The most valuable of these will be made available shortly in a paper I am preparing on the subject of the Midnapore wolf children and Feral Man.

Chapter One

1. The *Statesman*, 14 May 1908.
2. Calcutta Diocesan Council Reports, Midnapore and Kharagpur, 1916.
3. ibid., 1915.
4. ibid.
5. *Calcutta Diocesan Record*, October 1915, No. 2.
6. Interview: Dr K. C. Sarbadhicari, 29 March 1975.
7. Zingg Collection, Rev. J. A. L. Singh, *The History of the S.P.G. Mission Santal Evangelization of the Jungle Tracts, Midnapore*, 10 February 1936.
8. Calcutta Diocesan Council Reports, Kharagpur, 1913.
9. Zingg Collection, Singh to Mrs Henry Pfeiffer, 21 May 1938.
10. Bishop's College Archives, *Ordination*.

Chapter Two

1. Zingg Collection, Singh to Pakenham-Walsh, 19 July 1937.
2. Rev. J. A. L. Singh and Robert M. Zingg, *Wolf-Children and Feral Man* (incorporating *The Diary of the Wolf-Children of Midnapore*), Harper, 1942, Introduction, p. xxxi.
3. J. A. L. Singh, 'Among the Aboriginals', *Calcutta Diocesan Record*, November 1933.
4. Singh and Zingg, op. cit., Introduction, p. xxxii.
5. Interview: Nangi Hembron, 22 April 1975.

Chapter Three

1. Bishop's College Archives, *Midnapore*.
2. Singh and Zingg, op. cit., p. 4.
3. ibid., pp. 5–6.
4. ibid., p. 6.
5. ibid., p. 7.
6. Interview: Lasa Marandi, 1 May 1975.

7. Singh and Zingg, op. cit., p. 8.
8. ibid., p. 8.
9. ibid., p. 8.
10. ibid., p. 9.
11. ibid., p. 9.

Chapter Four

1. ibid., pp. 11–12.
2. ibid., p. 18.
3. ibid., p. 23.
4. ibid., pp. 29–30.
5. ibid., p. 6.
6. ibid., p. 19.
7. ibid., p. 45.
8. ibid., p. 45.
9. ibid., p. 35.
10. ibid., p. 15.
11. ibid., p. 15.
12. ibid., p. 21.
13. Bishop's College Archives, *Gandhi*.

Chapter Five

1. Singh and Zingg, op. cit., pp. 43–4.
2. ibid., p. 38.
3. Jana MS.
4. ibid.
5. ibid.
6. ibid.
7. ibid.
8. ibid.
9. Singh and Zingg, op. cit., p. 41.
10. Jana MS.
11. Singh and Zingg, op. cit., p. 52.
12. ibid., p. 54.
13. ibid., p. 59.
14. ibid., p. 97.
15. 'Order for the Burial of a Child', *The Book of Common Prayer* (according to the use of the Church of India, Pakistan, Burma and Ceylon).

Chapter Six

1. Jana MS.
2. *Medinipur Hitaishi*, 24 October 1921.
3. Singh and Zingg, op. cit., p. 65.
4. Jana MS.
5. The *Statesman*, 23 December 1921.
6. *Calcutta Diocesan Record*, December 1921, Vol. X, No. 9.
7. ibid.
8. Zingg Collection, Singh to Mrs Henry Pfeiffer, 21 May 1938.
9. Calcutta Diocesan Council Report, 1922–3.
10. Singh and Zingg, op. cit., p. 58.
11. ibid., p. 66.
12. ibid., p. 76.
13. ibid., p. 73.
14. Jana MS.
15. ibid.
16. ibid.
17. ibid.

Chapter Seven

1. Interview: Louise Mani Das,12 April 1975.
2. Jana MS.
3. Singh and Zingg, op. cit., p. 90.
4. Jana MS.
5. ibid.
6. Singh and Zingg, op. cit., p. 101.
7. Jana MS.
8. ibid.
9. Singh and Zingg, op. cit., p. 102.
10. Jana MS.
11. *The Book of Common Prayer*.

Chapter Eight

1. Bishop's College Archives, *Gandhi*.
2. Jana MS.
3. ibid.
4. ibid.

5. Arnold Gesell Papers, Statement by the Rt. Rev. Pakenham-Walsh, 2 May 1942.
6. ibid.
7. *Westminster Gazette*, 23 October 1926.
8. ibid.
9. The *Statesman*, 13 November 1926.
10. Zingg Collection, Pakenham-Walsh to Zingg, 14 March 1940.
11. ibid., Singh to Dr R. Ruggles Gates, 7 March 1940.
12. Singh and Zingg, op. cit., p. 87.

Chapter Nine

1. Jana MS.
2. Letters in possession of Mrs Jana.
3. Arnold Gesell Papers, Mrs Singh to Gesell, 6 July 1942.
4. ibid.
5. Interview: Mrs Geeta Mallik, 15 May 1975.
6. Singh and Zingg, op. cit., p. 108.
7. Arnold Gesell Papers, Mrs Singh to Gesell, 6 July 1942.
8. Interview: Rt. Rev. R. W. Bryan, 12 May 1975.
9. *American Journal of Psychology*, Vol. 46, 1936, p. 149.
10. ibid.
11. Singh and Zingg, op. cit., Preface, p. xxvi.
12. ibid., p. 89.
13. Interview: P. C. Ganguly, 9 May 1975.
14. Bishop's College Archives, *Midnapore*.
15. W. F. Ogburn and N. K. Bose, 'On the trail of the wolf-children', *Genetic Psychology Monographs*, No. 60.
16. Singh and Zingg, op. cit., p. 112.
17. Arnold Gesell Papers, Mrs Singh to Gesell, 6 July 1942.
18. ibid.
19. *The Book of Common Prayer*.

Chapter Ten

1. Bimal Dasgupta, 'Tale of Peddie Murder Yet Untold', *Midnapore College Magazine*.
2. ibid.
3. The *Statesman*, 9 April 1931.
4. Sir Robert N. Reid, *Years of Change in Bengal and Assam*, 1966.

5. Dasgupta, op. cit.
6. Subodh Chandra Bose, 'Peddie Greeted with Bullets', *Midnapore College Magazine.*
7. The *Statesman*, 10 April 1931.
8. Bishop's College Archives, Midnapore, Molony to Westcott, July 1932.
9. ibid., Hewitt to Molony, 14 August 1932.
10. Zingg Collection, Singh to Pakenham-Walsh, 26 April 1941.
11. Bishop's College Archives, Kharagpur.
12. Arnold Gesell Papers, Singh to Gesell, 4 April 1933.
13. Zingg Collection, Singh to Pakenham-Walsh, 26 April 1941.
14. ibid., Zingg to Eugene F. Saxton, 3 February 1941.
15. Arnold Gesell Papers, Squires to Zingg, 30 August 1942.
16. ibid.
17. *American Journal of Psychology*, Vol. 46, 1936, p. 149.
18. Zingg Collection, Kellogg to Zingg, 11 October 1938.
19. Singh and Zingg, op. cit., Frontispiece.
20. Zingg Collection, Singh to Ruggles Gates, 2 April 1940.
21. ibid.
22. ibid., Pakenham-Walsh to Zingg (quotes Goffin), 26 February 1938.
23. ibid., Zingg to Singh, 20 January 1937.

Chapter Eleven
1. Zingg Collection, Zingg to Professor R. Innkerjee, 18 January 1938.
2. ibid., Zingg to Singh, Easter Day, 1938.
3. ibid., Zingg to Redfield, 5 April 1938.
4. ibid., Pakenham-Walsh to Zingg, 30 July 1938.
5. ibid., Zingg to Pakenham-Walsh, 29 June 1938.
6. ibid., Pakenham-Walsh to Zingg, 25 May 1938.
7. 'Night-Shining Eyes', *Nature*, 14 September 1940, Vol. 146, p. 366.
8. *Current Biography*, 1940, Vol. 1, No. 11.
9. Arnold Gesell, *The Documentation of Infant Behaviour and its Relation to Cultural Anthropology*, 8th American Scientific Congress, 14 May 1940.
10. ibid.

11. Arnold Gesell, *Wolf Child and Human Child*, Harper, 1941.
12. Zingg Collection, Pakenham-Walsh to Zingg, 19 March 1939.
13. ibid., Ruggles Gates to Singh, 19 January 1940.
14. ibid., Singh to Ruggles Gates, 7 March 1940.
15. ibid.
16. ibid., Singh to Ruggles Gates, 2 April 1940.
17. ibid.
18. ibid., Pakenham-Walsh to Zingg, 15 March 1940.
19. ibid., Zingg to Singh, 1 May 1940.
20. ibid., Gesell to Singh, 27 March 1940.
21. ibid., Gesell to Singh, 30 September 1940.
22. ibid.
23. ibid., Zingg to Gesell, 9 October 1940.
24. *Time*, 3 March 1941.
25. Arnold Gesell Papers, Evans to Miss K. Gauss, 19 January 1941.
26. ibid., Mandelbaum to Zingg, 21 April 1941.
27. ibid., Singh to Gesell, 23 June 1941.
28. *Journal of Social Psychology*, July 1941.

Chapter Twelve

1. *Calcutta Diocesan Record*, November 1941.
2. Zingg Collection, Zingg to Gesell, 24 February 1942.
3. ibid., Zingg to Gesell, 29 May 1942.
4. ibid.
5. ibid., Gesell to Zingg, 3 June 1942.
6. *American Anthropologist*, Vol. 45, p. 468.
7. Arnold Gesell Papers.
8. ibid., Zingg to Gesell, 1948.
9. ibid., Gesell, 12 February 1947.
10. Zingg Collection, Zingg to Gesell and Ruggles Gates, 1944.
11. ibid.
12. ibid.
13. Arnold Gesell Papers, T. Campbell Rogers to Zingg, 1944.

Epilogue

1. Interview: Dr J. M. Sarma, 28 May 1975.

Index

321

Khatua, Bhagobhat, 14, 51–2, 54, 56–9, 75, 241, 260
Khatua, Jageswar, 14, 86, 301
Khiroda, 111
Kipling, Rudyard, 72
Kosdia, 64
Krogman, Wilton, 251–5
Kuarh, 44

Lefroy, George, Bishop of Calcutta, 15, 25
Lithuanian bear boys, 246
Long, Rev., 98
Lowman (Inspector-General), 224
Lytton, Lord, 198, 207

Macmillan (publishers), 249, 252, 258
Madan Theatres Co., 198
Mahato, Ghambir, 68–9
Mahato, Mr, 68–9
Maitra, Aswini Kumar, 227
Maiwana wolf boy, 202
Maji, Motra, 64
Mallik, Geeta, 202–3
Mandelbaum, David, 269–70
Manica, 200
Maran, Buru, 50
Marandi, Gita, 64
Marandi, Lasa, 64, 299, 301
Mayurbhanj, 33–4
  Dewar of, 62
  Maharajah of, 46–7
Mead, Margaret, 268
Medinipur Hitaishi, 136, 140, 141, 262
Midnapore, 9, 12, 221
Midnapore City Press, 196
Midnapore Zamindari Co., 97, 140
Mills, Lady Dorothy, 191
Molony, A. C. B., 231–2, 235, 274, 278

Mondhal, Haripada, 296
Montague, Prof. Ashley, 281–2
Mozufferpore, 11
Murray, Major, 228

Nalgoja, 62–3
Narajole, Rajah of, 21, 133, 211, 278
Nathaniel, Dr, 101
Nayagaram, 52, 299
New-Haven Journal Courier, 258–9
New Republic, 268

Ogburn, William, 294–8
Orphanage, *see* 'The Home'
Oxford Mission, 26
Oxford University Press, 242

Pachu, 155
Pakenham-Walsh, Herbert, 187, 191, 196, 204, 216, 235–6, 240–44, 248, 250–51, 258, 261, 263–4, 284, 298
Parsons, Herbert, 254
Patherdogra, 63
Pattanaik, Gopabandha, 49–50, 55, 62, 64, 70
Pattanaik, Umakanta, 301
Payne, Russell, 159, 231
Peddie, James, 221–9, 289
Pfeiffer, Annie, 245, 270, 279
Pilibhit, 39
Pioneer, 202
Prince of Wales, 140, 143, 219
Psychological Society of New York, 213

Redfield, Dr, 246, 248–9, 253
Reid, Sir Robert, 10, 186, 198, 226
Richards, Henry, 57, 61–4, 66, 68, 74, 133, 240–41, 259–60, 280